The Miracle at Coogan's Bluff

THOMAS KIERNAN

Thomas Y. Crowell Company
New York   Established 1834

Acknowledgment is made to Little, Brown and Company for permission to quote from *It's Good to Be Alive* by Roy Campanella, copyright © 1959 by Roy Campanella. Reprinted by permission.

Acknowledgment is made to the Baseball Hall of Fame for the team photo of the New York Giants, 1951. All other photos are credited to Wide World Photos.

Endpapers: The Miracle at Coogan's Bluff. Bobby Thomson hits his historic home run at the Polo Grounds, October 3, 1951. (Courtesy, the San Francisco Giants)

Designed by Ingrid Beckman
Manufactured in the United States of America

Library of Congress Cataloging in Publication Data

Kiernan, Thomas.
    The miracle at Coogan's Bluff.

    Includes index.
    1. New York (City). Baseball club (National League Giants) I. Title.
GV875.N42K53   796.357'64'097471   74-28081
ISBN 0-690-00440-0

1   2   3   4   5   6   7   8   9   10

*For Padraic and Joshua, who never saw
Coogan's Bluff.*

Contents

"Understand that we were a group of rational people. We knew that a home run can not be produced at will; the right pitch must be perfectly met and luck must ride with the ball . . . nevertheless, there will always lurk, around a corner in a pocket of our knowledge of the arts, an indefensible hope, and this was one of those times, which now and then you find in sports, when a density of expectation hangs in the air and plucks an event out of the future."

—John Updike

Prologue

"Positively No Ball-Playing Allowed"

COOGAN'S BLUFF IS a craggy, rock-faced cliff that rises abruptly from a curving ribbon of flat land bordering the Harlem River on the northerly end of the island of Manhattan. Running parallel to the river's course for about half a mile, its height is approximately equal to the distance, on a baseball diamond, between home plate and first base.

In a sense, Coogan's Bluff is a sacred place. For it was at the base of this steep palisade in early October of the year 1951 that, in the minds and imaginations of many, a miracle transpired. The miracle occurred within the oddly shaped baseball stadium that filled much of the narrow flat between the bluff and the river. The stadium was called the Polo Grounds, and it was the home of the New York Giants of the National Baseball League.

Today the Polo Grounds is nothing more than a memory. What remains of the events that took place there in 1951—particularly the seven weeks of increasingly unbearable tension that stretched over the suffocating dog days of a late New York summer and exploded in a nationwide catharsis on an early autumn afternoon—lies etched, one imagines on visiting the place today, in the scarred and striated face of Coogan's Bluff itself.

Unlike Lourdes, Golgotha, or Guadaloupe, there is to be found at

Coogan's Bluff no monument, grotto, or cathedral commemorating the miracle. Pilgrimages are not made to the site, and the solitary visitor finds no hawkers of souvenirs and holy relics, no supplicants crawling painfully along on their knees in sacrificial gratitude. Indeed, the visitor is hard-pressed even to locate the bluff itself amid the collection of tacky modern high-rise apartme*t* buildings randomly spotted like huge chess pieces on the land where the Polo Grounds once stood.

Discovering evidence of the one-time existence of the stadium—a landmark in its time—is equally difficult. A small sign at the entrance to the housing project informs the visitor that he is gazing upon the ''Polo Grounds Towers.''

A reminder that baseball was once played here is tucked into a distant corner of the housing complex. It is an ersatz baseball diamond set at one edge of a macadamized playground enclosed by a high cyclone fence. The simulated diamond is tiny, barely big enough to contain a peewee game, its tarmac chipped and rutted with neglect, its painted bases and foul lines long faded, barely perceptible. Often the diamond lies empty in the hot, sooted sunlight, while along the borders of the playground a dozen furious games of pick-up basketball are in progress.

On the walls of all the buildings, a few feet above the reach of the graffiti artists, ten or twelve yards apart, are affixed small neat rectangular signs that admonish, ''Positively No Ball-Playing Allowed.''

The miracle of Coogan's Bluff differed from more conventional miracles. It roundly defied the miracular tradition by taking place in America's largest city rather than in some remote mountain clearing. It was a totally public event, one whose unfolding the entire nation shared. Indeed, thereafter, and until the time of the assassination of a president twelve years later, the flight of a baseball—that tiny, stitched sphere which streaked with the suddenness of lightning through the gathering dusk below Coogan's Bluff on October 3, 1951, and upon whose trajectory the miracle stunningly unfurled like a banner from heaven—was the single most commonly recalled event in the American experience since the death of yet an earlier president in 1945.

It was the event most of us set our emotional watches by, about which the where-were-you-when question was most frequently asked for more than a decade.

There is no monument at Coogan's Bluff. Except for the stony facade of the bluff itself, which from the visitor's adult perspective now seems a shrunken, shoddy ghost of its former majesty, there is nothing to remind him of the incredible coming-together of the fruits of human industry and the abstractions of impersonal fate—except for those neat, faded signs whose message, when pronounced aloud, ring hollowly in his ear, "Positively No Ball-Playing Allowed."

PART I
The Miracle

1

A Baseball Autobiography

WHEN I WAS a young man, I thought it would be a very fine thing to become a professional baseball player. My most cherished vision was to someday patrol the vast, beautiful center-field greensward of the Polo Grounds in the crisp white flannels of my beloved New York Giants.

The New York Giants were, of course, a well-known major-league baseball club, most celebrated for their exploits in the decades between the great wars. They had been playing at the Polo Grounds, their home turf at the foot of Coogan's Bluff, for what seemed like eons. Through the layers of time they had accumulated a vast fandom.

This was still in the days when loyalties to baseball teams were passed on from father to son like religious beliefs. A boy's first visit with his father to the Polo Grounds, Ebbets Field, or Yankee Stadium—depending on the dogma subscribed to—represented something comparable in form and substance to a youngster's First Communion or Bar Mitzvah.

By virtue of such inheritance, I grew up a Giant fan. Unfortunately, in those days of the forties, adversity was more often than not the sole lot of the New York Giants. By the time I reached the age of fourteen, my devotion was of the rabid and unyielding variety.

My initiation into the Giant religion came when I was nine. To this day I remember my first visit to the Polo Grounds more vividly than my first trip to the altar to swallow the holy wafer. In fact, the whole process of my growing up could be described as a continuing war between instilled religious doctrine and ingrained belief in the New York Giants. Sad to say, perhaps, but I lost my religious faith long before my devotion to the Giants was wrenched away by a combination of maturity and distance.

Devotion to the New York Giants had been almost as much part and parcel of my family's tradition for three generations as their belief in a righteous and redeeming God. Being the only male issue, I was naturally commissioned to carry on the tradition and pass it on to my own sons.

By the time my first son was born, the Giants had long since moved west to San Francisco in search of sunnier, more lucrative climes, abandoning the rusty old Polo Grounds to South American soccer matches and six-day bicycle races—sports foreign to my Celtic-American sensibilities. My sons are now New York Mets fans.

They will forever be innocent of the awesome mystery, for a young boy, of the mammouth, misshapen, double-tiered, soot-encrusted edifice called the Polo Grounds. They will go through life without ever having explored the secret corners and remote caverns of its interior, without ever having raced and frolicked up and down its innumerable ramps and through its maze of corridors. And without ever having sat in its unique air, a blend of the smoke of twenty thousand cigarettes (on a good day) and the aroma of hundreds of gallons of beer gone stale—a mix that compacted and hung like a soggy blanket over the field and gave you a headache by the fourth inning.

A wealth of documentation exists testifying to the fact that there was never any polo played at the Polo Grounds. Nevertheless, as I was growing up, legend had it that at one time in its history the piece of land upon which the stadium was eventually erected was the private polo preserve of the wealthy Coogan family, who owned most of the property in the area and after whom the bluff was named.

It was a credible story within my own family, whose senior

member had partially broken out of the standard Irish stereotype and was upwardly mobile in the Anglo-Protestant New York establishment of the thirties and forties. It was especially reassuring to know that people with the name Coogan were able to dally at polo in a day when the Irish of New York were society's lepers. Certainly the terrain on which the stadium was built lent credence to the theory. It was a narrow, level, semirectilinear parcel of land bounded on the west by the curving face of the bluff and on the east by the rushing Harlem River. One could easily imagine privileged polo enthusiasts driving up from their stately homes in lower Manhattan in smart carriages to watch the matches from the excellent vantage points atop the bluff, while down below the clean wind off the river cooled the graceful horsemen and evaporated their careening ponies' lather.

But the real story was something else. When professional baseball was in its infancy in the 1880s, New York was represented by two teams. One was the New York Metropolitans of the then fledgling American Association, the forerunner of the American League. The other was a National League team called, simply, the New Yorkers. Both clubs were co-owned by two gentlemen named John B. Day and James Mutrie. Day took care of business matters while Mutrie, himself a former player, did the field managing.

In 1883 the teams were new to New York. They each played their first game in April of that year on a baseball diamond at 110th Street and Fifth Avenue, opposite the northeasternmost corner of Central Park. The property on which the diamond was set was owned not by an Irishman, but by James Gordon Bennett, the patrician publisher of the New York *Herald*. Bennett had been using the land, along with his society cronies, for polo. Hence the baseball field came to be called the "polo grounds."

The Metropolitans lasted only a few years in New York. In 1885 Day and Mutrie sold the club to concentrate their energies on the New Yorkers, who were a stronger team in a more established league.

The New Yorkers started out in 1883 as a team made up of players from the defunct Troy, New York, club, which had played in the National League the year before. The area around Troy, a shabby town across the river from Albany, had been the terminus of thousands of

Irish immigrants fleeing the great potato famine of 1846–48. Cheap labor, they built the Erie Canal single-handedly.

So down from Troy in 1883 came the likes of Mickey Welch, John Ward, James "Tip" O'Neill, Buck Ewing, Roger Connor, Mike Dorgan, Pat Gillespie, Tim Keefe, Bill Brown, Pat Murphy, Jim O'Rourke, Mike Slattery, George Gore, and Silent Mike Tiernan— big men all. When they took the field for one of their early games at James Gordon Bennett's polo field, manager Mutrie was heard to shout, "Come on, you giants!" Some of the fans, hearing Mutrie's exhortation, found the name particularly suited the team, and it spread through the stands. The newspapers adopted it the next day, and from then on the team was known as the Giants.

The year 1888 saw the Giants win their first National League pennant. It was also the year they began to look for larger, more permanent quarters. The leasing arrangements for Bennett's polo field were no longer satisfactory to owner Day, so he started the 1889 season by moving the club briefly to Jersey City, then to Staten Island. Day quickly deduced from the drooping attendance figures, however, that Staten Island was not the place to be. So on July 9 he moved the Giants, who were on their way to a second pennant, to a field at 157th Street and Eighth Avenue in Manhattan. A grandstand was hurriedly erected, and the place, shoehorned between Coogan's Bluff and the Harlem River, was quickly dubbed the "new polo grounds." When successive enlarged wooden grandstands were replaced by a horseshoe-shaped concrete and steel structure a few years later, it became, officially, the Polo Grounds.

The stadium accumulated a mythic history in its 60-odd years of existence. During the first two decades of the century it was the capital of major-league baseball. By the mid-thirties the stadium's 52,000 hard-bottomed seats had been witness to the feats—both brilliant and boneheaded—of countless legendary baseball figures. The Giants had become, with almost boring annual regularity, the powerhouse of the National League. The Polo Grounds was one of those places to which people went to see and be seen. It became a kind of outdoor Stork Club. Financiers, underworld luminaries, society leaders, political figures, stars of stage and screen, rich and celebrated industrialists—all flocked to the Polo Grounds, more to ogle each other than to watch the John McGraw–managed Giants display their considerable skills.

It was not until World War II was drawing to a close that I began to cultivate my dream of a baseball career in earnest. Of the illustrious history of the Giants I knew little and cared less. For me the Giants went no further back in time than the early forties, when I got my first exposure to them.

It was the worst possible time to be initiated into the society of Giant fandom. With the war on, the Giants were hardly more than a pick-up team of draft rejects. Between 1941 and 1946 they finished last twice; the best they could do was in 1942 when they came in third.

I was more than happily willing to wait until the end of the war, when they would reassemble and once again ascend to the pinnacle of the National League. In the meantime I was content to worship such heroes as Mel Ott, Buddy Kerr, Sid Gordon, Danny Gardella, Johnny Mize, and Van Lingle Mungo. The great but aging Mel Ott was also the manager.

The postwar resurgence never took place. At the war's conclusion, most of the returning ''name'' players had passed their prime. In 1946 the Giants finished a hapless last. In 1947, despite hitting a collective record-breaking 221 home runs, they finished fourth. The next year saw them slip back to fifth place.

Nevertheless, they were still my team. And with the postwar addition of new heroes—players like Walker Cooper, Bobby Thomson, Bill Rigney, Larry Jansen, Willard Marshall, Clint Hartung, Dave Koslo, and Montia Kennedy—there was hope.

The Giants had last won a pennant in 1937, and by the time 1950 rolled around, hope had been transformed to despair. Their championship skills, it was clear, had long since vanished, and with them a great number of their followers. Not even the addition of the once-hated Leo Durocher—a proven winner—as manager two years earlier seemed to help.

Indeed, by 1950 the Giants were held in the lowest esteem of the three New York baseball clubs. They were considered beyond salvation. During the forties the Yankees won six pennants, the Brooklyn

Dodgers three, while the Giants remained mired in the lower depths. To remain a diehard Giant fan, as I did, meant continued exposure to the cruel jibes and insults of Dodger and Yankee followers. Yet I was more than just a fan. I had my dream, and the time was coming for me to put it to the test.

My dream helped carry me through my high-school years. I caught and played the outfield for my school team and even got in a valuable summer of pass-the-hat semi-pro baseball in Vermont, where I led the Shoreham Champlainers in almost all of the few statistics kept.

But the more I pressed my ambitions on my father, the more adamant he grew in opposition. As far as he was concerned, it was one thing to be a baseball fan, altogether another to aspire to be a baseball player. Ballplayers were all right to watch by way of an afternoon's diversion, but other than that they were barely a step above convicted felons in social worth. I, my father decreed, would go to college and pursue a civilized vocation.

I learned to keep my dream to myself. Although not a deer, I could run the bases, had a strong, accurate arm, and could hit with power and consistency—at least against the kind of pitching I encountered in high school. In addition, I had what my high-school coach called the smarts, which was his way of saying I had good instincts for the game.

And then there were the scouts. Every major-league club had what they called bird-dogs, men who worked in other fields but spent their spare time making the rounds of high-school ball fields on the lookout for promising baseball talent. To have a bird-dog—some old fogy who was probably half in the bag and partly senile to boot—come up and say something complimentary to you after a game was enough to make your week.

The bird-dogs, if they liked a kid's looks, would drop a note to the big club, and if the big club got enough enthusiastic input, it would send one of its full-time scouts out to take a look.

The first scout who came by to inspect me during my last season in high school was from the Boston Braves. Unfortunately, someone let me know before the game that he was there. I never played worse. So much for the Boston Braves.

There were a couple of other scouts that spring—one from Cincinnati, as I recall, another from the St. Louis Browns (or was it the Cardinals?). But no one from my beloved Giants. My parents had connections with some of the people involved in the Giants' front office, but by this time I knew it would be futile to ask my father to use his influence.

I graduated in June of 1951 with nothing more than an indifferent nibble from the Cincinnati man. It was an offer of a contract to play with their Class D farm team somewhere in the wilds of East Texas—Lubbock, as I recall.

My father was polite to the Cincinnati man. He was not as polite to me. I had been accepted at college, that's where I was going two months hence, and there was to be no more talk about a baseball career. Period!

As a veteran Giant fan I was used to the bitter pill of disappointment when it came to baseball matters. So I swallowed it whole and began to ruminate on the virtues of Notre Dame, the university that had pledged to take me in. It wasn't Texas, I knew, but Indiana was far enough away to get me out from under the wings of an oppressive family. And there was always football.

No sooner had I resigned myself to four years on the Indiana prairie than a letter addressed to me arrived at my house from the New York Giants. "Dear Prospect," it started. I swear I was ready to change my name to Prospect. "We have been receiving outstanding reports on your baseball talents. In the event that you haven't already executed a contract with another major league club, we would be pleased to have you join us. . . ."

My God, the New York Giants were asking me to join them! Then I read on.

". . . join us for a tryout at the Polo Grounds on Wednesday, June 20, at 10 A.M. Please bring a pair of spikes and a uniform, if you have one. Also bring some lunch. Show this letter at the club-house gate. Sincerely, [signed] John Schwarz, Administrative Secretary, Farm System."

Well, it was better than nothing. A tryout. OK. But what about my father?

I showed him the letter, then did a lot of pleading. It was only a tryout, I assured him. Probably nothing would come of it, but at least

I would be able to say that I once actually played baseball at the Polo Grounds.

To myself I was saying, this is it! I was convinced of my destiny. My dream was going to come true. If they offered me a contract, no matter how lowly, I would run away from home in order to accept it. Screw my old man! If he didn't like it, he could lump it. Of course I didn't stop to think that I was underage and needed his signature to sign.

With his grudging approval I set out for the Polo Grounds on the appointed morning from our home in Orange, New Jersey. I carried my threadbare high-school uniform, along with two gloves and a couple of sandwiches, all stuffed in an old pillowcase. My freshly polished spikes were slung like a talisman around my neck.

Two hours later I emerged from the sweltering subway station at 155th Street and Eighth Avenue. It was still early in the morning, but the temperature was already in the high eighties, with the humidity not far behind. As I turned into Eighth Avenue I saw the familiar green wall of the Polo Grounds gleaming in the thick sunlight. The sweet anticipation that had been building up during the long subway ride abruptly turned to heart-throbbing anxiety. Suddenly my warm flesh was a moonscape of goose bumps, and I wanted to disappear back into the the subway.

But I pressed on. I presented myself at the clubhouse gate and tried to act properly casual. How often during the past few years had I stood outside that gate after a game, aquiver with expectation and hope, hungering to catch a fleeting close-up glimpse of the gargantuan Johnny Mize, the sleek and swarthy Sid Gordon, the willowy, pock-marked Buddy Kerr, the smoothly handsome Willard Marshall!

Now, here I was, with the possibility looming—at least in my mind—that I was to become one of them. I showed my letter to the guard at the gate, and presto! I was in the New York Giants' clubhouse, a place I had entered only in my daydreams.

I was assigned a spare cubicle at one end of the large locker room. As I changed in the solemn silence of the place (there were twenty-five or thirty other hopefuls there, all equally awed to find themselves in the shrine of shrines), I surveyed the names taped to the cubicles assigned to the regular Giant players.

Stanky, Dark, Lohrke, Thompson, Rigney, Wilson—infielders all—clustered at one corner of the room. And Irvin, Monte Irvin, a guy from my home town. If he could make it, especially with the strikes he had had against him, so could I!

My eyes roved further—Thomson, Mueller, Lockman, Hartung. Hartung—the Hondo Hurricane. And Mays, the rookie outfielder I hadn't seen play yet. I memorized the location of the outfielders' cubicles so that when I next walked into the clubhouse, after being called up from Minneapolis or some such farm team, I'd know right where to go to dump my stuff.

Desire and envy gnawed at me. No matter that these guys were not the heroes of a few years earlier, when I was *really* impressionable. No matter that they were not as skilled and dynamic and colorful as their despised rivals in Brooklyn. No matter that they had lost eleven games in a row at the beginning of the season and were still floundering around in the cellar while the ruffians from Brooklyn were enjoying high tea in the drawing room. This was my team, these were my guys, and one day soon I would be part of it all.

I thought I had performed rather well out on the field, and was bursting with satisfaction at the end of the tryout. I had hit the fairly tough pitches of one of the scouts with ease, putting two of them in the left-centerfield seats—both in the upper deck! I had covered the outfield gracefully and well, caught all the balls that were fungoed my way, and made the plays a centerfielder is supposed to make. I had showed off my arm to advantage with a pair of right-on-the-money one-hoppers to the plate. And although I was not the fastest hopeful there, I was not too far behind the jack-rabbit leaders in the timed sprints around the bases.

Understand my feelings then, when the men conducting the tryout invited a handful of fellows to stay behind for a further look and dismissed the rest of us with a polite thank you.

At first I was sure they'd made a dreadful mistake. After all, I wasn't fantasizing all this. I *had* stood out—a lot more than some of the guys that the scouts had selected to stay. How could they be sending *me* away without a contract discussion? Or at least a further look?

But the head scout made it clear, when I summoned up the courage to question him, that they'd seen enough. They weren't interested.

A kid I had played against in high school was among the few chosen to stay behind. He was Joe Burke, an all-state pitcher. I'd gotten two hits off him the last time I'd faced him in a game about a month earlier. I could hear him laughing as I took the long walk back to the Polo Grounds clubhouse.

Stinking with sweat, I didn't even bother to shower. I quickly got back into my clothes and, before leaving, took one last look around. All those names taped up on the cubicles were suddenly cold, distant, mocking epitaphs engraved on the mausoleum of my disappointment. I couldn't get out of there fast enough. I never wanted to think about the New York Giants again.

When I got home and told my father what had happened, he grunted noncommittally behind his newspaper. It took me several weeks to learn that he was using the paper to conceal a carefully planned conspiracy to thwart my ambition.

Later that summer I found out that he had contacted one of his acquaintances in the Giants' front office after he heard that I had been invited for a tryout. He prevailed upon his friend to put out the word to the scouts who would be conducting the tryout: discourage the Kiernan kid. His parents won't let him sign even if we do like him.

But until I learned of my father's machinations I turned completely sour on the Giants. As a result, I blessedly missed most of their early-season flounderings that year. I stayed away from the Polo Grounds for almost two months, although I had been practically a weekly visitor for the previous three or four seasons.

I ignored their box scores in the papers. I turned to another station when the baseball results were announced on the radio. And I exulted at the news of every loss that did filter through my various censorship devices.

Like an unrequited lover I sulked and agonized. I burned with the rage of the cuckold. I even tried to strike back with an infidelity of my own—I secretly tried to become a Dodger fan. I tried hard, too—for several weeks at least—even going so far as to travel to Ebbets Field on a couple of occasions.

But it was no use. There was no way I could bring myself to root for the Dodgers, whether sincerely or just to balance the books. I ex-

perienced a guilt that bordered on self-revulsion each time I journeyed to Brooklyn.

Time passed. My agony began to wear thin as my rage dissolved.
Then I learned about my father's role in the whole business. Today I
have to admit that he was probably a wise judge of baseball talent.
He must have known that I would never be able to hit the big-league
curve ball, a fact that I was already subliminally aware of but refused
to admit.

But at last I was freed from the bondage of my misplaced suspi-
cions. I was sure now that the Giants didn't want me because my old
man had engineered it; they themselves had not failed to appreciate
my talents. I thus felt free to return to the Giants.

And so I did. After a hiatus of almost ten weeks, I found myself
back in my regular seat in the upper deck of the Polo Grounds,
halfway between third base and home plate. I preferred sitting on the
visitors' side of the stadium so that I could see into the Giants' dugout and get a clear view of the bench action, which in those days was
often more exciting than the action on the field.

The date of my return was August 12, 1951, a Sunday. It was Wes
Westrum Day, with the good burghers of Poughkeepsie, New York,
honoring the Giant catcher, their fellow townsman, with a new Mer-
cury. And it was the day after another Giant defeat had dropped them
13½ games behind the league-leading Dodgers. The loss, to the
previous year's champion Philadelphia Phillies, had stripped even the
Giants' most fanatical advocates of the illusion that the Polo
Grounders had any chance of gaining the pennant.

Since the Giants obviously were not going anywhere, I wasn't expecting much as I watched them take batting and fielding practice.
Although it was Wes Westrum Day, I chose that afternoon to end my
boycott because it was a doubleheader and I wanted to have plenty of
time for my first look at the rookie who had been called up from (of
all places) Minneapolis and who was creating a sensation among
Giant fans during my self-imposed exile.

As I watched fielding practice, I quickly discovered why, even
without my father's intervention, the Giants weren't especially interested in recruiting centerfielders the day I had my tryout. There on the

broad lawn of the outfield crouched Willie Mays. Although he was just beginning to show his fabled power at the plate, center field was already his playground. He glided smoothly across acres of emerald grass to convert towering, far-reaching drives into routine outs and make impossible catches with the graceful economy of a panther. The Giants would not be needing another centerfielder for years to come.

That Sunday was a suffocatingly humid day—a typical August afternoon in New York. After I left the stadium and threaded my way through the sweating crowd to the clubhouse exit for a close-up look at Mays, I was struck by the odd fact that the Giants had won both ends of the doubleheader. Surely a fluke, I thought. A perfect example of how a team that has lost all hope feels no pressure, relaxes and loosens up and is thereby able to play decent baseball. Sal Maglie and Al Corwin, a rookie new to the Giants, had both pitched well, and the fielding had sparkled for a change. But the Jints, as the tabloids called them (the nickname seemed to symbolize the Giants' abbreviated talents when they were doing badly), were still swinging bats with holes in them, as they had all season. That they were able to put together back-to-back wins in honor of my return to the fold was a pleasant prospect to savor on the long trip back to New Jersey. But at that moment I was interested only in getting a closer look at this kid Mays.

The Giants, for whom many springtime prognosticators had predicted a banner, even pennant season, had started the year with a whimper. Losing twelve of their first fourteen games, playing like men with their hands tied behind their backs, they were quickly given up for lost. The sports-page pundits turned their attention elsewhere. Giant fans, conditioned by years of false expectations and shattered hopes, and now finally at the peak of disgust with their hapless heroes, did likewise. By the third week of the season $45,000 worth of season tickets had been cashed in—enough money to pay the salaries of the starting outfield.

Throughout May the Giants languished deep in the second division while their abhorred rivals, the Brooklyn Dodgers, sprinted away from the rest of the league.

This was a surprise to no one. With three pennants in the last five years under their belt, the Bums appeared to be on their way to wrapping up the fastest pennant in history. Gil Hodges, Jackie Robinson, Roy Campanella, Carl Furillo, Duke Snider, and later, Andy Pafko supplied them with a collective arsenal of almost atomic power in the Shaker box that was Ebbets Field. Pee Wee Reese and Billy Cox, along with Robinson and Hodges, provided incomparable slickness afield, and pitchers like Preacher Roe, Don Newcombe, Ralph Branca, Carl Erskine, and Clem Labine made them seem virtually invincible.

With the Giants so far behind then, and given no chance of overtaking the Dodgers—or even making the National League race look interesting—there appeared that dripping August Sunday, as in a masterfully plotted whodunit, the first foreshadowing of the events that would culminate in the most breathtaking climax to any baseball season in history. It would be a climax so incredible that Arthur Daley, the sports columnist for the New York *Times,* would write, "A demented Hollywood script writer in the last throes of delirium tremens would not have dared pen anything so completely fantastic as the way this dizziest of pennant races has finished."

Baseball, though a game of infinite possibilities, operates within a narrow framework of percentages and probabilities. And no one thought that the law of baseball probability permitted the possibility of a team coming from 13½ games behind, with only 44 games left to play, to win the pennant. Such a feat had never been achieved. Indeed, there had been nothing close to it in the eighty-year history of major-league baseball. And the way the Giants had been playing all summer, no same man would have tolerated the suggestion that *they* were capable of doing it.

2

Omens and Portents

Salvatore Anthony Maglie glared in at Edward Stephen Waitkus and toyed with the idea of putting his next pitch in the Philadelphia first baseman's ribs. It was midafternoon of the Sunday that marked the end of my self-imposed exile from the Polo Grounds, and the heat and humidity rising through the day had finally coagulated into a steamy atmospheric glue.

I remember wondering what Maglie was thinking about as he stood there on the mound, still as a statue, glowering at Waitkus. The heat was enough to put any man in a bad mood. Maglie, a man whose mood seemed perpetually bad, peered in malevolently at Waitkus.

It was the ninth inning of the first game of the Giants' doubleheader with the Phils. The visitors had shut out the Polo Grounders the day before, dropping them 13½ games behind the Dodgers. The Phillies themselves were now only a game and a half behind the Giants and were lusting after second-place money. They had jumped on Maglie for two runs in the first three innings of this game, with a Waitkus home run doing most of the damage. The Giants had come back with three runs in the last of the third on a Monte Irvin home run and had held their 3 to 2 lead into the ninth. But Waitkus had touched Maglie for two more hits in the interim. Now, with two Phils out in the top of the ninth and Waitkus at the plate, Maglie was fulminating to himself. He had gone to no balls and two strikes on Waitkus and, one out from wrapping up the game, now considered "hitting the bastard."

"There was no love lost between Waitkus and me," Maglie recalls. "Yeah, I remember it. He was a left-handed hitter. He wasn't having too good a year that year, but he was hittin' me pretty good."

Waitkus was a solid batsman—usually up near .300. He was a low-ball hitter. Maglie was a low-ball pitcher. "He *always* hit me pretty good," Maglie says today. "But he was a loudmouth, you know. He always liked to let everybody know about it."

Maglie riveted his glare on Waitkus for the longest time. There were about 17,000 fans in the Polo Grounds that day—mostly there to honor Westrum—and some of them began to pick up vibrations from the tableau. "Hit him, Sal baby, stick it in his ear!" shouted a rotund, shirtless character a few rows away from me. "Knock the fuckin' bastard down!" came another voice through the dense, steamy air.

Down on the mound Maglie let a sinister smile slowly curl his mouth—a mouth that was usually set in a permanent scowl beneath his long curving hawklike nose and dark baleful eyes. When Maglie smiled at you it gave you an eerie feeling, like an undertaker silently estimating your coffin measurements.

Waitkus, as contentious a man as the Giants' pitcher, suddenly felt a stab of pain knife through the scar tissue in his abdomen. The scar tissue was the residue of a bullet wound he had suffered two years before at the hand of an unrequited lover, a crazed girl who had knocked on his hotel-room door with a gun in her purse. The pain always came back whenever Waitkus sensed that something bad was about to happen to him. As Maglie finally set himself to start his wind-up, the smile still curling his lips, Waitkus suddenly jumped out of the batter's box. The plate umpire held up his hands and called time.

Waitkus turned his back to Maglie, bent over, and rubbed some dirt on his fingers. Maglie continued to glower at his back while Westrum, the Giants' catcher, scanned the area in front of the plate for pebbles. When Waitkus stepped back in and hefted his bat, he found Maglie's hooded glare still riveted on him.

Maglie was well known around the league as a pitcher who would throw at a hitter without qualm, and he knew he had Waitkus thinking now. To embellish the psych-job, he did an elaborate bit of business shaking off his catcher's signs, then flashed a dummy sign back at Westrum that was supposed to make Waitkus think some special kind of pitch was coming up. Westrum did his bit by calling out to Maglie, "Aw c'mon, Sal, let's get this game over with."

"Go ahead, you fuckin' wop!" Waitkus shouted at Maglie. He waved his bat toward the mound. "Go ahead, I'm ready for it!"

Maglie said nothing, just widened his smile a millimeter as Waitkus made a show of digging in at the plate.

"C'mon, Sal," rasped the impatient voice of Manager Leo Durocher from the Giants' dugout. "It's gettin' late."

Maglie ignored Durocher and tightened his scowl. Then, as he started into his wind-up, Waitkus again backed out of the box.

The umpire was growing impatient, too. "Play ball," he said to Waitkus.

"He's the one's takin' all the fuckin' time," Waitkus protested.

"Play ball!" came the stern rejoinder.

Waitkus moved defiantly back into the box. "By now I decided not to hit him," Maglie remembers. "I figured I had him good and worked up and he'll be lookin' for the ball to be coming straight at his head. He'd be duckin' out of there soon's the ball left my hand. Besides, if I hit him it puts the tying run on base. So I give a fast ball on the outside corner, figuring to get him on a called strike and that would be the game."

Maglie chuckles, almost a hint of admiration in his deep, dry voice. "Be damned if the son of a bitch didn't hang in there and pole the pitch down the right-field line into the upper deck. Lucky for me it was a few feet foul. Had to hand it to him, though. Maybe once you've been shot in the gut you're not afraid of anything. I understand he gave me the finger comin' back to get his bat, but I wasn't lookin' at him. Got him out on the next pitch. We won the ball game."

Maglie, the ace of the Giants' staff, was pitching for himself that day. With the Giants' pennant hopes seemingly out of the question, he was out there with only one thing in mind—next year's salary. He had been banned from organized baseball for five years for having jumped to the Mexican League in 1946, a move which was considered akin to high treason. When he was finally readmitted to baseball in 1950 it was like starting all over again, at least financially. He came back at practically the salary of a rookie. An outstanding year in 1950 resulted in a modest raise for 1951, but he was still far behind most other pitchers in the league—few of whom had his record or skills.

His win over Philadelphia in the first game of that Sunday's twin bill left him with a won-lost record of sixteen and four and further strengthened his bargaining position for the 1952 season. The last thing he was thinking about was the prospect of pitching in the World Series, and he certainly had no inkling that his win that day was the beginning of something.

The year 1951 was not a pivotal year in the relentless and colorful course of American history. Yet looking back through the smudged lens of time, one cannot help but tremble slightly with a sense of *déjà vu.*

The major headline stories in the early part of the year revolved about our involvement in the Korean War. Harry Truman was our president that year, himself the beneficiary of a minor miracle three years earlier when his contender for the Oval Office, Thomas Dewey, managed to snap defeat from the jaws of victory in an election in which not even the most reckless of gamblers would take odds on the doughty, "give 'em hell" man from Missouri. But now Truman's popularity was at an all-time low. And when a week before the beginning of the 1951 baseball season he crankily stripped General Douglas MacArthur of his supreme (some said divine) command in the Far East, there was talk of impeachment.

As summer faded into autumn a voice in the U.S. Congress—a voice which in three years would become the catalyst for one of the nation's most shameful periods—was making itself heard loudly for the first time. Joseph McCarthy, freshman Senator from Wisconsin, announced one afternoon in Washington that he held in his hand a document. . . .

And in Cincinnati, Ohio, in a rush of patriotic fervor, that city's major-league baseball team was seriously considering a change in its nickname. The Cincinnati papers ran a contest inviting all fans to submit their choices for a new name—one that would be exciting, dynamic, hopefully mellifluous, yet would preserve the flavor and image of the Cincinnati team. The winning name was the Barons, a moniker that was understandable in view of the fact that Cincinnati was predominantly German in heritage. The new name failed to catch on however, and to this day the Cincinnati team has remained the Reds.

For fans of the New York Giants the depression that stemmed from living in America that spring was deepened by the performance of their team. Leo Durocher had confidently, loudly, repeatedly predicted a pennant before the beginning of the season. He finally had his kind of team, he asserted to reporter after reporter during spring training, and the Giants, under his crafty and inspired leadership, were going to go all the way in 1951.

Not that his optimism was without any justification. The Giants had finished fast the year before and almost sneaked in to steal the flag while the Phillies and Dodgers were quarreling over it during the last weeks of the 1950 season.

In April 1951 more than a few sportswriters wholeheartedly agreed with his estimate of the Giants' chances. Arthur Daley, the day before the 1951 season officially started, wrote in the *Times:*

> For the first time since their last pennant-winning days in '36 and '37, the Giants toe the mark a definite pennant contender. Durocher, in the face of severe criticism from all sides, does seem to have achieved the objective he had in mind when he dismantled the power-laden but otherwise inept array that for so long failed to bring a pennant to the Polo Grounds. In its place he has developed a talented, fine-spirited group of players. The Polo Grounders do look primed for a quick getaway this spring.

Durocher had been eating his words from the very start of the season, and by the time Sal Maglie won over Philadelphia that August 12 he was even having trouble getting up the courage to show his face around Toots Shor's. With his club 13½ games behind the

Dodgers—15 behind in the loss column—he was able to read nothing into Maglie's victory that sweltering Sunday afternoon except to note that it had staved off the Phils' rush and enabled the Giants to maintain their grip, however tenuous, on second place.

The Giants went on to win the second game 2 to 1 behind the pitching of Al Corwin, who had been promoted from their Ottawa farm club only a few weeks before. Durocher recalls seeing nothing significant about this victory either, except that he was a bit surprised over Corwin's pitching.

The twenty-four-year-old rookie had spent an undistinguished year in Ottawa and an even less distinctive season the year before in Jacksonville, where he lost 18 games and compiled a 4.57 earned run average. The right-hander was not a very promising prospect, but the Giants had called him up anyway—mainly on a Durocher hunch. In his first outing two weeks earlier he lost the tail end of a double-header in Pittsburgh, giving up five runs. Durocher was feeling a bit better about having brought Corwin up after the rookie followed Maglie's first-game win over the Phils with an even tighter win of his own. The twin victories kept the Phils off the Giants' neck, at least temporarily.

Don Mueller, the Giants' rightfielder, today says he went home that night and made plans over the phone with his brother in St. Louis to embark on a hunting trip the day after the regular season ended. He had no desire to hang around New York to watch the Dodgers in the World Series.

Leftfielder Monte Irvin wasn't going to stick around for the World Series either, and that day's double win over Philadelphia gave him no cause to reconsider his postseason plans. "I'd been watching the Dodgers beat the crap out of us all year. I sure as hell didn't feel like seeing any more of them. That night, after we beat the Phils two, I remember I got home and discussed with my wife about going to California. She'd never seen the coast, and I'd promised in July to take her soon's the season was over. We had reservations for San Francisco October 2."

Bill Rigney, the Giants' busy utility infielder and probably the most knowledgeable baseball "thinker" of all the players on the club, was another who experienced no portents that Sunday. Hating the stale, sweltering air of New York, he was already thinking of an October of clean, sunny skies in his native California.

Alvin Dark, Eddie Stanky, Whitey Lockman, Larry Jansen, Maglie, Mays, Dave Koslo, George Spencer—none of the Giants' regulars had any notion that their twin victories presaged anything significant. Not even Bobby Thomson, the man who would become the penultimate hero of the miracle. Only Wes Westrum recalls the day with crystal clarity. And that's because it was Wes Westrum Day.

"I'll never forget that afternoon. It was my big day, and a whole lot of people came down from Poughkeepsie to honor me. They gave me a new car and lots of other stuff. And then I rewarded them all by striking out five times."

Not even I, the most determined of all prophecy-mongers amongst Giant followers, read any significance into that signal Sunday. I recall the long journey home that evening and remember that I felt happy for the Giants and happy for myself. I was back in the fold, the team had won two, and all was right with the world. Even the bitterness of my fractured dream was abating.

But then, waiting late that night for sleep to come, I found myself reflecting on something I had overheard coming down on the subway from the Polo Grounds. "You know," a man standing near me had said to another, "the way the Giants played today, they're gonna catch the Dodgers."

The other man scoffed. I wanted to leap up, grab the first fellow by the lapels, and shake some sense into him—warn him against these delusions of grandeur, the number-one disease of Giant fans. Not only did it attack the senses of otherwise sensible men, it was also highly contagious.

During the rest of the trip home I put the thought—one that at that point would not have crossed my mind unassisted, even in my wildest dreams for the Giants—out of my head. But as I lay drifting off to sleep that night it crept back with the insistence of a mosquito's buzz. What if . . . ? I began to wonder as I slipped into the presleep netherworld. What if . . . ? It was only 12½ games.

All that night and into the morning, I dreamed it.

3

"These Guys Who Grabbed Our Hearts . . ."

BOBBY THOMSON WAS BORN Robert Brown Thomson in the city of Glasgow on October 25, 1923. He came to this country at the age of two and grew up in Staten Island. His father's passion for cricket found no outlet on the playing fields of Staten Island, so young Bobby took up its nearest cousin, baseball. When he entered high school he discovered he had a talent for that most difficult of arts— making square contact with a cylindrical bat against a round ball.

Not that the young Scotsman was a natural hitter. He wasn't, but he worked diligently throughout his days as a high-school ballplayer and put together a respectable enough reputation to interest several major-league teams, the Giants and Dodgers among them. Being a Giant fan, he signed with the Polo Grounders in 1942 and had an unspectacular year in their farm system before the war intervened. Four years later, with a stint in the Army Air Corps in California behind him, and the Giants starving for talent, he found himself at spring training with the mother team in Florida. A year later he was the Giants' regular centerfielder.

The physical trait one remembers most about him from those days was his loping gait. He ran on his toes, his whole torso tipped slightly forward, and although he was able to cover a fair amount of ground in a given amount of time he never gave the impression of straining. He modeled his style on that of Joe DiMaggio. Despite the fact that he never quite possessed the Yankee Clipper's skills, he was held in great esteem by Giant fans.

Bobby Thomson was a shy, diffident, almost phlegmatic young man. As a baseball player he was steady, fairly consistent, but unexciting—in personality and character the personification of the Giant team as a whole. Though more interesting to watch than, say, Don Mueller or Whitey Lockman, he was less exciting than Eddie Stanky, Monte Irvin, or Willie Mays. He was the one player on the team capable of an occasional spectacular play between days and often weeks of routine, journeyman work. That he should have been responsible for the most breathtaking moment in sports is fitting. For Thomson was the quintessential New York Giant.

When Thomson came up from Jersey City to join the parent team late in 1946, Mel Ott was the Giants' manager. In those days the Polo Grounders were the lumberjacks of the league—big men, power hitters but slow afoot. They could hit home runs by the gross, but they couldn't, in spite of all their power, win pennants. The team was the projection of the personality and philosophy of its manager, Ott, who in his career had hit more home runs than any other left-handed hitter in the National League.

In 1948 Leo Durocher, fired in midseason by the Dodgers after a stormy career at Ebbets Field, was immediately hired by the Giants to replace Ott. It was the managerial coup of the decade, and the garrulous, bellicose Durocher, known in the press as the Lip, quickly made his presence felt in the clubhouse of his once-hated rivals. His first declaration to reporters, after excoriating the Dodger management, was to announce his intention to remold the Giants in his own image. That meant a scrappy, fighting baseball team—the kind the Polo Grounds hadn't seen since the days of John McGraw.

Durocher moved fast. First he got rid of Johnny Mize, the behemoth first baseman who had hit 51 home runs in 1947 and 40 in 1948. Then he dumped another Giant favorite, heavy-hitting Walker Cooper, the catcher. And then, at the end of the 1949 season, he sent three more Giant regulars—third baseman Sid Gordon, outfielder Willard Marshall, and shortstop Buddy Kerr—to the Boston Braves in exchange for Alvin Dark and Eddie Stanky, shortstop and second baseman respectively. Giant fans were stunned. "Dark and Stanky are my kind of ballplayers," Durocher rasped in defense of the trade, perhaps thinking wistfully of Jackie Robinson and Pee Wee Reese, the scrappers he had left behind in Brooklyn.

The wholesale housecleaning didn't seem to help, and Durocher's 1948 promise to turn the Giants into overnight winners appeared particularly empty at the end of the 1950 season, when the club finished third despite the presence of Dark and Stanky.

In the beginning Durocher had wanted to get rid of Thomson too, for the diffident Scotsman symbolized the old Giants. Besides which, the cantankerous manager didn't like him. Thomson was the kind of fellow who never let you know what he was thinking, and that was anathema to an ebullient spirit like Durocher. But the Giants were unable to make a deal for Thomson, so he stayed—and remained always, in the mind of Leo Durocher, on probation. Thomson was the first man Durocher would bench at the hint of a slump, and he was always the last to go back into the line-up. While other players would be sat down for a day or two's rest, Thomson would sit for weeks while Durocher plugged up center field with everyone but the batboy.

But Thomson persevered, and when the 1951 season started he was again in center field. Not for long, however. Durocher, the Patton *cum* Clausewitz of the baseball world, the supreme tactician and ruthless shuffler of personnel, still was not satisfied with the Scotsman as his centerfielder. With the laconic Don Mueller in right and the bland Whitey Lockman in left, the Giants' outfield seemed like a trio of morticians.

Durocher remembered his Brooklyn aggregation—the hot-tempered Carl Furillo, the explosive Duke Snider, the antic Gene Hermanski. So, as the Giants blundered their way through the opening month of the season, the manager made a move. To begin, he switched Lockman to first base and sent Monte Irvin, a natural outfielder, back to left field. Then he called up the hot-hitting Willie Mays from Minneapolis and installed him permanently in center field in place of Bobby Thomson. Later, to replace the troubled, slumping Henry Thompson at third base, he brought Bobby Thomson off the bench.

These moves turned out to be strokes of managerial genius. And although he didn't realize it at the time, the switch to third base was to be Thomson's salvation and his ladder to immortality. The New York *Times,* in reporting the Giants' loss to Philadelphia the day before they won their August 12 doubleheader, noted that "Bobby Thomson's hitting has picked up tremendously since he took over third base. He has been banging the ball at a .300 clip over the span of the last three weeks, which is in contrast to his feeble .200 average during the first half of the season. His home run production is mounting as well, and he is playing like a new Thomson." It was yet another foreshadowing of what was to come.

When Willie Mays was sixteen years old his dreams were, perforce, considerably more modest than mine at the same age. He grew up in the slums of Fairfield, Alabama, near Birmingham. By the time he was sixteen he was whiling away the hot Alabama afternoons on the streets and sandlots of the ghetto. A black youngster brought up in the epicenter of "know-your-own-placeness," Mays was just another cipher in the vast Negro populace of the Birmingham area. He was thinking about looking for a job as a presser in a cleaning shop— the trade he had learned at Fairfield Industrial High School.

But this timid, idle kid with the Aunt Jemima manner had another talent—he could play baseball. Soon he was signed by the Birmingham Barons—one of the dozens of all-black baseball teams that existed in another world throughout the South. They put the wide-eyed Mays in center field, and within a year the 18-year-old was tearing up the Negro National League.

During Mays' second season with the Barons, the New York Giants were scouring the South for Negro talent. The Dodgers had broken the ban on black players in organized baseball four years earlier by grabbing off Jackie Robinson and sending him to Montreal for grooming before bringing him up to Brooklyn. The Giants' management, mindful of the fact that their home park stood on one of the main thoroughfares of Harlem, and painfully aware that the Brooklyn coup had helped knock their already sagging attendance figures for a further loop, saw the light. By 1948 the Giants had started scouting black players throughout the South.

In 1950 a report came in from Giant scout Eddie Montague in Birmingham. It was a rave report and the name on it read Willie Mays. Owner Horace Stoneham tried the name out in his mind. Willie Mays . . . Willie Mays. Sounds like a shoeshine boy over at the Biltmore. Could a kid with a name like Willie Mays ever make it to the Polo Grounds? Stoneham didn't know it, but this black boy he had never seen would keep him in freshly shined shoes for many years to come.

Mays played parts of two seasons in the Giant farm system, first at Trenton, then at Minneapolis. The Giants wanted to keep him down for a year or two more—by now they already had four black players on their roster. Although attendance was up—even in those terrible days of 1951—they didn't want to overdo a good thing. But there was Mays sitting in Minneapolis with a phenomenal batting average of .477 through April and May of the American Association's season, and here were the Giants with a disastrous 6-won and 20-lost start to what was supposed to be the season they would win it all under Durocher.

Durocher had had his problems with blacks. Indeed, it was falsely rumored that he was fired by the Dodgers because he had cursed out Branch Rickey for the Robinson caper and swore to him that he would never work for the Dodgers as long as there was a Negro on the team. Robinson came up to the Dodgers in 1947. Durocher got his walking papers in 1948.

Durocher's attitude toward blacks was no secret during his years as a player and early reign as Dodger manager. Perhaps his switch to the Giants mellowed him. He was always a man to know on which side his bread was buttered, and he was not one to let opportunity go unanswered when it knocked. In Monte Irvin and Henry Thompson, the two talented black players the Giants had promoted earlier as a hasty counterpunch to Jackie Robinson and Roy Campanella, he knew he had a good thing. And though he never got close to Irvin and Thompson he played them. And strangest of all, he sang their praises.

The Giants, having stumbled and fallen down at the start of the season, were crawling across the month of May on their knees. No one but Alvin Dark was hitting, and the pitching staff was unable to subsist during the offensive drought. Durocher looked at his outfield day after day and could see nothing but a combined batting average of .203 and a total of 16 runs batted in, a level of performance that wouldn't qualify the Giants for contention in a Class D League. The reports coming in from Minneapolis about Mays were getting better each day. Durocher could stand it no longer. "Get me Mays!" he finally demanded of Horace Stoneham. "No, we've got too many already," came the reply. "Get me Mays," Durocher countered, "or I quit!" Mays was called up on Thursday, May 24. He was given the number 24.

The American South used to be to baseball what Australia was to tennis. Professional baseball rosters were perennially filled with more players from below the Mason-Dixon line than from all the other regions of the country combined. If you stood around the clubhouse of any major-league baseball team the great majority of accents you heard would be from the near or far South.

The most obvious explanation for this was the climate, which for most of the year was clement, allowing youngsters that much more time to hone the various skills required by the game. Another had to do with cultural and economic factors peculiar to the South. The heavy concentration of lower economic classes, both white and black, created a greater pool of potential talent from which baseball rosters could be filled than any other single region of the country. Furthermore, baseball, an anachronistic game based on out-of-date verities, found its principal source of attraction in the one part of the nation where anachronistic attitudes and values still broadly prevailed.

Willie Mays was from the South, but he was never thought of as a Southerner. He was, in the beginning, a Negro. And because he had a face and demeanor that Americans have been able to cherish as the last of the unaffectedly accommodating black ones, he was always a "credit to his race." Later, he became a "black man." But never was he considered a Southerner.

Eddie Stanky was born in Philadelphia but had settled in Mobile, Alabama. Because he was from Mobile and was white, he was considered a true Southerner. Stanky, who had come to the Giants with Alvin Dark from the Boston Braves the year before, was a little man with a little man's personality. He made up in pugnaciousness and bellicosity what he lacked in skill. His name was more than just a name, it was a description of the man himself. When they made Leo Durocher, it was as if they didn't throw away the mold until Stanky was born. Stanky could have been Durocher's son, except that Durocher was from Massachusetts and Stanky from Alabama. Though they spoke with different accents, their behavioral responses to any given stimulus were almost identical.

Stanky had bitten, ripped, and clawed his way into the major leagues in 1943 at the age of twenty-six. His promotion from the minors to the Chicago Cubs was largely brought about by the dearth of baseball talent during the war. Having gained such fortuitous entree into the big time, from then on it was purely a matter of survival for Stanky, who quickly became known as the Brat.

He was traded to Brooklyn in 1944 and played three seasons under Durocher. Then, when the Dodgers decided to make Jackie Robinson their second baseman, he was sent to the Boston Braves. There he joined with rookie Alvin Dark to help lead the Braves to a pennant in 1948. When Durocher came to the Giants that same year, he vowed to get Stanky back. By 1950 he did.

Stanky was the man who would "spike my mother if it meant being safe on a close play." The newspapers had settled on the word "scrappy," as in "scrappy little second baseman," but this was nothing more than a journalistic euphemism. Stanky was scrappy the way Adolph Hitler was anti-Semitic—the adjectives don't even begin to tell the story.

Eddie Stanky was among the most unpopular players in baseball in the late forties and early fifties. On the field he was cruel and surly—unswerving in his pursuit of nastiness. Yet in spite of his sparse skills, and in spite of his temperament—or perhaps because of it—he was a hell of a baseball player. He was a man who could find more ways to beat you than four bribed umpires.

Stanky was a good-looking man. At thirty-two, he had a benevolent—almost altar boy's—cast to his face. His features were smooth and deceptively bland. All except his eyes, which were cold, blue, and ever agleam with hidden demons.

His most notable offensive skill was getting on base, more usually by walking than by means of his bat, although he hit .300 in 1950. He was the Giants' leadoff hitter and would drive pitchers loony with frustration. He would wangle walks the way a con man bilks a rich widow. He led the Giants in runs scored in 1950, courtesy of the batters who hit behind him—especially courtesy of his partner at shortstop and follow-up batter, Alvin Dark.

Dark was also a Southerner, a handsome, odd-bodied gentleman with Indian features. He came out of Comanche, Oklahoma, where he was born in 1923, to become a three-sport star at Louisiana State University—captain and quarterback of the football team, captain and high-scoring forward of the basketball team, captain and star shortstop of the baseball team. It seemed that Al Dark would be forever known as Captain, for that's what he became with the Giants—their official field captain.

Dark had another nickname. Perhaps because he swung a black bat, or because he was dark-complected and had coal black hair, he was known around the league as Blackie. But I've heard it mentioned that the tag was originally put on him by Jackie Robinson during a bench-jockeying session in 1949 when the Dodgers were playing the Braves—in tribute to Dark's early and well-known animadversions against the Negro players who were popping up on rosters throughout the league. Tragically, Dark's racism would almost be his ruin later in his career when he began to manage.

At five feet eleven and 185 pounds the 28-year-old Dark, with his wide-waisted, high-hipped, short-torsoed physique, was more like an outfielder. Yet he was a shortstop. Not a great one, but one who got the job done with a minimum of fuss.

As a hitter he was the same way. The hit-and-run play was his specialty, and few right-handed batters in baseball were more adept at maneuvering a pitch into right field behind the base runner. With the wily Stanky as leadoff batter and Dark following him, the Giants would often open a game with runners on first and third before anyone was out. This combination was the key to Leo Durocher's batting-order strategy; it was up to the following batters to deliver them home.

Stanky and Dark did their job consistently all year. But in the early part of the season they were stranded by the futile efforts of the hitters behind them.

Don Mueller, the Giant rightfielder, followed Dark in the order, and it was around him that both the initial failures and the final success of the Giants revolved during 1951. For the first three months of the season Mueller was not hitting anywhere near his potential, and because of this the Giants had a great deal of trouble winning. That the other middle-of-the-order hitters were also struggling was not insignificant, but Mueller's role in the batting order that Durocher had so carefully crafted was especially crucial.

Mueller was 24 and a native of St. Louis. He was a left-handed hitter who became the Giants' regular rightfielder in 1950 after proving his ability to stroke singles through gaps in the infield with the precision and consistency of a diamond cutter. His job in the batting order was to get Stanky home and Dark around to third so that, theoretically, the Giants would still have two men on with none out, a run in the bargain, and their big guns coming to the plate.

On paper, Durocher's 1951 batting-order theories looked like a dream. There was only one thing wrong: Mueller, who was supposed to be the first-run-producing transition between the get-on-base men, Stanky and Dark, and the sluggers who followed him, found his well dry during the early part of the season. Usually a .300-plus hitter, by June 1 he was floundering at an anemic .185. Durocher, at his wits' end over the collapse of the logic of his batting-order theories, was forced at first to drop Mueller down to seventh in the order—a virtual trip to Siberia for a man who quietly prided himself on his hitting consistency—and then to bench him. It was not until August 2 that the man the newspapers called Mandrake, but who was known among his teammates as Mule, was able to lift his average over .200. He had started hitting those soft, artful bounders and liners again as a pinch hitter. When Durocher noticed that they were dropping in, he returned Mueller to the line-up. Shortly after that, the Giants went on their incredible tear.

Mueller, like Thomson, came up through the Giants' system in the mid-forties, but until Durocher took over the team no one connected with the organization would have given much for his prospects of making it to the Polo Grounds. Although he was calm and collected in the Giant tradition (one often wonders if these personality traits weren't the single most important criterion the Giants used in signing young prospects in the forties), he was not an Ottian power hitter and was therefore thought to have little chance of making a team that so assiduously sought to pack its roster with muscle—owner Horace Stoneham's notion of the key to selling tickets. Yet Mueller put together a string of seasons in the minor leagues in which he hit in the high .300s. So he had earned his ticket to the Polo Grounds by the time Durocher took over from Ott.

The Giants started the 1951 season with only one genuine power hitter other than Bobby Thomson. He was a man who, because of baseball's racial barrier, had not gained entrance to the big leagues until he was 30. A superb natural athlete, the "greatest high-school athlete ever to come out of New Jersey," Monte Irvin was born in Alabama but raised in the black ghetto of what was once the fashionable suburban town of Orange, New Jersey. Blessed from the start of his life with athletic instincts, talents, and grace second to none, he carved a brilliant career in the late thirties as a high-school athlete. He was all-state in everything a boy could be all-state in. If it was possible for a black teenager to be a household word in those days, he was one in North Jersey.

Irvin was a streamlined man, slope-shouldered and thick-bodied like a boxer, yet lithe and smooth, with flattened facial features that gave him the look of a lean mahogany Buddha. He was solid enough so that when he walked his feet left imprints; but when he ran his legs were those of a gazelle. He was extremely conscious of his body—it was to him what a violin is to a Heifitz. When he moved, whether swinging at a pitch, chasing a line drive, or simply kneeling down in the on-deck circle, he did so with deliberate grace.

Irvin had been the Giants' great black hope for the two years prior to 1951, and more than any other player, with the possible exception of Maglie, he had been responsible for the improving attendance figures at the Polo Grounds the year before. Yet he never lived up to his potential. Age, bitterness over some of the attitudes toward him by less talented teammates, cynicism over his function as a Giant, and a long-standing resentment over his early exclusion from organized baseball, all served to divert him from the full expression of his excellence. Despite these distractions he was still a superb baseball player. One can only wonder how much more brilliant he would have been had he been able to play in the majors five or six years earlier.

Appointed Willie Mays' proxy older brother by Durocher, Irvin read the assignment as a mandate to become an example to Mays. Irvin was an outfielder by both instinct and desire. Most of the time, however, Durocher had him playing first base, a position Irvin hated. But when Mays made his appearance on the scene in May, Durocher became convinced that Irvin belonged back in the outfield where he could tutor the green but talented rookie.

Irvin not only accepted responsibility for Mays, he took the move as a challenge. For the first time as a Giant he had a teammate who, it appeared, was every bit as talented as he was. More than 10 years older than Mays, Irvin was suddenly confronted with the likelihood that his own skills and reputation were about to be eclipsed. He was running out of years, whereas the ebullient Mays had his entire career in front of him.

So Irvin took Willie under his wing, and when the two men were in the outfield together Mays was Eliza Doolittle to Irvin's Henry Higgins. Irvin would instruct Mays on game situations, shout out which bases the rookie should throw to, position him against each enemy hitter—to make it easy for Mays to turn what would be extra-base hits with anyone else in center field into outs.

In baseball, the great outfielder not only knows the opposition's hitters—where they're most likely to hit the ball if they get a good piece of it—he also knows his own pitchers. He knows what a certain pitcher is going to throw to a certain hitter in a given situation, and through such knowledge gains a defensive edge to which he can then apply his natural skills. Irvin was this kind of outfielder; Willie Mays, when he first came up, was not. All Mays had going for him was his glorious range and his crack-of-the-bat instincts. It has been said that during 1951, Mays' first season, center field at the Polo Grounds was covered by two people. It was Mays' body out there making all those fantastic catches and throws, but it was Monte Ir-vin's wisdom and experience that made the majority of them pos-sible.

The advent of Mays was the rejuvenation of Monte Irvin. Returned to his natural habitat in the outfield, and responding to his responsi-bility, he was no longer the aging, bitter, sullen man of the previous season. It was as if Mays' sparkling innocence was a massive am-phetamine injection to Irvin's competitive spirit. As the clean-up man in the Giants' batting order, Irvin had been hitting a feeble .216 through the first month and a half of the season. He was supposed to be Durocher's trump card—the man who would, more often than not, bring both Dark and Mueller home with booming triples and home runs and thus turn modest threats into big innings. But until Mays' arrival, the dispirited Irvin had been a distinct disappointment.

Irvin ended the season leading the league with 121 runs batted in and built up a batting average of .312 after almost two months of consistently popping out. These feats were comparable to the Giants' finish itself, and a tribute to the effect Willie Mays' presence had on him.

Suffering a broken leg the following spring, Irvin would never have quite another season like 1951. Mays would spend most of the following two years in the Army, leaving the Giant slugger to his own devices again. With Mays' return to the club in 1954 Irvin would already be, as ballplayers go, an old man. His speed and reflexes would be gone, his skills withered, and he would be reduced to playing in Willie Mays' shadow.

It has been observed, often piously since the advent of Jackie Robinson, that baseball teams are a microcosm of America because their rosters reflect the broad cross-section of ethnic and racial strains "that have made America great." The New York Giants of 1951 put the lie to that cliché. To a foreigner it might appear that the Giants, judging from the names that dominated their spring-training roster, were a German soccer team rather than an American baseball club. Stanky, Mueller, Lockman, Hartung, Bamberger, Rufer, Pavlick, Kramer, Kolwe, Gettel, Lohrke, Bowman, Hofman, Hearn, Jansen and Jorgensen. Almost one-half of the Giant team was of German extraction, an overbalance that lends credence to the theory that Horace Stoneham admired more than anything else in his ballplayers the qualities of obedience, thoroughness, and discipline, however colorless they might be. Stoneham had been trying for 15 years to resurrect the Giants in the image of the great teams of the thirties, whose brightest star was the thorough and disciplined Mel Ott. And wasn't Ott a good German name?

Had someone pointed out to Durocher, whose forebears were hot-blooded Frenchmen, that he was managing a regiment of Germans, he might have swooned on the spot. One of his Krauts, as Durocher used to call them, was the man who followed Monte Irvin in the batting order—Carroll Walter Lockman. Handsome, sleek, pale blond, a young man who could have been playing sympathetic Nazi *Oberleutnants* in Hollywood, Whitey Lockman was an outfielder by training and inclination. He was another of those desirable prospects—calm, measured, and earnest—who had come up through the Giants' farm system. Like Thomson and Mueller, he played baseball proficiently but without any particular sparkle. And like them, he was a favorite of the fans—most likely because Giant fans, fed for years on Teutonic efficiency, mistrusted excitement and flare.

The Giant batting order was not a static one during 1951. As Durocher desperately sought during the early months to breathe some life into the club's offense, he abandoned the neat theories he had developed at the beginning of the season and juggled the order without let-up until the last month. It was no small vindication, though, that with the exception of latecomer Mays' place in it, the order with which the Giants ended the season was exactly the one they started it with.

Lockman was the fifth hitter in the line-up. Durocher's logic for this was based on the fact that the 25-year-old North Carolinian was another of those consistent line-drive hitters whose average usually flirted with .300 and whose exceptional speed afoot ensured a high yearly harvest of extra-base hits. With Irvin the clean-up hitter having driven Dark and Mueller across with a double or triple, Lockman would often enough, it was thought, follow with a blow that would get Irvin around.

Lockman had been signed in 1943 at the age of 18. He was

brought up to the Giants in 1945 from their Triple A farm team in Jersey City and immediately impressed everyone by hitting .341 during the last month of the season. He was then drafted into the service for a year and suffered a leg fracture the next, but when he came back in 1948 he became a regular in the outfield and was invariably among the leaders on the club in singles and doubles. A left-handed swinger, he was a spray-hitter who had a gift for lining pitches over third base and into the left-field corner.

Despite Lockman's proven talent with a bat, he hit a meager .207 the first month of the season. With Mueller at .160, Irvin at .239, and Bobby Thomson, who followed Lockman, hovering around .200, the middle of the Giant batting order was like jello. And there was no relief to be found at the bottom of the order, traditionally the place a manager stuck his least consistent hitters.

The Polo Grounders started the season with Henry Curtis Thompson at third base and batting seventh. Thompson, one of the club's two original black players, came from Oklahoma City. He had been with the club for two years, having been signed along with Irvin while both were playing in Cuba in the winter of 1948. Thompson came to the Polo Grounds, again along with Irvin, in 1949. Playing second base, he hit a creditable .280. In 1950 he played most of the season at third base and hit an even more impressive .289, with 20 home runs.

It looked to Durocher as though he had solved his third-base problems. Unfortunately for the Giants, and even more so for Thompson, he was never able to solve his own problems. When sober, he was a solid, dependable hitter and a flashy fielder. When drunk or hung over, he was erratic at the plate and ten thumbs in the field. More often than not, he was hung over.

Thompson could have been a real success during those first years after the racial barrier came down. Born into poverty, he passed his early youth on the streets and back alleys of various cities in the Southwest. He left school in the seventh grade and spent his teens alternately pursuing the rewards of petty crime and the game of baseball. After a series of skirmishes with the law, Thompson's talents and energies were directed exclusively toward baseball by a benevolent probation officer. In 1945, at the age of 20, he was already one of the standout performers in Negro baseball.

In 1947, the year Jackie Robinson made his debut as the first black man in the majors, Thompson was signed by the St. Louis Browns of the American League. Although he hit well in the few games he appeared in that year, he couldn't handle the catcalls and racial jibes of the St. Louis fans—a city then, as now, more Southern than Northern in its attitudes. The chilly atmosphere in the previously lily-white St. Louis clubhouse was even more disturbing to the sensitive but inarticulate Thompson.

In response he drank, he cursed, he fought, and in no time he was dropped by the Browns. He was out of baseball for a year, then resurfaced in Cuba where he was discovered playing with Irvin and several other future major-league black stars. Alex Pompez, a Giant scout, recommended him to the Polo Grounders along with Irvin. The Giants were eager to get Irvin. They weren't so sure about Thompson because of the unfavorable reports they'd had on him from St. Louis. Pompez pressed the point until finally Horace Stoneham said OK, let's take a chance.

Thompson was still only 23 when he was signed, considerably younger than most of the other players coming out of Negro baseball. With his talents he should have had the brightest future. He was short but was thickly muscled through the chest, shoulders, and forearms. A left-handed hitter, he handled the bat like a lightweight sledgehammer, swooping it around with an ease and economy that were surprising in so small a man. Long before the coming of Henry Aaron, Thompson was given the nickname Hammerin' Henry. By 1951, one would have thought he had it made in the big leagues.

But he didn't. During that season, still unaccustomed to the inequities and oppressiveness of life in Harlem after a boyhood in the Southwest, he drank heavily. Twice that year the Giants sent him back to the minors, more to discipline him than to improve his playing. True, he came back to the Polo Grounds and had a couple of good years after 1951, but he never gave himself the opportunity to play up to his potential.

Nor did he lose his taste for larceny—the criminal, not baseball, variety. After the 1956 season, in which he played only sporadically,

Thompson was caught by police while participating in an armed hold-up. A series of other armed robberies were traced to him. It was off to prison for Hammerin' Henry, still only 31 years old.

By the time he got out, the Giants had moved to San Francisco. Horace Stoneham was well known for taking care of old Giant ballplayers he fancied, giving them sinecures in the organization. He especially fancied drinking men and liked to surround himself with old cronies over a couple of bottles of scotch. Henry Thompson was an ex-Giant and a drinking man. He was also black and an ex-con. He went to Stoneham, a brusque, rotund drinking man. Stoneham could sympathize with a man like Thompson. No, there was no job available in the organization. Stoneham found him employment elsewhere however, using his influence to get him on the payroll of the city of Fresno, California, where he worked with wayward youngsters. Thompson seemed to be rehabilitating himself quite nicely. Then he keeled over—from a heart attack, it was said—and died.

When Willie Mays was brought up from Minneapolis, Durocher inserted him into Thompson's seventh spot in the batting order—benching the long-slumping Mueller, putting Thompson in Mueller's place, and shuffling others around. Behind Thompson and then Mays in the line-up came the Giant catcher, Wesley Noreen Westrum, from Clearbrook, Minnesota, and Poughkeepsie, New York.

Following three years of seasoning in the Giants' farm system, Westrum first came to the Polo Grounders in 1947 at the age of 24. After two more years as a back-up catcher, he became the Giants' regular receiver in 1950 and hit 23 home runs. Westrum was a stocky, ruddy, fair-haired block of granite. He handled the tools of ignorance with a competence that was a model for other catchers. Trouble was, he couldn't hit with any regularity. Oh, he stroked a home run here and there, and would even come through in the clutch now and again, but no one realized the accidental nature of his offensive limitations better than Westrum himself.

Defensively, he was a pearl. His 1950 fielding average was .999, which means he made only one error all season—in 140 games behind the plate. In 1951 he constantly came up with broken or jammed fingers, the prime occupational hazard of catchers. He played anyway, but his already uncertain hitting suffered even more as a result. There was barely a day he could grip a bat. At the beginning of the season Durocher told him, in effect, "Look, you're my catcher. I'm not going to worry about your hitting as long as you can do the job you did last year behind the plate." So, except for a couple of short periods when Westrum's bat got hot, he hit eighth in the order.

Nevertheless Westrum was the glue that held the Giants together, and through the years he has been given more and more credit by his teammates for the club's astonishing comeback during the last few weeks of the 1951 season. He finished the year with a lowly .220 batting average, but that doesn't even begin to tell the story of his contribution. His value must be measured by his effect on the pitching staff. Although technically not in charge of the staff (pitching coach Frank Shellenback was), he took a swarm of squabbling, stumbling individualists and turned them into a tight-knit dedicated group which might have leaped en masse off the Polo Grounds' roof had he demanded it. Westrum, a tentative and not altogether self-confident man until 1951, suddenly, inexplicably, came alive with authority. He had been Durocher's pet scapegoat for several years, and whenever things got particularly bad the loud-mouthed manager would pointedly shout across the clubhouse to a reporter: "If only we had a Campanella on this club!" The fact that Durocher also publicly picked on his pitchers probably created the symbiosis that was eventually to arise between Westrum and the pitching staff.

However it happened, this melding together of empathy and purpose was, more than anything else, the key to the Giants' comeback. While Durocher was busy taking all the credit for the sudden and seemingly mysterious turnabout of the club's pitching, Westrum was quietly going about his business. He had begun to hang out with the pitchers, more as an older brother than as a buddy (although he was younger than most of them), and would spend endless hours talking about the art. Soon Jansen, Hearn, Jones, and Koslo, all of whom had faltered through the beginning months of the season, began to win. Even the spot starters—Montia Kennedy, George Spencer, and later Al Corwin—were turning in stellar performances. It was as if, instead of delivering the right pitches at the right time, the pitchers were having them reeled in by Westrum. The Giant catcher would call for a slider, put up his mitt for a target, and here it would come—a perfect slider, breaking just at the right moment and thudding into his mitt. Westrum would flash the curve sign, and the same thing would happen. Fast ball, again the same. Suddenly the pitchers were throwing like Hall-of-Famers.

The Giants set out on their remarkable comeback streak through August and September mainly by throttling their opponents' bats. Starting on August 12 and running right through to the last game of the regular season, the average number of earned runs given up by Giant pitching in 44 games was 2.26. This was in contrast to the first four months, when their average was 4.91. In the hail of statistics later rained on Giant fans by way of explaining their team's unexpected turnaround, this one was generally overlooked. In retrospect it was the vital statistic.

There was one pitcher who remained exempt from the statisticians' arithmetic. Sal Maglie, the scowling, controversial Giant ace, had started out the season as though he were a member of another team. During the early months, while the rest of the Giants were acting like beached whales, Maglie was winning—pitching shutouts and one-run victories. By the time August 12 came around, he had already compiled a 15 and 4 won-lost record. An aloof and private man, Maglie was like a time-efficiency expert hired by management to come into a factory every four days. He put things right, then departed to let things run on their own until he was called in again.

Maglie had signed with the Giants as a young pitcher in Niagara Falls, New York, shortly before the war. He worked his way through the farm system and was about to succeed to the big team when he decided in 1946 to jump to the Mexican League, which was luring American ballplayers with huge bonuses and doubled salaries.

Maglie went to Mexico and, like several others, was immediately banned from organized baseball for five years by Commissioner Harold Landis. Mexico proved to be less than Mecca, however, and when the Mexican League went bankrupt the following year, Maglie and his fellow expatriates found themselves out of work. Maglie remained out of baseball for three years. Then, late in 1949, the Supreme Court declared that the Commissioner's ban was unconstitutional, and the maverick players were unenthusiastically welcomed back to their former teams. Older now by four years, their skills rusted by inactivity, most didn't make it. But Maglie did.

Giant fans were lustily disapproving when Maglie made his first appearance in the Polo Grounds at the start of the 1950 season. But when he finished the year by winning 11 games in a row and pitching 46 consecutive scoreless innings, all resentment was forgotten—at least on the part of the fans. Maglie never forgot, though, and from that time on he toiled for the Giants with an arrogant and contemptuous disregard for the fans and the club. He did his work—most of the time magnificently—but remained wrapped in his own cocoon.

He became known as Sal the Barber in the manner that Mafia gangsters are known as Tony the Trigger or Nino the Knife. Although a sportswriter had given him the nickname as a tribute to his razor-sharp curve ball, the fans quickly converted it into a metaphor for what they saw as Maglie's inherent ruthlessness.

Maglie thrived on the myth of his meanness. He began to refrain from shaving the day before a start so that his surly countenance would be enhanced on the mound, hopefully striking even further fear and helplessness into opposing batters. The fans loved this new wrinkle, and Maglie became permanently installed in their hearts as the Giants' number-one hero.

1951 was his best season in a Giant uniform. He finished with a 23 and 6 record, though in his greatest test—the last game of the playoff, the game the Giants had to win to finally take the pennant—he would fail. Ironically, that failure would enable the miracle at Coogan's Bluff to take place.

If Maglie was a loner, Larry Jansen, the other ace of the staff, was the perfect organization man. A tall, raw-boned Oregonian, Jansen was a rear-back-and-throw pitcher whose lively fast ball complemented the crafty curves of Sal the Barber. But Jansen had no nicknames. He was a hard-throwing and fairly consistent right-hander given to neither tantrums nor sulks. He did his job and derived his satisfaction with quiet maturity.

Overshadowed by the garrulousness of Durocher and Stanky and by the dark mysteries of Irvin and Maglie, Jansen was another of those team members who seemed to have been cut from the traditional Giant mold. He had come to the club in 1947 after a brilliant season in the Triple A Pacific Coast League where, pitching for the San Francisco Seals, he won 30, lost only 6, and compiled an incredible earned run average of 1.57. He more than fulfilled his promise when he put together a 21 and 5 record in his rookie year with the Giants, and over the next three campaigns he won 52 games. He got off to a bad start at the beginning of the 1951 season however, mainly as a result of Durocher's mistreatment of his placid but proud nature. But with the help of Westrum's benevolent and sympathetic handling he quickly righted himself, forging an eventual 22 and 11 won-lost record.

The rest of the staff during those last seven weeks of the season was a projection of Westrum, and on the few occasions a breakdown occurred the Giant catcher would react as though he were personally to blame. He coaxed and cooed Jim Hearn, a handsome right-hander the Giants had picked up for a song the year before from St. Louis, and Hearn produced several key wins in the Giant drive. He barked at Dave Koslo, a previously inconsistent left-hander of uneven temperament, and Koslo responded. He was stern with Sheldon Jones, another journeyman pitcher of uncertain skills, and Jones came up with a string of vital victories. He nursed George Spencer and Al Corwin, two rookies, into temporary respectability. He calmed Montia Kennedy, a gifted but unpredictably mercurial southpaw, into giving uncharacteristically even performances.

Although not one of the obvious heroes of the Giants' miraculous finish, Wes Westrum more than anyone else among the players was the day-to-day force behind the team's resurgence. It was Westrum who was the calm, knowing mediator between the insensitive Durocher and his hypersensitive pitchers; it was Westrum who by turns scolded and cajoled all his teammates and eventually infected each of them with his confidence and belief in his dream that the

Dodgers could be caught; it was Westrum who continued to play with broken fingers, aching legs, and a perforated ulcer; it was the battered Westrum, in the end barely able to hit the ball out of the infield, who was the template upon which the miracle ultimately unfolded.

There are few among the members of the 1951 Giant team who today, once noting the extent of their own contribution, do not give a large share of the credit to Westrum. One of these is Bill Rigney, and perhaps his reasons derive from the fact that he believed, even before Westrum, even before anyone else, that the Giants could do what they did.

Not that he takes any credit for himself, for by 1951 he was hardly more than a utility infielder and occasional pinch hitter. In his eyes, the lion's share of the credit goes to Durocher.

Rigney was 32 in 1951. He had come to the Giants in 1946 from California after a five-year career in the minor leagues followed by a three-year wartime stint in the Navy. For four seasons he was, more or less, a regular infielder on the Giants, playing third base, shortstop, and second. Tall, bespectacled, graying, slender as a sparrow's leg, Rigney was a modestly accomplished baseball player. When Stanky, Dark, and the power-hitting Henry Thompson were acquired in 1949, Rigney saw the writing on the wall. Sure enough, he was relegated to utility work in 1950. But instead of sulking over the obvious end of his career as a regular, he turned his energies to rooting, encouraging, and consoling. By 1951 he was the chief cheerleader and unofficial tactician of the Giants—a role he played most of the time from the bench—and he never doubted for one moment that the Giants would win the pennant.

By 1951 Rigney was nurturing an ambition to continue in baseball as a manager; thus, he began more and more to watch Durocher.* Indeed, when he did become a manager a few years later, he modeled his style after Durocher's. With his explosive temperament and hyperactive baseball mind, he had a colorful, if only moderately suc-

---

* As it turned out, six members of that Giant team (Rigney, Westrum, Dark, Lockman, Stanky, and coach Herman Franks) went on to become major-league managers. All of them attribute much of their ambition and success to their exposure to Durocher.

cessful, managerial career. He lacked Durocher's intimidatory gifts. But he did gain a keen appreciation for the difficulties of managing and for the damned-if-you-do, damned-if-you-don't bind that every manager finds himself in. He learned that a good manager cannot make a poor ball team play well, but that a bad manager can make a superior team play poorly. He learned in short that a manager does not make a baseball team, but that a baseball team makes a manager.

4

The Lion

LEO DUROCHER WAS, and is, a bundle of contradictions. Born Leo Ernest Durocher on July 27, 1905, in West Springfield, Massachusetts, he grew up with one objective in life—to get out of West Springfield, Massachusetts, any way he could. He discovered early on that the only way one achieved this was through guile and daring. How much of these he inherited and how much he acquired on the streets and in the pool halls of his home town is a matter of conjecture, but by the time he was 20 he was playing baseball for the New York Yankees and was that club's more or less regular shortstop during its halcyon Ruthian era in the late 1920s. While with the Yankees he was awarded the nickname "Fifth Avenue" in honor of the garish clothes he wore.

From New York he went to the Cincinnati Reds in 1930, was their weak-hitting but slick-fielding shortstop for three years, and then was traded to the St. Louis Cardinals. At St. Louis he was a full-fledged member of the fabled Gashouse Gang and one year even hit .286, high in a career that was dominated by averages in the .220s.

Durocher was traded to the Brooklyn Dodgers late in 1937. The Dodgers had not won a pennant in 17 years; indeed, the very mention of their name among baseball cognoscenti was the occasion of much derisive whooping and guffawing. But the arrival of Durocher marked the dawning of a new day for Brooklyn and its beleaguered fans. Shortly thereafter Larry MacPhail was named general manager and he began at once to restructure the Dodgers. In his first move he purchased slugging first baseman Dolph Camilli from the Phillies. Then, in quick succession, he acquired pitcher Kirby Higbe from Philadelphia, purchased shortstop Pee Wee Reese from the Boston Red Sox organization, obtained outfielder Joe Medwick and pitcher Curt Davis from the Cardinals, and reclaimed an aging hurler named Whitlow Wyatt from the minors. Relief pitcher Hugh Casey was brought up from Memphis. Fat Freddie Fitzsimmons, the aging star pitcher of the Giants for 13 seasons, came over to the Dodgers and began to win again. MacPhail hired Babe Ruth as a coach in June 1938 and at the end of the season named the 33-year-old Durocher to replace Burleigh Grimes as manager of the club.

The Dodgers climbed from seventh to third in 1939. In 1940 they finished second, and in the following year they won their first pennant in 20 years. The outspoken, controversial Durocher was hailed as a genius, although the Yankees beat Brooklyn in the World Series.

There followed another five-year drought during the war years, but in 1946 Durocher's club almost made it again, losing a playoff for the pennant to St. Louis. With the addition of Jackie Robinson to the team in the spring of 1947, the Dodgers were the clear choice to go all the way—despite the dissension among many of the players over Robinson. Durocher, however, was not going to be around to guide his club to the championship. He was suspended for one year just before the start of the 1947 campaign by Commissioner A. B. "Happy" Chandler for "conduct detrimental to baseball." The suspension came about as a result of a dispute between Larry MacPhail, then with the Yankees, and his successor in Brooklyn, Branch Rickey. In a sense Durocher was the fall guy in the affair, although it was not without some pleasure that he jumped at a chance to embarrass MacPhail.

The two had developed a long-smoldering feud since the day in 1939 when MacPhail named Durocher to manage the Dodgers. MacPhail was basically a promoter—loud and raucous, but skilled. In Durocher he thought he had discovered a man after his own heart.

But as in every situation in which two egocentrics are forced to share the same limelight, camaraderie turned to scorn. By the time Mac-Phail went over to the Yankees in 1945—driven out of Brooklyn at least in part by Durocher's swifter tongue—he and the Lip were barely on speaking terms.

During the spring of 1947 the Dodgers and Yankees played a series of exhibition games in Havana—then a watering hole for Mafia types. After one game the puritanical Rickey announced that Mac-Phail, the Yankee president, had entertained two known gamblers in his box. The irony here was that Durocher had long been known as a friend of similarly colorful figures—a fact which already had some sanctimonious bigwigs in and out of baseball after his scalp. When challenged, Rickey asked Durocher to back up his statement. Durocher did. The outraged MacPhail immediately demanded a hearing before Commissioner Chandler. The impetuous Durocher thereupon shot back with some further choice descriptions of MacPhail.

There were two hearings at Sarasota, Florida. At the second one, Chandler dismissed everyone but Rickey, Arthur Mann, who was Rickey's assistant, and Walter O'Malley, another Dodger executive who would succeed Rickey as Dodger president four years later. According to Mann's account of the proceedings in his book *Baseball Confidential,* Chandler then asked Rickey, "How much would it hurt you folks to have your fellow out of baseball?"

"Happy," Mann quoted Rickey as saying, "what on earth is the matter with you?"

Chandler responded only by producing a letter from "a big man in Washington" who was advising him to kick Durocher out of baseball.

What occurred behind the scenes after that is anybody's guess. The "big man in Washington" was never identified. But Durocher was notified a few weeks later that he was officially suspended from baseball for a year. The suspension, coincident with the elevation of Jackie Robinson to the Dodgers, convinced many that it had been secretly arranged by Rickey to get Durocher out of the way so that the Dodger boss's pet project—Robinson—could go forward unhindered.

Such was not the case however. Durocher, in fact, had been working closely with Rickey to ensure the Brooklyn team's acceptance of Robinson. Many of the Dodgers were hinting at a team rebellion if Robinson was brought up. At Rickey's request, Durocher talked to each player individually during the spring, patiently pointing out the ways in which Robinson would help the team. In addition, again at the behest of Rickey, he gave interviews to the newspapers praising Robinson and insisting that the black star had every right to play in the big leagues.

Durocher had not been entirely convinced of the proposition before then. But the fact that he was receiving a good deal of favorable newspaper publicity as a consequence of his public promotion of Robinson probably did more than anything else to change his racial attitudes. A social rebel at heart, he delighted in swimming against the tide. He had so often been publicly castigated for his actions before, that to be praised and admired for taking a dangerous stand on Robinson really charged his ego. He began to enjoy the role Rickey had cast him into.

The suspension didn't surprise Durocher. But he was disillusioned with Rickey for failing to support him publicly. For his part, Rickey was disillusioned with Durocher. He had seen the evidence. He decided to keep his own counsel and became determined to remove Durocher permanently from the Dodger organization at the first opportunity.

That opportunity presented itself the following year. With Burt Shotton, an organization functionary, brought in to manage Brooklyn in Durocher's absence, the Dodgers won the 1947 pennant. Rickey was contractually obliged to give the team back to Durocher at the end of his suspension in the spring of 1948, which he did. Meanwhile he was secretly trying to peddle him.

By 1948 the New York Giants were pennant-starved and continuing to slip at the gate. They hadn't finished anywhere near first place in the past two years, and with manager Mel Ott continuing his same old ways the prospects for the future were bleak. Besides, Ott, who came from the deepest reaches of the South, was not kindly disposed to the employment of black ballplayers, although with the success of Robinson in Brooklyn the Giant management knew it was going to have to come up with something to match the Dodgers.

As the Giants got off to their usual poor start in April and May of 1948, Giant owner Stoneham began to contemplate the prospect of removing Ott. It was nothing more than contemplation however, until one day in midseason when he received a phone call from Branch Rickey.

"Now listen, Horace," the conversation is said to have started, "isn't it about time you thought about making some changes on your ball club? Judas Priest, every time you boys visit Ebbets Field our attendance drops like a lead ball."

"Well," Stoneham is supposed to have answered, "to tell the truth I've been thinking of making some changes, but you know, they're hard to find."

"Who's hard to find?"

"Negroes. Good Negro ballplayers."

"Hah!" was Rickey's rejoinder. "They're a dime a dozen. But I'm not talking about ballplayers, Horace."

"Then what?"

"Your manager. Now I know Mr. Ott has a treasured place in all your hearts, but——"

"Oh, I've been thinking about that, too," Stoneham supposedly interjected. "But who the hell am I going to find in the middle of the year? My idea is to wait until the season's over and then see who's available."

"I know a man who's available, and he's just right for your club."

"Who's that?"

"How would you like Durocher?"

"Eh?"

"Durocher," said Rickey. "How would you like to have him?"

Stoneham still wasn't sure he'd heard right. He glanced out his office window, which looked out on the Polo Grounds from behind center field. All he saw were empty seats. "You mean you're willing to let him go?"

"Do you want to make a deal?" Rickey asked.

"Well, let me think about it," said Stoneham, his mind already made up. Of course he wanted Durocher. "When would we announce it, after the World Series?"

"World Series nothing," Rickey said. "He's yours right now."

Garry Schumacher, who was then the head of promotion and publicity for the Giants, recently told me the rest of the story. "I remember Horace called me into his office to tell me Durocher was
coming over to us. It was one of the big sports stories of the year,
and I was going to have to handle the press on it. Of course, at first I
thought, hell, I've got plenty of time on this, I mean, I was thinking
Horace was talking about the end of the season. Then he tells me,
nope, Leo's coming the next day and we've got to make the announcement in the morning.

"Well, I'll tell you, it came as quite a shock, don't you know. The
Dodgers were playing out of town somewhere—I think they were in
Montreal playing an exhibition against their farm team up there—and
not even Leo knew about it yet. The first thing we did was go over to
his apartment on Park Avenue. He was living there with his wife,
Laraine Day. We went over to break the news to her. When we were
let in she was listening to the Dodger game on the radio. We told her
the news about Leo, and I'll be damned if she didn't walk over to the
radio and switch it from the Dodgers to the Giants. 'Now that we're
with the Giants,' she said, 'I only listen to Giant games.' She was a
corker, all right. Why, she became one of the Giants' biggest
boosters. I never knew a dame like her.

"Well, Leo got back to New York that night or the next morning.
By now he knew, and was really delighted. Of course, I was still
pretty upset. I hated to see Mel Ott go that way—so abruptly, you
know. Everyone loved him, he was such a fine gentleman. But the
deed was done, and my big worry now was getting the story out. A
lot of Giant fans were going to be upset, we knew. After all, they'd
been programmed for ten years to hate Durocher. It was quite a
shock."

It was true, the shock waves rolled over New York for weeks.
Giant fans were stunned. It was almost as if they preferred ineptitude
to excellence. I can recall my own mystification at the astonishing
turn of events. Even I preferred the second-division team of Mize,
Cooper, Gordon, and Marshall—placid, lead-footed sluggers all—to
the kind of team Durocher announced he intended to form. "My kind
of ball club!" he proclaimed upon assuming command. "I intend to
make the Giants winners, and I'll do it with my kind of ballplayers."

Which meant scrappy, loud, daring athletes. I wasn't sure I was ready for that. A lot of other Giant fans were equally doubtful. It was like turning a church into Minsky's.

The Giants finished the 1948 season in fifth place, 10 games behind the pennant-winning Boston Braves. Since Durocher had only taken over in July, the finish could be excused on the grounds that the Lip had not had enough time to work his magic. Curiously enough, attendance at the Polo Grounds dropped by about 150,000 from the previous year.

In 1949 the Giants again finished fifth, this time 24 games behind the winners—who else but the Brooklyn Dodgers? Some improvement! Now Durocher could have no excuses. He had mouthed, bragged, boasted, and cleaned house, and look what he gave us. Attendance sagged by another 250,000.

As the 1950 season opened, the Giants presented an almost entirely new face to the world. Gone were the mastodons of the Ott era. In their place we found Eddie Stanky, Alvin Dark, Monte Irvin, Henry Thompson, Don Mueller, and Wes Westrum. Yet Bobby Thomson and Whitey Lockman remained from the previous year. Optimism, however cautious, ran high.

Naturally, the Polo Grounders got off to their usual horrendous start. Durocher had infused the offensive line-up with new faces but had not yet solved the other problem plaguing the Giants since the thirties—their pitching. With the exception of Larry Jansen, the pitching staff was as potent as a cap pistol in hunting season. Koslo, Jones, Kennedy—all long-time Giants—and Jack Kramer were the other starters behind Jansen, with Kramer and the newly returned Sal Maglie working in relief.

Jansen was winning twice for every time he lost, and most of his defeats were complete-game, low-scoring cliff-hangers that needed only another run or two to reverse the outcome. He pitched gamely into July, almost single-handedly keeping the Giants respectable, while the rest of the staff bumbled about. With the Giants descending through sixth place on July 21, the desperate Durocher decided to give Sal Maglie a start against the St. Louis Cardinals.

Durocher had little faith in the sullen, aging right-hander from Niagara Falls, the Giant front office even less. When Maglie showed up at spring training earlier that year after being allowed back into baseball, he was no stranger to the club. Of all the major-league teams in 1946 the Giants had been hardest hit by the blandishments of multimillionaire promoter Jorge Pasquel, organizer of the Mexican League and owner of many of its teams. Several front-line players defected to Mexico along with a number of promising prospects. Horace Stoneham was convinced that Maglie had been the ringleader of the Giant defectors, and his belief was no less certain when the pitcher returned to the Giants in 1950. Stoneham had Durocher convinced as well, so Maglie was earmarked for the manager's doghouse from the very beginning. Durocher's shaky faith in the pitcher was further compromised when he gave him a starting assignment against Cincinnati early in the season—Maglie was knocked out in short order by the cream-puff Reds.

But when the Giants were midway through 1950, Durocher could no longer afford to indulge his boss's prejudices. Continuing to use Maglie to mop up lost causes, as Durocher had been doing for three months, would have been understandable if the Giants had been blessed with a top-drawer staff. But the pitching had gone from bad to worse, and Durocher's choices were now being made out of desperation.

And here is where managerial genius came into play. From the day of that Maglie outing on July 21 against St. Louis—which he won— the Giants became the hottest team in the league. They won 49 games, lost only 22, and finished in third place behind the Dodgers and Phillies, who were tied for first on the last day. So hot were they in the final month, many believed that if the season had lasted another week they would have swept past both Philadelphia and Brooklyn and taken the pennant.

Maglie was absolutely dazzling after his win over St. Louis. Made a regular starter, he won eleven straight games and compiled an overall record of 18 and 4. Almost as brilliant was Jim Hearn, a young but failed pitcher fobbed off on the Giants by St. Louis in midsummer for the paltry price of $25,000. He won eleven games and sculpted a glittering earned run average of 2.49. Jansen continued to win his two games out of every three, and even the rest of the staff began to become infected by all the excellence around them.

With the sudden turnaround of the pitching staff, the Giant hitters came alive too. Stanky, Irvin, Dark, Henry Thompson, Mueller, Lockman—all slammed the ball at well over .300 during the final two months of 1950. Only Westrum and Bobby Thomson struggled at the plate, although between them they produced a total of 48 home runs for the entire year.

Durocher could begin crowing once again. And he did—setting the stage for 1951, which, in his words, was going to be the year "the Giants take it all." The second half of the 1950 season had proved, he said repeatedly over the winter, that "I can win anywhere when I have my kind of team." He rhapsodized over all the new young talent coming from the minors to the Giants in spring training the following March and served notice on the sportswriters, "If we don't win it all next year, boys, you can have me. You can write whatever you want about me and you'll get no complaints. Because if we don't win it by at least six games, I don't fuckin' belong in baseball."

For a man who had been in baseball for as long as he had, it was an uncharacteristic challenge. It was even more so coming from a man who had made an avocation of warring with sportswriters. But then, at the age of 46, Leo Durocher—the man who was celebrated for claiming that "nice guys finish last," but who had done friends and strangers extraordinary unpublicized kindnesses—was a man of endless contradictions.

5

The Lion Roars

THE 1951 BASEBALL SEASON OPENED for the New York Giants on Tuesday, April 17, in Boston—the same day the dismissed General Douglas MacArthur, like a returning emperor, arrived in San Francisco. It was a gloriously sunny day in Northern California. Millions came out for his homecoming, and the event was a monumental triumph for the soon-to-be "old soldier." In Boston meanwhile it was cold and dreary, and only 6,000 people turned out at Braves Field to watch the home team open against the Giants. It was but a footnote to that historic day, but Larry Jansen, seemingly in mid-season form, spun a lovely five-hit shutout, and the Giants won 4 to 0. It was the last time they would be in first place for months to come.

When the Polo Grounders had convened in St. Petersburg seven weeks earlier it certainly looked as if they would fulfill Leo Durocher's off-season prophecies. Not only did they have everyone back from the previous year—that red-hot second-semester club—but they were practically drowning in ultratalented rookie prospects.

There was willowy Artie Wilson, another black man from Alabama, who had hit .312 at Triple A Oakland in 1950 and who Durocher predicted would take Eddie Stanky's job away from him.

There was Davey Williams, another second-base hopeful who had hit with power the year before at the Giants' Minneapolis farm and whose fielding was as slick as Durocher's sharkskin suits. There was Bobby Hofman, still another infielder who hit .296 at Oakland and was as accomplished afield as Williams. There was Rafael Noble, a catcher from Cuba who had hit .316 and pounded 15 home runs at Oakland. According to Durocher, he was a cinch to send Westrum back to warming up pitchers in the bullpen. And there was Billy Taylor, an outfielder who had hit an amazing .345 during a full season with the Sioux City farm team.

Things looked even brighter for the pitching staff. Rookie George Bamberger had won 17 games for the Jersey City Giants in 1950 and led the International League in strikeouts. Charlie Bishop had won 16 at Sioux City. Roger Bowman had also chalked up 16 at Jersey City. Allen Gettel, though not a rookie, had won 23 while losing only 7 the year before at Oakland. And George Spencer had 11 wins to his credit at Jersey City. With Jansen, Maglie, and Hearn set as his first three starters, all Durocher had to do was find one more starter out of these five talented newcomers and the Giants would be well nigh invincible. No one had seen Durocher so pleasant and amiable in ten previous springs.

"Leo Durocher is more confident than ever that his club will make that quick start that he's been saying is so vital to success in the 1951 flag race," wrote John Drebinger in the New York *Times* as the Giants ended the Florida phase of their spring training. As they barnstormed north, the New York writers finally became full-blooded believers and sent back dispatches all but predicting outright that the Giants would win the pennant in a breeze.

Opening day at Boston did nothing to still their enthusiasm. Jansen's exquisitely crafted shutout and the Polo Grounders' 10 base hits were like self-fulfilling prophecy. With the Dodgers losing their opener in Philadelphia, the first day of the season was, many felt, a harbinger of things to come.

There was only one element of foreboding in the Giants' defeat of the Braves. Monte Irvin, who had been installed as the Giants' regular first baseman in 1950, made two errors on plays that would be routine for an ordinary first-sacker. Irvin hated playing first. But since he was the best athlete on the Giants and Durocher had no one else who could hit, the position was his. Irvin could never learn to feel comfortable there however, and his constant anxiety about fielding the position not only pressured the proud New Jerseyan into damaging defensive lapses, it also adversely affected his hitting.

On Wednesday, April 18, MacArthur arrived in Washington to be greeted by another blizzard of confetti. In Boston, still chilly and dank, Sal Maglie collapsed in the sixth inning and the Giants lost 8 to 5. The big gun for the Braves was Walker Cooper, the very same Walker Cooper that Durocher had scorned two years earlier. One writer attributed the loss to the Law of Avenging Gods and excused Maglie's ineffectiveness by blaming it on the cold. Even the best teams lose baseball games, and early-season performances are not a true indicator of a club's quality due to the ever present vagaries of the weather. The fact was that the Giants came back to tie the game in the top of the ninth inning only to lose it in the end, averred the writer. The game should have been called on account of darkness, he claimed. But even if they had to lose, they had kept it close all the way and made 11 base hits. Not to worry.

The next day, Thursday, was Patriot's Day in Boston, and the Giants, rounding out their opening series with the Braves, split a doubleheader. Jim Hearn scattered seven hits in the first game and won 4 to 2. In the second the Giants exploded for 12 runs, paced by Monte Irvin's grand-slam home run. But shades of yesteryear—the Braves went through six Giant pitchers and won the match 13 to 12.

Jack Kramer, a journeyman hurler the Giants had picked up from the Boston Red Sox the year before, started. The Braves jumped on him for five runs in the first inning. Thereafter Durocher called on three of his bright pitching newcomers—George Spencer, George Bamberger, and Allen Gettel—all to no avail. He then brought in Montia Kennedy, one of the holdovers from the Giant team's past. He was a fireballing lefty from the Richmond, Virginia, area whom the Giants had been holding on to since 1946 in the hope that he would eventually fulfill his Feller-like potential. By now he was an old face on the Giants, one of those veteran pitchers for whom you pulled with a passion each time he made an appearance, but whom you knew was destined to fail. He had shown a few flashes of Fellerian brilliance during the Giants' strong finish the year before, but that day he reverted to his usual form, giving the Braves three runs before getting a man out.

With the Giants still ahead 12 to 11 in the last of the ninth, Durocher summoned Dave Koslo, another old face (he first came to the Giants in 1941), to preserve the lead and assure the Giants of a double victory. Koslo was somewhat of a hard-luck pitcher. A stocky left-hander from Menasha, Wisconsin, he was a good deal better than his past won-lost records would have indicated—indeed, he led the National League in earned run averages in 1949. But whenever he pitched, the Giants invariably failed to hit. They had hit plenty that day in Boston, and all Koslo had to do was get three Braves out to send the club back to New York with a 3 and 1 record. It was not to be, though. The Braves got to Koslo immediately, and before anyone else could warm up in the Giant bullpen they pushed across the tying and winning runs. The Giants were now at 2 wins and 2 losses.

Friday saw them back at the Polo Grounds for their home opener, and 30,000 souls turned out to watch them do battle with the Dodgers. The attendance might have been larger but for the fact that on the same day General MacArthur was playing to millions of New Yorkers in a ticker-tape parade up Broadway after having delivered his "Old Soldiers Never Die" speech before Congress. In the District of Columbia, meanwhile, President Truman was being roundly booed by 25,000 people at Griffith Stadium as he tossed out the first ball for the Senators' home opener with the Yankees.

It was a day of festive celebration in New York, and with MacArthur getting most of the headlines few noticed or even cared that the Giants lost to Brooklyn.

Saturday was even more festive as 46,000 people came out to see Douglas MacArthur watch the Giants and Dodgers clash in the second game of their opening series. And clash they did. MacArthur, who had not touched foot on American soil in two decades, said on his arrival in New York that one of the things he had missed during all those years in the Far East was a good old-fashioned game of baseball. Well, here he was at the Polo Grounds, his second day in New York, basking in the adulation of the crowd. The game he watched must have warmed the cockles of his warrior's heart, for it contained almost as much combat as did the Korean War.

Before Durocher moved over from Brooklyn to the Polo Grounds, Giant-Dodger games were fiercely contended but usually remained within the rules established by Abner Doubleday. After Durocher made his switch, however, the Marquis of Queensbury's rules were often as vital a factor in the two clubs' frays as those of Doubleday. Pete Reiser, the gifted Dodger centerfielder who had served under Durocher in the early forties, once said that "playing for Leo is the most fun I ever had. I never saw a man who hates to lose as much as him. Every game is like a World Series game."

The only thing Durocher hated worse than losing was losing to his former employers, the Dodgers. Whenever the two clubs met, an air of incipient gang warfare hung over the ball park. It was said that as a youth the skinny, undersized Durocher always carried a shiv inside his shirt to give him an edge in the back alleys and poolrooms of West Springfield. In his later years as a manager, the bean ball was his shiv.

Durocher teams were always known as bean-ball clubs. By 1950, whenever the Giants went up against the Dodgers, the bean ball was a part of every Giant pitcher's repertoire. Under the field management of kindly old Burt Shotten, the Dodgers had been forced to grin and bear Durocher's tactics for three years. But 1951 brought a new manager to Brooklyn—a Durocher protege named Charlie Dressen. The Dodger players were overjoyed. Cut from the same mold as Durocher, Dressen had no hesitancy in having his pitchers return the compliments in kind—as quickly became obvious during the teams' second meeting of the young season before the exalted General MacArthur.

Larry Jansen, making his second start of the season, went up against Chris Van Cuyk of the Dodgers. Jansen was one Giant pitcher who abhorred Durocher's bean-ball notions. He was a fine control pitcher who year after year led the staff in the least number of bases on balls yielded. During the previous season he had hit only one batter in 275 innings (Maglie, in contrast, hit 10 in 69 fewer innings). In addition Jansen was a gentle man. Imagine his mood, then, when in the fifth inning Durocher ordered him to throw at Dodger catcher Roy Campanella, who had homered in the second to tie the game at 3 and 3.

In Durocher's view, Jansen's only pitching weakness was his lack of meanness. Enemy batters, confident of the Oregonian's sure-fire control, would dig in at the plate without fear of being hit. The result was that Jansen gave up many more home runs than a pitcher of his quality should have. Durocher had been trying for three years to get him to instill a little fear in the hitters by occasionally brushing them back. Jansen, a man of peace and good will, had resisted.

But now he was under specific orders to throw at Campanella. His first pitch was a strike. Durocher leaped up on the steps of the Giant dugout and shouted the order aloud. Of course Campanella heard him.

Jansen's next pitch was a pretty slider that broke across the plate for a second strike. Campanella, uncertain, had taken a step back, expecting the ball at his head. Furious now, Durocher shouted at Jansen again. "It'll be a C-note if you don't!" he added.

Campanella, confused, stepped out of the box and rubbed some dirt on his hands. "He gonna throw at me or not?" he asked Wes Westrum while bent over.

"Who, Larry?" Westrum said from under his catcher's mask. "He wouldn't throw at Adolph Hitler." Reassured, Campanella moved back to the plate and took his stance.

"Remember," Durocher barked out to Jansen. "It'll cost you a C-note."

It was the first time Jansen had ever been threatened with a fine for disobeying a manager's order to throw at a hitter. He considered it for a moment, weighing his personal ethics against a shrunken paycheck. Then he grimaced to himself, wound up, and let fly.

He took something off the pitch so that Campanella would have a chance to duck. Campanella, settled in at the plate, was astonished to see the ball coming straight at his shoulder. He spun away, but could feel the ball nick his shirt sleeve.

"Ball one," umpire Augie Donatelli declared.

"Ball one!" Campanella exclaimed, whirling to face the ump. "It hit me!"

"Ball one," Donatelli said.

Campanella was fuming. He didn't know whether to go on arguing with the umpire or challenge Westrum for having set him up.

"Get back in there," Donatelli commanded.

"But it hit me, right here." Much gesturing and gesticulating.

"It didn't hit you," said Donatelli. "Get back in or you're out of the game."

Campanella, a right-handed hitter, had a full view of the Giant dugout. As he stepped back in he saw Durocher grinning at him wickedly. "Westrum," he said through gritted teeth, "you gonna pay for that."

"I didn't call it," the Giant catcher protested.

"You told me he wasn't gonna throw at me."

"I didn't think he would."

"You gonna pay, buddy boy," Campanella said as he watched Jansen's next pitch nick the outside corner for a called third strike.

Sure enough, when Westrum came to bat in the bottom of the sixth the first pitch was right at his head, with nothing taken off. He hit the dirt, then came up squabbling with Campanella, his face pushed right into the iron of the pudgy receiver's face mask. The umpire quickly separated them, then strode over to the Dodger dugout and warned Dressen about any further incidents. This brought howls of protest from the Dodger bench. In the Giant dugout, Durocher was plotting his next move.

The score remained tied at 3 and 3 going into the eighth. Campanella was the hitter again. Jansen was again under orders, this time backed up by Westrum. His first pitch sailed in at Campanella's elbow—not a bean ball, but the best the mild-mannered pitcher could manage. Campanella came off the ground shouting and cursing at Westrum. Not content with that, he shoved the Giant catcher back into Donatelli. Westrum rebounded and delivered a shove of his own that propelled Campanella halfway to the mound. Campanella clenched his fists and charged back at Westrum, who had shed his glove and was tearing off his mask, ready to escalate the hostilities. Both benches emptied. The big crowd was roaring, everyone glancing down at General MacArthur in his box next to the Giant dugout to see how he was enjoying the fracas.

When order was restored Campanella stroked a double over Whitey Lockman's head in left field and the Dodgers went on to score three runs. They got another in the ninth to wrap up a second consecutive 7 to 3 victory. As the teams jogged toward their center-field clubhouses at the end of the game, Dressen shouted gleefully at Durocher, "Keep it up, Leo, keep throwin' at us, baby." Durocher gave him the finger.

The two clubs wrapped up their first series of the season the next day, Sunday, April 22. It was Sal Maglie versus Carl Erskine, and the Giants were leading 3 to 1 into the eighth inning when the Dodgers came up with two runs to tie after Maglie and Jackie Robinson had words over a fast ball that hit Robinson in the back.

The game went into the tenth inning before the Giants lost it on a Carl Furillo home run. The Giants had now lost four straight and at the end of the first week of the season were sitting in next to last place, three games behind the front-running Dodgers. So far, no one was calling Durocher on his promissory note of a fast start. A full week later, though, the entire world of Giant fandom was ready to foreclose, for the Polo Grounders continued to lose, dropping seven more in a row.

That Wednesday evening the Giants returned to New York from Philadelphia, where they had lost three straight to the Phillies. On Thursday, with the Chinese army only eleven miles from Seoul, the Giants dropped their eighth in a row to the Braves at the Polo Grounds, 3 to 0, Sal Maglie taking his third loss against no wins. Friday saw still another defeat at the hands of the Braves as Jim Hearn faltered against Warren Spahn. On Saturday the New Yorkers traveled to Ebbets Field to start their second series of the season with the Dodgers. The Giants lost 8 to 4, and on Sunday they lost 6 to 3 as the Bums routed Larry Jansen.

Panic was setting in. It was the club's eleventh straight loss and they now had a secure hold on last place, seven games behind the leaders. Bill Rigney recalls the mood in the Giant clubhouse just after the game. "The Lion let us have it. Eleven in a row, I mean it was unheard of. He tore into Eddie Stanky, Hank Thompson, Bobby Thomson, Jim Hearn, everybody. When he first came over to the club we'd all heard about his reputation for going into these maniacal rages, but this was the first time in the three years he'd been with us that we saw it. He was so hot you could've fried eggs on the language coming out of his mouth.

"Then something happened. He'd been going on for about ten minutes—motherfucking this, cocksucking that—you know how he talked. Everybody was hanging their heads, a lot of them wincing at the same time. A lot of the boys on that club, guys like Mueller, Thomson, Jimmy Hearn, Alvin, Larry Jansen—they were pretty clean-cut fellows. They didn't use that kind of language and it made them feel pretty uneasy. Anyway, Durocher was going on and on, berating each one of us in turn. He got to Hearn, I think it was, and was shouting at the top of his voice about how Jim couldn't hit a barn door from five yards away when the bat boy stuck his head in the door and asked somebody some inane question. Right in the middle of Leo's tirade and here's this kid asking—I think it was one of the coaches, Shellenback probably—here's this kid asking Shellenback where he should put the batting-practice balls. Well, all of us sort of looked over at the kid, taking our attention away from Leo. Shellenback sort of shakes his head at the kid, motions him to beat it, but the kid says something else. Now here's Leo ranting and raving—suddenly we're looking across the clubhouse at the kid. Durocher stops, turns around, and sees the kid. Now the kid, getting no answer from Shellenback, sees Durocher looking at him. So he asks Leo where the ball bag should go. Durocher lets out a howl, grabs somebody's glove and lets fly with it at the kid, who's standing in the doorway. Leo was so mad the veins on his forehead looked to explode, and he threw that glove at the kid as hard as he could. When the kid sees what's about to happen, of course he ducks out the door. Everybody's watching in fascination as the glove leaves Leo's hand. Now, he's throwing this glove from about six or seven yards away from the door. It misses the door completely and smashes against the wall about two feet off to the side.

"There's a silence for a second or two. Leo's just staring at the glove. Then a voice pipes up—as I recall it was Alvin. He says in that Southern drawl of his, 'Hey, Skip, five yards.'

"Well, none of us could see Leo's face, he was still facing the door. Then Stanky comes in with a remark. 'Yeah,' he says, 'shitty follow-through too.'

"Leo's whole body starts to shake. He turns around and he's howling with laughter. So then we all break up, everybody laughing out of control for—Jesus, it seemed like ten minutes. The Dodger clubhouse was right next to the visitors' at Ebbets Field, with only a door separating them. They must've been able to hear the Lion on his tear. Now they hear this hysterical laughter. They must have thought we were all gone crazy, like maybe we murdered Leo and were all celebrating over his body.

"Anyway, that moment did it. It was a turning point for us early in the season. You could feel the tension and pressure of those first dismal two weeks lift—like breaking through the clouds into clear sky when you're in an airplane. From the next day on we played fantastic baseball. And it had nothing to do with Leo's fabled managerial genius. It was a simple case of a bat boy being in the wrong place at the wrong time. Of course, later on, being the kind of guy he is, Leo claimed that he'd staged the whole thing—you know, instructed the kid beforehand to make his entrance just at that moment. That was Leo Durocher for you."

The next evening the Giants went out and beat the Dodgers 8 to 5 in the first night game of the season at Ebbets Field. They pummeled four Brooklyn pitchers for eight runs in the first two innings and then held off the Dodgers as they chipped away at the lead for the next seven.

It was another nasty game, with Maglie making his fourth start of the season for the Giants. On Jackie Robinson's first time up, Maglie knocked him down with a pitch at his head, then got him on a called third strike. Next time up, Robinson laid a perfect bunt down the first-base line, but instead of sprinting toward first, he held back. Maglie pounced off the mound to field the bunt. As he bent over, a foot away from the line, Robinson speeded up and, barely staying within the base path, smashed into Maglie's backside, sending him sprawling. Robinson then made it to first before the Giant pitcher could recover and throw.

A furious argument followed, to the delight of the 33,000 people in attendance. Durocher, famous for his histrionics in his almost daily beefs with umpires, was like a spastic hornet as he flew about the three umps, claiming Robinson had left the base path to interfere with Maglie. While that imbroglio was going on, Maglie and Robinson were having heated words in the vicinity of first base, separated only by pulling and tugging teammates. When peace was restored and Durocher finally stalked back to the Giant dugout, his profanities warming the chilly April air, the booing could be heard in Long Island.

Nevertheless, as cruel April came to an end, the baseball pundits were beginning to write the Giants off. In his column of May 1 in the New York *Times,* Arthur Daley recalled:

> In St. Pete two months ago, Leo Durocher was brimful of confidence as he spoke in an it-can't-happen-to-us-again fashion [referring to the first month of the 1950 season]. . . .
>
> This year, everyone said well in advance of opening day that the first fortnight of competition could very well decide the National League pennant race because it pitted the four strong Eastern teams against one another. . . . But as far as the Giants are concerned, the damage has already been done. It would take a miracle for them to win the pennant now. . . .
>
> The losing streak of the Polo Grounds' tenants represents a far greater disaster than the faltering start a year ago. At that time Durocher was fumbling for the right combination in order to get his lineup set. But at this time he knows he has his best possible variety on the field. And still he's deeply and incomprehensibly embedded in last place.

The Giants beat the hapless Chicago Cubs the first two days in May. And they added a psychological victory of sorts. The previous Monday's brouhaha between Maglie and Robinson had reached the office of the National League president. "I'm getting tired of Robinson's popping off," Ford Frick was quoted as telling an assemblage of sportswriters. "I have today warned the Brooklyn club that if they don't control Robinson, I will."

Robinson fired back, "And I'm getting tired of being thrown at. Let Mr. Frick change the color of his skin, put on a baseball uniform, and go out and hit against Maglie.'' It was a clear charge of racism against Maglie.

Reading the stories in the Giant clubhouse during the Chicago series, Maglie smiled.

During the following three days, while MacArthur was suggesting under oath in Washington that the Truman administration was soft on communism, and the beleaguered state of Israel was fending off an invasion from Syria, the Giants lost a close game to Pittsburgh in extra innings, then beat the Pirates two straight for five wins in their last six games. Had they righted themselves? John Drebinger, covering them for the *Times,* wasn't sure. Of the second of the two wins over Pittsburgh he wrote:

> For a time it seemed the Giants wouldn't fare so well. Out of seemingly nowhere the Bucs came up with a 6'4" righthander named Bill Koski—a Class D hurler in the Kitty League last year, and a dead ringer for our own Clint Hartung. The Giants seemed so taken up with this singular aspect that it took them all of four innings before they got around to thinking of something else, and it almost cost them the ball game.

The reference to Clint Hartung, for anyone reading that report, had to stir memories even in 1951. Clint Hartung—a name that would forever be a metaphor for the perennial optimism souring into disappointment that all Giant fans learned to endure in the 1940s. By 1951 it could be described as a syndrome, a chronic affliction that appeared in early spring and spontaneously remitted sometime around the end of September.

Clint Hartung was the man among all men who was going to transmogrify the New York Giants after the war. A six-foot-five, 220-pound greyhound of a young man, he came out of the service in late 1946 at the age of 23 with the reputation of having been the most fabulous of all the G.I. ballplayers—every manager's dream come true. He was, in short, the next Babe Ruth; indeed, the feats of Ruth would pale into insignificance once Hartung had a few seasons behind him. He could hit the ball 700 feet on the fly, had a bazooka for an arm, could run like the wind—there was absolutely nothing he couldn't do on a baseball field. He was a gift from the heavens, and the Giants had him!

When Hartung arrived at the Giants' 1947 spring training camp, skeptical sportswriters came out in droves to inspect him. At first he did nothing to disappoint his advocates in the Giant publicity office. His very first time up in an intrasquad game he hit a home run that had the writers inventing new words to describe indescribable power. When he threw from the deepest reaches of the outfield the ball was a four-hundred-foot blur. And when he took a turn on the mound—for he could pitch, too—he was eyeblink fast.

Pretty soon the word got out in the New York papers—the Giants had a superman on their hands. Even the most wizened of writers became believers those first few weeks of spring training. The big floppy-eared Texan was the pheenom of all pheenoms, and he quickly became known as the Hondo Hurricane in honor of his home town in Texas.

But then (and there was always a "but then" when it came to the Giants) Hartung, as both an outfielder and pitcher, began to face major-league hurlers and hitters as the spring exhibition schedule got under way, and the edges of the myth began to fray. He did a respectable enough job for an ordinary ballplayer but was simply unable to live up to his billing as the new Captain Marvel. He clearly could have benefited by a year or two of seasoning in the minors.

The Giants, however, were anxious to capitalize on his double-threat reputation, so they brought him to the Polo Grounds. Pitching and playing the outfield in 1947, he did a surprisingly good job—all things considered. He compiled a pitching record of 9 wins and 7 losses in 23 outings, although his earned run average was a not so respectable 4.57. As an outfielder, he hit .309 in 34 games.

In 1948 the Giants, loaded with outfielders, decided to make him a pitcher exclusively. That season he was in 36 games and finished with an 8 and 8 record, although again his earned run mark floated above respectability. In 1949 he won 9 and lost 11, and finished with an ERA of 5.00.

By 1950 it was apparent that Clint Hartung would never make the

Hall of Fame as a pitcher, and his one last season on the mound proved it as his earned run average skyrocketed to 6.65. Durocher finally gave up on him as a hurler and turned him into a pinch hitter and utility outfielder. In 1951, Giant fans were seeing less and less of Clint Hartung. The Hondo Hurricane had been reduced to an ordinary drizzle, but hopes for him still beat strong in the hearts of a few diehard fans. And as poetic justice would have it, Hartung would get to play a role in the final miracle at Coogan's Bluff.

The Giants moved toward the second week of May still in last place while the Dodgers, Cardinals, and Braves fought it out for first. With five wins in their last six games however, and the pitching tightening up, they looked indeed as though they might be recovering from the disaster of the first two weeks. But then there occurred an incident, so typical of the Giants, that had to make one think twice.

On Sunday, May 6, the Polo Grounders were trailing the Reds 4 to 1 in the late innings of the first game of a twin bill, but had a rally going. With one out and men on second and third, Whitey Lockman doubled the two runners home to make it 4 to 3. Lockman was the tying run as the still sizzling Dark stepped to the plate. As the Cincinnati pitcher looked in for his sign, Lockman took a short lead off second—short because the Reds' second baseman, Connie Ryan, was himself only a foot or two from the bag. Why are they playing me so close? Lockman wondered. Before he had a chance to further contemplate the question he found out. Ryan, the ball hidden in his glove, took two quick steps to his right and tagged Lockman. The umpire, who knew Ryan had the ball, cried ''Yer out!''

Lockman was dumbfounded and automatically started to protest. Before he could get a word out, Durocher, who had been in the third-base coaching box, was all over the umpire, screaming at the top of his voice. A 46-year-old man, Durocher could move like greased lightning when the occasion called for it.

As far as Durocher was concerned, this was one occasion that called for it, for Lockman's being suckered like that was more Durocher's fault than the outfielder's. When a runner is on second base, it is always the third-base coach's responsibility to ensure that everything is as it should be on the field before a runner takes a lead. This was a lecture Durocher had given repeatedly during spring training. The hidden ball trick was one of the oldest ploys in baseball. Though perfectly legal, it was so dog-eared it was seldom ever attempted any more except in sandlot games.

In any event, it worked on Lockman, and Durocher was in a rage at having been shown up. Lockman recalls, "Sure, I remember that day. I was trying to get my two cents in, this 'n' that, but you wouldn't have been able to hear an air raid siren the way Leo was bellowing at that umpire. He was kicking dirt and cussin' like there was no tomorrow. Finally the ump threw him out of the game. You remember, to get to the clubhouse at the Polo Grounds you didn't go through the dugout but had to go all the way out through center field. Well, I forget exactly what Leo was protesting about—I mean, I was out, sure as shootin'—but later on we figured he was putting up such a fuss so's he'd be sure to get the boot. That way, he'd have to go straight to the clubhouse and not come back to the dugout. He knew what everybody'd be thinking after all those talks he gave us about watching the third-base coach. Hell, I'd looked at him before stepping off second, and he had no more idea Ryan had the ball than I did." Lockman pauses, then laughs to himself. "Y'know, that's odd. I've been with Leo a lot the last few years and I never thought to ask him if he deliberately got himself thrown out that day."

So, with Lockman called out at second, the tying run did not score when Alvin Dark singled to right field. And instead of one out, there were two. The long-slumping Monte Irvin, now batting eighth in Durocher's revised order, popped out. The rally was killed and the Giants lost the first game of the doubleheader 4 to 3.

They won the second game, though, and proceeded to win three more in a row over St. Louis the following week to pull themselves out of the cellar and into seventh place.

As they prepared to leave on their first western road trip of the season, they had won 11 of their last 14 games, were poised on the threshold of sixth place, and were creeping up on .500 with an overall record of 13 wins and 15 losses. All, it appeared, was not yet lost.

By the end of the Giants' road trip, the National League race had suddenly drawn tight as a knot, with all eight teams in contention. As an illustration of how bunched the standings were, the Giants were in fourth place, two games behind, while Philadelphia, in last place, was only three games behind. First place was changing hands almost hourly between Brooklyn, Boston, and St. Louis. The Dodgers had stumbled after their quick start in the first two weeks—a start that was mainly courtesy of the Giants—and as the Polo Grounders returned to New York to begin a long home stand against the Braves the sportswriters were changing their tune.

Two significant events occurred during the previous week. On Sunday, May 20, the Giants lost to the Cardinals in St. Louis 8 to 7. Durocher and Eddie Stanky were thrown out of the game after a prolonged and violent argument with umpire Lon Warneke. (The next day Durocher was fined $100 by Ford Frick for his "vile, abusive words" to Warneke.)

While Durocher sat fuming in the clubhouse, listening to the game on a radio, the Giants lost a three-run lead in the last of the seventh. The Cards put five runs across, helped in large part by two errors by Monte Irvin at first base. Irvin was not hitting anywhere near his potential—he was limping along at .260—and his play at first base was growing more atrocious by the day.

In the eighth inning the Giants scored a run to make it 8 to 7, Cards leading. The Giants had runners on first and third with one out and Irvin up. A base hit, even a long fly, would tie the score. An extra-base hit could put them ahead. It was a situation made to order for Irvin, according to Durocher's early-season batting-order philosophy. Irvin promptly rapped into an easy double play, snuffing out the Giant rally.

In the privacy of the clubhouse Durocher cursed his hapless first baseman. "That's it!" he roared at Stanky. "Gotta do something with that big buck. He's hurtin' us more'n he's helpin'."

Durocher began to think aloud. He had no one else on the club who could play first. Oh, he had Hartung, but that was even worse. "What about Tookie Gilbert down at Minneapolis?" suggested Stanky. "Nah," said Durocher, "hits good in the minors, but a .220

hitter up here. This other kid, Blaylock, at Ottawa—what's he hitting, .150? Shit, I'm horse-collared.''

"Well then," said Stankey, "how about puttin' Hank Thompson on first and moving Rig in at third?"

"That's like putting a Band-Aid on a gut wound.''

"Then what about Rigney on first? He's agile, and he's smart.''

"Nah, another Band-Aid.''

As the game outside went into the ninth inning, Durocher and Stanky, both with an ear cocked to the radio, discussed other possibilities. With two out and none on, Whitey Lockman singled to left. Rafael Noble, filling in at catcher for Westrum, who had broken a finger two weeks earlier, was the next hitter. "Thataway, Whitey," Durocher said to the radio. "Okay, Noble, get him around!"

Suddenly Durocher's mind clicked. "Lockman," he said to himself. He turned to Stanky and said it louder. "Lockman! That's it.''

"What about him?"

"He fooled around at first down at St. Pete. Looked pretty good, too. That's it, goddamnit. I put him on first. I sit Mueller down for a while and move Irvin to right.'' The juice began to flow now as Durocher began remaking his line-up. "Yeah, it's perfect. Get Irvin off first and he starts to hit. Whitey can't be no more worse at first, he'll be better. Then I move Thomson over to left. See if that doesn't start *him* hittin'.''

Noble fouled out to end the game. Durocher paused to growl "Shit," then picked up a first baseman's glove and went to the clubhouse door to meet the returning players. As Lockman entered, Durocher handed him the glove and said, "Whitey, take this to bed with you. Tomorrow you're at first.''

Lockman blinked, his bland face frowning into puzzlement. Before he had a chance to say anything, though, Durocher had moved away and was intercepting the sulky Irvin. "Monte, tomorrow you go in right," he barked. After thinking about it for a second, Irvin's face brightened. He was expecting a chewing out from Durocher.

The next day Lockman opened at first base and Irvin in left field. Durocher had a small change of heart overnight and decided to give Mueller another day or two in right, especially since the Giants were expecting to face a string of right-handed pitchers. Mueller hit from the left side, and maybe a diet of righty pitching would get him out of his slump.

On the occasion of the Lockman-Irvin switch, the Giants lost to the Cards 5 to 2, but Irvin stroked three hits and knocked in both Giant runs. Their next game was in Chicago and Irvin hit a home run to win it 2 to 1 for Maglie. It was the Barber's sixth straight victory.

In the meantime Durocher managed, after three days of phone calls to New York, to hector Horace Stoneham into agreeing to bring up Willie Mays. The quid pro quo was as expected—send down one of the other black players, a marginal one like Wilson or Noble. Durocher protested mightily. The Giants would have to send some-one down to make room for Mays on the roster, that went without question. But why not somebody like Hartung or Gettel, both of whom had been of little use to the club?

No dice, came the answer from the front office. Did Durocher real-ize that all five blacks might be in the line-up at the same time? Five Negroes to four whites!

Durocher had imagined it. The idea rather appealed to him. To be the first manager to put more blacks on the field than whites—he could already taste the controversy.

He laid out his plans to Stoneham. The Lockman-Irvin switch was already made and was working. But Mueller wasn't hitting. Who could he put in Mueller's place, Hartung? No, Hartung had already lost two games in right field misplaying easy fly balls. Jorgensen? Strictly utility.

"What about Hank Thompson?" came the reply.

"Not a bad idea," Durocher said, playing all his cards now. "But who do I put on third?"

"Rigney."

"Rigney, shit. He's gettin' old and he don't hit. I put Wilson on third."

"So then?"

"So then I got a half-assed outfield and a half-assed infield, I got a third baseman playin' right field, and a second baseman at third. Be-sides that, with Noble in the line-up, you got four darkies on the field."

"Yes, but that's better than five."

"So you'll go for four?"

"If it's necessary."

"Then gimme Mays, goddamnit! With him in center I move Thomson to left and Irvin over to right and I got an outfield that'll make some noise. With Noble in there and Thompson at third, we got four bucks on the field, which you say you'll go for. But at least they're playin' where they should be."

"Then you agree to drop Wilson?"

"Like hell I agree. We keep Wilson to spell Stanky and get rid of Hartung. Or Gettel. Or Kramer. They ain't doin' me no good."

"Rigney can spell Stanky."

"Wilson'll hit rings around Rigney."

"Then we'll bring up Davey Williams from Minneapolis. He's over .300. The best second baseman in the organization."

"A good prospect," Durocher replied. "But who do you send down for him?"

"One of the pitchers—say, Kramer."

"Bring him up then," Durocher said, refusing to be cowed. "But Wilson stays. He can play short too, behind Dark. When you bring up Mays, let Hartung go, or Gettel. Or Rigney even."

"Sorry, Leo."

"Goddamnit, I want Mays!"

The long-distance battle seesawed for three days until, finally, Durocher gave in. He got his Willie Mays, but in the end agreed to send the 30-year-old Wilson to the Giants' Ottawa farm club.

It was a bitter pill for Wilson to swallow. He was another of those immensely gifted black athletes who had found the door to organized baseball opened only after they had reached the peak of their talents, and it was the end of his brief shot at the major leagues. The bitterness was compounded by the fact that he was the one who had first recognized Willie Mays' potential. Three years earlier Wilson had been playing in Birmingham and was unofficially recruiting black talent for the Dodgers. When he saw the then 17-year-old Mays play, he immediately urged the Dodgers to go after him. The Dodgers hesitated, and the Giants stepped into the breech. Now Artie Wilson was being shunted aside so that Willie Howard Mays could make his entrance into big-league baseball.

6

"The Giants Is Dead"

MAYS ARRIVED in New York while the Giants were en route from Chicago to Philadelphia for the concluding three games of their road trip. He showed up at the Giants' offices near Times Square with only the clothes on his back and his spikes, glove, and favorite bat. Garry Schumacher recalls his arrival, "I was by the front door talking to someone when in walks this Negro kid carrying a bat and wearing the most bizarre looking cap you've ever seen, something like the old motoring caps, a plaid affair with a bill in front and a tiny belt in back. Now we always had kids coming in asking for tryouts and at first I thought this was just another one of them. Then he says who he is and I say to myself, well, we're going to have to get this kid dressed up. After he met Horace we went out and bought him some clothes and then sent him on down to Philadelphia to join the club. Even with the new clothes, though, he refused to take off that cap."

That night Mays was in center field against Philadelphia. Durocher moved Thomson to left and put Irvin in right. He finally had his outfield, he thought. Then, in the third inning, Eddie Waitkus lofted a soft fly to right-center. Mays and Irvin both chased it. The two bumped into each other, and the ball fell in for a double. An auspicious beginning for Willie Mays. In left field, Bobby Thomson, whose pride was stinging as a result of his transfer, nodded sagely.

In the dugout between innings, Durocher jumped on Irvin. He had watched Mays in pregame practice and marveled at his range and speed and the jump he got on the ball. He realized immediately that Mays was a natural. So after venting his spleen on Irvin, he sat his outfielders down in the far corner of the dugout and calmly told them that from then on in, any ball hit in the general direction of Mays was his. Irvin's and Thomson's jobs were primarily to protect the lines. With Mays in there, the outfield could spread out more, and the occasional ball that got by Mays up the alleys would be more than compensated for; by playing closer to the foul lines, the right- and left-fielders would be able to hold many potential extra-base hits punched or sliced down the lines to singles. "That's what I liked about Durocher," Monte Irvin says today. "He liked to yell at a man a lot. But he never held a grudge. He'd yell at you, then a minute later he'd have his arm around you telling you how you could do better."

The Giants beat Philadelphia 8 to 5 that night, and although Mays failed to hit safely and misplayed Waitkus' fly, he hit two long drives that were caught, and made a pair of sparkling catches himself after Durocher's dugout lecture.

The next day the Giants won again on a Jansen seven-hitter, 2 to 0, Thomson belting a two-run homer. On Sunday they followed with Maglie's 2 to 0 win to sweep the series and put them over the .500 mark for the first time.

On the train back to New York Durocher spent most of his time commiserating with Mays, who had gone hitless through the series. He was 0 for 12 and sulking mightily. "I told you I wasn't goin' to hit this pitchin'," he kept telling Durocher.

"Listen, man," said Monte Irvin, sitting with Mays, "we won three in a row without you hitting. Now figure it out. As long as *you* don't hit, *we* win. Only trouble'll be if you get a hit."

On Monday, May 28, the Giants opened a home stand with a night game against the Braves. Mays, batting third in the order, came up in the first inning and hit a towering home run off Warren Spahn—a drive that bounced off the left-field roof of the Polo Grounds. It was a prodigious clout and the customers went wild with joy. It was Mays' first base hit as a Giant. The Giants lost 4 to 1.

At the conclusion of a Memorial Day doubleheader with the Braves, which they split, the Giants were sitting in fifth place, 4½ games behind the Dodgers. The standings had spread out over the past two weeks, and with three Brooklyn players—Robinson, Reese, and Abrams—among the top five hitters in the league, the Dodgers had a firm hold on first place. The only Giant hitting over .300 was Alvin Dark. The rest of the regulars were in the mid-.200s except for the benched Mueller, whose average remained an uncharacteristic .197. Mays was now at .043, but everyone realized, or at least hoped, that that was no gauge of his real potential.

Despite the Giants' sickly hitting, most observers were optimistic about the club's chances going into June. The optimism derived mainly from the performance of the pitching staff. Maglie had won seven in a row, Jansen and Hearn were throwing effectively, and George Spencer had developed into a top-notch reliever. Even Dave Koslo was showing some consistency for a change, and many believed that once the Giant bats heated up for real the New Yorkers would make a run at the Dodgers.

In June, Mays was still complaining to Durocher about his inability to hit big-league pitching—indeed, at one point in tears, he begged Durocher to send him back to Minneapolis.

"Now look here," Durocher rasped, grown tired of Mays' self-pitying. "Ya coulda won me a ball game tonight, but ya didn't. So what? Ever occur to ya, tomorrow's another day? And yer going to be playin' center field tomorrow, got that? And the day after that. And the day after that. So get used to the idea and stop all this goddamn bitchin' and cryin'!"

Durocher turned to leave, then spun around. "And by the way, who do ya think y'are? Hubbell?"

"What yo' mean?" said Mays balefully.

"The way ya wear the legs of them pants a'yours, down t'the ankles like that. Pull 'em up!"

"Whut fo'?"

"Because," said Durocher, "you're makin' the goddamn umpires think yer strike zone's down where the knees of yer pants are.

They're hurtin' ya on the low pitch. Pull up yer pants. If ya do, ya'll get two hits tomorra.''

Mays pulled up his pants. Durocher also dropped him from third to eighth in the batting order, and the next day, in the Giants' 14 to 3 win, Mays got two hits—a single and a triple.

Things were looking up for Giant fans as their favorites moved into July and the halfway mark of the season. Then, in their true fashion, they were steamrollered in Boston—19 to 7. The Braves knocked Maglie out in the first with four runs (Maglie had never beaten the Braves), but the Giants came back with five in the third and two more in the fifth to lead 7 to 4. So far, so good. But alas, the Braves got eight in the seventh and seven more in the eighth. At the time, nurturing my grudge, I secretly rejoiced when I heard the news.

However, they were not to be cowed. On July 1, while Bobby Feller was pitching the third no-hitter of his career against Detroit in the American League, the Giants came back behind Larry Jansen and polished off the Braves 4 to 1. They won again the next day with Jim Hearn and then returned to the Polo Grounds to beat the Phils in the thirteenth inning 9 to 8. They had to come from behind five times to do it, and Durocher was so anxious to win the game he used Jansen in relief, with Maglie and Hearn warming up in the bullpen. In the top of the thirteenth the Phils broke the 7 to 7 deadlock with a run; in the home half, Mays hit a solo homer to tie it, then Irvin doubled, and Lockman singled him home with the winner. Lockman, having settled in at first base with the help of some special tutoring by ex-Dodger Buddy Hassett, was beginning to raise his batting average toward .300. The vital victory still left the Giants 4½ games behind Brooklyn and set the stage for their traditional July 4 series. If the Giants, who were sizzling along with 26 wins in their last 33 games, could sweep the three-game set, they would be only a game and a half behind the Bums as they approached the midseason All-Star break.

It was not to be. On July 4 the two teams met in a doubleheader at Ebbets Field. The games could not have been more exciting and raucous, but the Giants dropped both, falling back to 6½ games off the pace.

During the All-Star break the Giants brought up second baseman

Davey Williams from Minneapolis. It was, in a sense, as though they were conceding the season.

Williams had been earmarked as the next Giant second-sacker. The St. Louis Cardinals were, at the same time, looking for a new manager to succeed Marty Marion in 1952. They were after Eddie Stanky, and Stanky wanted the job. Realizing that Stanky would probably be gone in 1952, the Giants promoted Williams so that they could get a good look at him during the second half of the season against major-league pitching. A .280 hitter at Minneapolis for the past two seasons, he didn't figure to help the Giants much on offense, but he could certainly hold his own as a fielder.

As the Polo Grounders gathered after the All-Star break to begin the second half of the season with a long home stand, the New York sports pages were not only writing them off again but were even suggesting that they had written themselves off. Durocher protested. When Louis Effrat of the *Times* asked him if he thought the Dodgers could be caught and, if so, by whom, Durocher "placed his right index finger above his thumb, a sixteenth of an inch apart. 'Not even that much do I concede the Dodgers,' he said. 'Sure, we're second, 8½ out right now, but there's still a long way to go.'

"The New Yorkers started to move fast just about this time last year," Effrat went on, "and are even better off now than they were at the corresponding stage in 1950. Willie Mays has been a big help and the bats of Mueller and Irvin are booming. But bringing up Williams at this point and saying he's going to be playing a lot of second base has to make Giant fans wonder about their intentions, despite what Durocher says."

True, Effrat wrote, Mays, Mueller, and Irvin had all hit well over the previous month. Irvin was up to .306 with 55 runs batted in. Mueller had come from .167 to .312. Mays was at .273; he had already hit 10 home runs and was getting Giant pitchers out of trouble time after time with circus catches. Dark was still slugging the ball at a .322 clip, and even Bobby Thomson, playing semiregularly again, had 15 home runs—five in his last seven games—although his .230 average was still way below normal. With the exception of Maglie, the pitching had tailed off somewhat, but was still adequate.

But the team, with an overall record of 43 wins and 36 losses versus the Dodgers' 50 wins and 26 losses, seemed to have played up to its full potential after its early-season debacle of eleven straight losses. It had won 41 and lost only 24 since then—superior baseball for any ball club. How could it possibly play better than that?

On Wednesday night, July 18, while Jersey Joe Walcott was knocking out Ezzard Charles in Pittsburgh to win the heavyweight boxing championship at the age of 37, the Giants lost to the Cubs before 8,500 customers at the Polo Grounds (even Giant fans seemed to be conceding). During the game, Hank Thompson, back in the line-up for another chance, was spiked in the foot on a rough-and-tumble play at third base by Chicago pitcher Frank Hiller. He needed a couple of stitches in the clubhouse to close the wound, and while he was being attended to by the team doctor, Horace Stoneham was upstairs in the press room announcing that he was farming Thompson out to Ottawa. At first blush it seemed like a cruel reward for Thompson—a man who always gave his best, although his best was often diluted by an alcoholic haze. Actually the Giants had been planning the move for some days to get Thompson away from the saloons of Harlem so that he might regain his batting eye. In his place they wanted to bring up a young hurler, Al Corwin, whose low earned run average at Ottawa indicated that he might be of some help to the faltering pitching staff. Only the timing of the announcement was cruel. Of course Stoneham, never famous for his tact, took another bad rap in the papers, but Thompson went—dejectedly but obediently.

Corwin came down from Ottawa and played an important role in the events that ensued. But that was not the only egg hatched by Thompson's demotion, no indeed. The Giants were now without a regular third baseman. They had Bill Rigney, but they were not going to go anywhere with the man the fans called the Cricket. And they had Hank Schenz, a journeyman from Pittsburgh, but he was strictly a low-.200 hitter.

Durocher looked around his clubhouse and saw Bobby Thomson. Thomson had been signed by the Giants in 1942 as a third baseman but had been turned into an outfielder in the minors to make use of his speed. (Even in 1951, with Mays and Irvin aboard, Thomson was still the fastest man on the club.)

Durocher had a hunch. He called Thomson into his office and said,

"Hoot mon (Thomson's nickname around the clubhouse), yer hittin' home runs, but in between ya ain't hittin' shit."

Thomson was a mild-mannered fellow most of the time, and when he was around authority he was used to obeisance. He nodded sheepishly.

"Now ya been with this club fer what—five, six years? I know yer popular with the fans, but they don't know somethin' I know about ya. Ya know what that is?"

"What's that, Skip?"

Thomson's indifferent response irked Durocher. How once, just once, he'd like to really rile him. He didn't realize that Thomson was quivering inside, fearing that Durocher had called him in to tell him he was being sent down or released. He knew that the Giants were thinking about next year and that they had a bevy of outfielders in the minors they were interested in bringing up for a look. Or maybe they were trading him for a third baseman—there had been some talk about him going to the Braves with Koslo and Kennedy for Bob Elliott, Boston's all-star corner man. And Durocher's tone seemed to be leading up to something that was sure to be unpleasant. He could already see the headline on the back page of the *Daily News:* JINTS DUMP THOM-THOM DUO.

"What is it?" he said as Durocher continued to glare at him.

"Ya really wanna know?"

"Sure."

"Awright, it's this—ya ain't half the ballplayer ya could be."

Thomson gulped. He shook his head in bewilderment. "I don't get it."

Durocher didn't bother explaining. Instead he waved Thomson to the door. "G'wan, get outta here!"

"What?"

"Get outta here!"

Thomson, more confused than ever, looked at Durocher for a second as the manager began to leaf through a newspaper. Then he got up and started to leave. Is this all? he thought.

"By the way," Durocher said as Thomson opened the door. "Tomorra take infield. From now on yer gonna play third. But I'm warnin' ya, it's yer last chance ta stay with this club."

The Giants were rained out the next day, but on Friday, July 20, they beat the Reds 11 to 5, Sal Maglie gaining his thirteenth win against four losses. Thomson started at third base, and although he made an error, he collected three hits. Surprisingly, the Dodgers had hit a slump. They'd won only three of nine games since the All-Star break, but the other first-division teams had played so poorly that the Dodgers had lost only a game and a half of their lead.

The Polo Grounders closed out their home stand over the July 22 weekend by taking two from the Reds and losing one. The successful series got them back into second place, and Thomson stroked seven hits in fourteen trips to the plate.

As the club started another western trip, Durocher announced to the press that the "Thomson experiment" would continue. "Oh how that man loves to 'experiment,' " wrote Joe Williams in the *World Telegram and Sun*. "But then, the 'experiment' with Lockman has worked pretty well. And if you can say that sticking it out with Willie Mays when the rookie appeared unable to hit his way through tissue paper qualified as an 'experiment,' then you have to say Durocher has a pretty good track record—experiment-wise. But if the Giants had any genuine qualifications for overtaking the Brooks, there wouldn't be any need for experiment. All they have going for them at this late date is hope, and there's not a Giant fan alive who hasn't had his fill of that. No siree, ladies and gentlemen, you can count the Giants out. The best they can hope for is to finish the season a respectable second again."

News from the West was good. The Giants took two out of three in Pittsburgh and then swept four straight in Cincinnati as Bobby Thomson continued to pound the hide off the ball, making up for his more than occasional miscues at third base. But the Dodgers, also traveling the western cities, had snapped out of their slump and were on an eight-game winning streak. The Giants were thus still 9½ games behind and beginning to feel the lusting breath of the Phillies on their neck.

After playing scintillating ball on the first half of their western visit, the New Yorkers reverted to their more usual style of play, returning East on Monday, August 5, with only four wins in the last eight games of the trip. The writers traveling with them all agreed in print that the Giants were looking tired, both defensively and offensively. One scribe even suggested that after winning six of seven at the beginning of the trip and finding they had not gained a centimeter on the Dodgers, they had simply lost interest. They were losing games they should have won because they were suddenly playing sloppy, indifferent baseball.

For example, on August 3 at Sportsman's Park in St. Louis, Alvin Dark led off the third inning with a double up the right-centerfield alley, then fell on his face overrunning second base. The relay throw from the outfield beat him back to the bag and he was an easy out. Mays then singled, but of course Dark was not on second to score. The Giants lost 5 to 4.

Even so, the Polo Grounders were a handsome 10 wins and 5 losses for the trip, but they came home infected with a lackadaisical attitude. The only bright spot was Bobby Thomson. "Since Thomson took over at third," wrote James Dawson in the *Times* of August 6, "the Staten Island Scot has been hitting at a .345 clip through 17 games, with 5 home runs and 17 RBIs."

Coming up was a three-game series against the Dodgers at Ebbets Field. The first game, on August 7, was rained out, so instead of reporting on the game the local sportswriters analyzed the pennant race, such as it was. "Leo Durocher's second-place Giants, 9½ games behind, are the only rivals who still have a ghost of a chance of flagging down the pace-setting Brooks," Roscoe McGowen explained in the *Times*. "If the New Yorkers fail to gain ground in this three-game set, the indicated pennant runaway of Charlie Dressen's Dodgers will be just about assured."

The rained-out game was rescheduled for the next day, and the habitues of Ebbets Field were treated to an unexpected midweek doubleheader—or so they thought. The Brooklyn management, especially the pecunious Branch Rickey, had always been stingy in scheduling twin bills at Ebbets Field, even on Sundays and holidays. Indeed, the Dodgers traditionally played the fewest doubleheaders at home of any club in the majors. "Let them schedule all the doubleheaders they want when we're on the road," went the Rickey rationale. "It will keep our boys busy and out of the bars. But at home, every game we play should be as an individual product, paid for separately and in full. That is the free enterprise system, and two for the price of one merely demeans your product.''

When two teams play a pair of games on the same day, they usually comprise a doubleheader. Not the way Rickey handled things. Much to the consternation of Giant and Dodger fans alike, he dictated that the previous day's rained-out match would be played in the afternoon, and the scheduled single game for that afternoon would be played at night. The ball park would be emptied after the first game, and anyone wishing to see the second game would have to buy fresh tickets.

Tempers were high, then, not so much on the field as in the packed stands, as the Giants and Dodgers prepared to start play on the afternoon of August 8, a Wednesday. Giant aficionados, rechanneling their frustration over their heroes, complained loudly and profanely about the Dodger management. Dodger loyalists, although themselves grumbling over Rickey's fiat, could in good conscience brook no outside criticism of their team's front-office leadership. Hence the stands were like a brushfire in a drought, with fistfights breaking out here, there, everywhere. In contrast, the mood on the field was relatively peaceful. Most of the spectators were too busy with the action in the stands to take more than passing notice of the Dodgers beating the Giants 7 to 2.

That night was altogether another story, however, as Sal Maglie took the mound against Clyde King of the Dodgers. By this point in the season the Maglie-Robinson feud had escalated into all-out warfare, and it seemed that every time Maglie was on the mound Robinson responded with a mercurial performance. From the fans' point of view, the confrontation was a good deal more fun than watching fistfights in the stands. It was no longer a matter of observing ballplayers from a distance going through the usual ballplayer motions. One could actually see Robinson at the plate or on the bases taunt Maglie or make a threatening gesture with his bat or his fist. One could actually see Maglie hunch his shoulders, turn his back in contempt, darken his scowl, and toss his head disdainfully. The two stars, sparring on the edge of homicide, lost their remoteness and became as human as those who had paid to watch them. So far throughout the season, Maglie still held the upper hand insofar as the outcome of their battles was concerned, although with the Giants now 10½ behind, it would be stretching a point to suggest he enjoyed the advantage. However, tonight was to be Robinson's.

In his first time up, Robinson, naturally, went down. He got up and took a few steps toward the mound, his thin, high voice piercing the thick, smoky air with obscenities. Maglie made a vulgar Sicilian gesture in response as Robinson marched back to the plate, then turned his back and stared into center field. The crowd went wild. On the next pitch Robinson hit a tremendous line drive over Willie Mays' head in center. The ball caromed off the wall—the place Maglie had been staring at. A brilliant fielding play by Mays held Robinson to a double. But then he stole third on Maglie's first pitch to Campanella and trotted home, laughing like a hyena when substitute catcher Sal Yvars threw the ball into left field. The Dodgers had their first run.

His second time up, leading off the fourth inning, Robinson dropped a bunt down the first-base line. Maglie, by now wise to Robinson's tactics, refused to come off the mound to field it. By the time Lockman got to it the Dodger second baseman was across first. Taking daring leads—even for Robinson—he drew four futile pickoff throws from Maglie. The partisan Brooklyn crowd was booing for all it was worth by the fourth. Maglie looked up into the stands and felt a wave of claustrophobia flow through him. Then the plate umpire shouted out to him, "Let's go, pitcher, speed it up!" Holding his right hand at his belt, Maglie extended his middle finger. The crowd was not one to miss a nuance, and the booing grew even more tumultuous.

Maglie stretched, looked, and again threw back to first, this time softly, contemptuously. It was his answer to the umpire. Robinson must have been reading his mind. As Maglie made his move, Robinson broke for second. The ball floated toward Lockman at first. By the time it plopped into his mitt Robinson was three-quarters of the way to second and starting his slide. Lockman didn't even bother to throw.

The amused Campanella waited dutifully in the batter's box as the next act of the drama unfolded. Maglie made a couple of bluff pickoff throws to second, not trusting himself to release the ball. Willie

Mays crept close in behind second to back up just in case. On Maglie's first pitch to Campanella the Dodger catcher hit a liner into center field. Normally it would have been an easy out, but with Mays playing in so close it settled beyond his outstretched arm, and Campanella had a double. Robinson scored easily, cackling at Maglie all the way and pausing at home plate to address a few more obscenities to the Giant ace. Maglie cracked an elbow back at his tormentor. The fans roared with glee as Robinson strutted back to the Brooklyn dugout.

"I was still new to the Dodgers then," remembers second-string catcher Rube Walker in his kindly North Carolina drawl. Walker had come to the Dodgers in the Pafko deal and is now a coach with the New York Mets. "I'd never seen a ballplayer as worked up as Robinson was that night—he was flyin' higher'n a kite, comin' back to the dugout practically frothin' at the mouth. Course, we was way out in front then and didn't have nothin' to lose with him foolin' around with Maglie like that. It was some exhibition, all right. And the crowd—well, they jes' worked him up that much more."

By the sixth inning the Dodgers led 3 to 2. Up again came Robinson, this time with men on second and third with two out. Maglie grimly threw two inside pitches that drove Robinson back. The Dodger turned to complain to the umpire. After getting his beef off his chest he bent down angrily to scratch some dirt. As he did, catcher Yvars himself gathered a handful of dirt and surreptitiously flicked it at Robinson's face. Robinson froze in his stooped position.

He had taken an immense amount of racial abuse in his first two years in baseball. More recently however, much of the abuse he was getting had lost its overt racial character and seemed directed more at Robinson the ballplayer than at Robinson the black man. For this he was grateful, but he was still hypersensitive to anything that might have a racial overtone. That night, four years after his debut in the big leagues, he felt free to react and respond like an ordinary ballplayer rather than swallow his rage for the sake of Branch Rickey's "noble experiment."

Still bent over, his face turning hard with barely controlled rage, he looked into Yvars' mask. "Listen, you chicken-ass motherfucker," he said through clenched teeth, "you ever do something like that again, I'll tear you apart. Understand?" He held his gaze on Yvars. The utility catcher averted his eyes, gave a weak laugh, and said, "Aw, c'mon, Jackie."

Robinson was satisfied. Yvars understood. Robinson straightened up and stepped back to the plate. "Okay, you bush pitcher," he called out to Maglie. "Why don't you see if you can't hit me this time."

Maglie checked the runner at third and delivered. It was the standard intimidating Maglie curve, spinning straight at the right-handed hitter's head, then abruptly dipping away across the outside corner of the plate. Robinson, his bat held high, refused to succumb to his instinct to pull back. He read the curve-ball spin and lashed out at the ball as it broke, slicing it into right-centerfield for a base hit. The two runners scored to make the score 5 to 2. Robinson, on first with two out, was practically beating the Giants single-handed. But that was not the end of it.

Durocher must have been enjoying the spectacle, for he allowed Maglie to stay in. This time the Giant pitcher made no attempt to pick his enemy off. So on the first pitch to Campanella, a swinging strike, Robinson stole second to the frenzied delight of the grandstand throng. Yvars throw wasn't even close. Maglie peered almost pleadingly into the Giant dugout. He seemed to be saying, "Hey, get me outta here."

Campanella, a right-handed hitter, was in on Robinson's game now. Robinson flashed the steal signal from second base, and as Maglie broke from his stretch to deliver, Robinson was off for third. The pitch was a fast ball down the pipe, a sitting duck for Campanella. He deliberately swung and missed and forced Yvars to throw over him to third. Bobby Thomson had to leap high over the sliding Robinson to keep the ball from again flying into the outfield.

"Going home on the next one!" Robinson shouted at Maglie. Maglie smiled and said, "Go ahead, see what it gets ya, showboat!" He had one last trick up his sleeve. If Robinson broke, he would fire the ball straight at him. He calculated the number of feet he'd have to lead him. He figured he'd have to put the ball four feet from the plate on the third-base side. Low. It would catch Robinson in the middle of his slide. There was no way anyone could prove it was deliberate.

As Robinson danced away from third the crowd was begging him to go. It wanted Maglie's humiliation to be complete. Maglie went into a long double wind-up, tempting Robinson to break. He watched him out of the side of his eye and said to himself, "Go, you bastard, go!"

As soon as Robinson saw his adversary go into his uncharacteristic contortions he knew the Maglie plan. It's a trap. The son of a bitch is gonna try and level me, he realized.

Maglie delivered the two-strike pitch as Robinson pulled up short. The ball, as if telegraphing Maglie's intentions, rocketed in at Campanella's knees but three feet behind them. Campanella yelped as he leaped into the air. Yvars lunged to his left. The ball glanced off the tip of his mitt and skittered toward the Giant dugout. Watching Yvars chase the ball, Robinson jigged toward the plate, pausing to draw the catcher's throw to Maglie, who should now have been dashing in to cover home. Yvars picked the ball up at the edge of the dugout steps, whirled, and got set to fire to Maglie. Only there was no Maglie. Yvars, astonished, raced back toward the plate. Robinson, still only two-thirds of the way home, turned and saw that Maglie was still on the mound, watching sourly. He laughed, the lights of Ebbets Field turning his teeth into a brilliant white gleam against his black skin. Then, as Yvars and first baseman Lockman converged on home plate, he quickly danced the rest of the way home and ceremoniously stomped on the plate.

The 41,000 customers went wild. When Durocher finally came out to remove Maglie their cheers abruptly shifted into a booing and stamping that caused the seismographic needles to squiggle at Fordham University, sixteen miles away in the Bronx. Maglie didn't wait for his relief pitcher. He handed the ball to Durocher and without a word marched toward the Giant dugout. Around him fell a rain of beer cups, hot-dog rolls, mustard globs and peanuts. Just before he disappeared into the dugout, he looked up and tipped his cap, his middle finger extended.

As if that wasn't excitement enough, the Giants came back in the top of the ninth to tie the score at 6 and 6. With Dave Koslo now pitching for the Polo Grounders the game went into the last of the tenth still tied. But with two out, the Dodgers rapped three straight singles—two of them infield squibblers—to load the bases. Next up was Billy Cox. After fouling off two strikes, Cox picked out a Koslo curve and drilled it past Bobby Thomson, driving home Robinson with the game-winning run.

Robinson had scored four and knocked in two more to account for six of the Dodgers' seven runs. Wrote Roscoe McGowen in the next day's *Times,* "It looks as though the Dodgers wrapped up the pennant last night in the 10th inning of a wild game at Ebbets Field."

After the game Jackie Robinson was outside the Giant locker room alternately shouting at his beaten tormentors and pounding on the clubhouse door with a bat. Bill Rigney remembers, "Finally there was a little bit of a pause, and Eddie Stanky and Alvin Dark and myself and—Monte Irvin was dressing right across from us—and then Eddie says, 'Stick that bat up your ass, you black sheepfucker!" Then we all realized Monte Irvin was there, right across from us. We all kind of sheepishly turned around to see if he'd heard. He had this cute little grin on his face, and he said, 'That's good enough for me, Eddie.' "

The Giants' next game was against Philadelphia at the Polo Grounds on Saturday, August 11, the start of a four-game series that the sportswriters now considered as deciding who would occupy second place. Robin Roberts beat the Giants 4 to 0 in the first game of the Series.

"The Lion was losing interest," Rigney recalls. "It used to happen a lot with him. If he wasn't in the thick of a race he'd lose interest, start letting the coaches run games, or even some of the players. Or else he'd put in players he knew were going to hurt the club—it was his way of telling Horace, 'Get me a better player.' Anyhow, I think I 'managed' that day, and of course it was like trying to manage a bunch of robots. Nobody cared any more—well, almost nobody. Everybody was playing for themselves, for their next year's salaries.

"The next day we were playing the Phils a doubleheader, and the people were giving a day for Wes. I looked at Wes in the clubhouse after the loss to Roberts and he was *really* down—you know what a sincere guy he is. Well, I said, 'Wes, what's the matter?' And he shakes his head and says, 'Jesus, Rig, all these folks are coming down from Poughkeepsie tomorrow, they've been planning this all year. And I feel ashamed to have to go out there and accept all those gifts and things. I mean, look at us. We'll go out there and play no-account baseball and probably lose both games, and those folks'll have to make that long drive back and they'll really be feeling sour. I'm gonna feel like a horse's ass.'

"I started talking to some of the other fellas about it and in a few minutes everybody's talking it up. It was like a groundswell right there in the clubhouse, you could feel it, everybody coming alive again, saying, 'Hey, let's go out there and do it tomorrow, guys. Can't let old Wes down in front of his people'—that sort of thing.

"Sounds corny as hell, I know, and it was only half-serious at the time and half in jest. But some of the guys evidently thought about it overnight—I know I did—because the next day we all came into the clubhouse really bent on making an effort for Wes. It wasn't trying to stay out of third place or thinking we could make another run at the Dodgers—hell, we'd all forgotten about that. It was strictly, 'Gotta do something for Wes.' "

7

"Let 'er Rip"

HAD I KNOWN that prior to taking the field the Giants had convened in the clubhouse and dedicated themselves to making the day a pleasant one for Westrum, I might have devoted more attention to the stocky but frangible Giant receiver. But I had ended my boycott for the sole purpose of getting my first look at Willie Mays, so he was the focus of my attention.

As I've already mentioned, the Giants won both games. Maglie concluded his battle of wits with Waitkus at the end of the first match, and rookie Al Corwin came back to pitch a four-hitter and win 2 to 1, thanks to a Bobby Thomson double with two men on. And so the Giants did their part to make the day a memorable one for Westrum—although he whiffed five times and came up empty in the hitting department.

The New Yorkers beat the Phils the following evening on a three-run Whitey Lockman home run. Then they edged out the Dodgers 3 to 2 behind George Spencer in what everyone thought would be a meaningless series with Brooklyn at the Polo Grounds.

It was Spencer's forty-fourth appearance of the year, but only his third start. With the Giant staff exhausted and only Maglie and Jansen anywhere near dependable, Durocher was desperate for starters.

Again the winning margin was supplied by a Lockman home run.

Jim Hearn, who had been struggling for the past month, came back the next evening and held the Dodgers to a run as the Polo Grounders won 3 to 1 on a Westrum homer in the eighth. Hearn got a lot of help from Willie Mays, who pulled off a play that snuffed out a Brooklyn rally—a play that has gone down in baseball annals as one of the truly unbelievable plays of all time.

With one out, the score tied 1 and 1 in the top of the eighth, and Billy Cox, a fast man, on third for the Dodgers, Carl Furillo hit a long fly into right-centerfield. Mays, shaded toward left-center, broke for it. For a moment it looked as though the ball might fall in for extra bases, but as Mays sped toward it Giant fans sighed in relief— he was going to reach it. Cox would tag up and score easily from third, sure, but at least Mays would prevent Furillo from getting on.

For an ordinary centerfielder it would have been an extraordinary catch. For Mays it was routine. It was what happened next that turned it into legend. Mays intercepted the ball at full gallop and going away, about 330 feet from the plate. Cox was poised on third in a semisprinter's stance, 90 feet away from the plate. The instant the ball touched Mays' glove, Cox was off for home. Westrum, not dreaming there would be a throw, didn't even bother to remove his mask.

"The thing everybody talked about later," says Mays, "was takin' the ball on my left, it was away from my throwin' arm. I'd have to come to a stop and get all turned around 'fore I could throw, and that'd give a turtle time to score."

What Mays did after catching the ball was let the momentum of its impact in his glove spin him completely around. As he came around he saw Lockman lined up with the plate as a cutoff man—standard first baseman's procedure on a ball hit into right field with men on base. With his hat twirling off his head, Mays spun around and without losing a shred of motion heaved the ball on a clothesline at Lockman's head 275 feet away.

Still spinning, now with his back to the plate, the centerfielder corkscrewed to the ground, then peered back under his armpit to the infield. He couldn't locate the ball. All he could see in the far distance was Cox racing toward home plate and starting to slide.

When Mays released the ball it took off as though it had a will of its own. In spite of his slingshot of an arm, Mays, throwing from such an awkward, off-balance position, could not possibly have put such velocity on it. Yet the ball streaked at Lockman with astonishing speed and unerring aim.

"I was absolutely astounded," Lockman recently recalled to me. "I'd had balls thrown to me by Stanky or whoever was playing second from only a few feet away, really hard—you know how it is, you hardly have time to react. Well, this ball was like that, only it was coming from, what, 250, 275 feet away. I remember seeing Willie throw, and the next instant the ball was on top of me. I heard Wes yell to let it come, but I ducked out of there more for self-preservation than anything else."

Westrum, his mask still on, took the throw right on top of the plate with the astonished sliding Cox still three feet away. After being tagged out, Cox simply sat there staring at the plate. The Polo Grounds erupted, according Mays an ovation that hadn't been heard there since Carl Hubbell struck out five American League sluggers in a row in the 1934 All-Star Game.

Mays trotted off the field looking a bit worried and bewildered. When his disbelieving teammates greeted him at the top of the steps, he shrugged his way through them. In those days of his rookie year he didn't like it when a big fuss was made over him. He didn't feel deserving—after all, he only did what came naturally. Later on in his career, when second nature began to desert him, he would learn to crave the big fuss.

As often happens when a player makes a sensational, inning-ending play, he was first up in the bottom of the eighth. There was another standing ovation as he emerged from the dugout with his bats. Still another as he lined a single to left. The next hitter was Westrum, and the Giant catcher powered a home run into the upper deck in left to put the Giants ahead to stay, 3 to 1.

The next day, in the final game of the series, Maglie fashioned a four-hitter to win his seventeenth, 2 to 1—despite three Giant errors. Suddenly, in five days, the Polo Grounders had won six in a row and were 9½ games behind the Dodgers. Was something cooking? As they left for Philadelphia on the morning of Friday, August 17, to

open a three-game weekend set with the Phillies, no one dared enter-
tain any hope—not at this late date in the season. All hope, all wishful thinking, had finally been abandoned. Not even the members of
the team gave it any thought.

"Nah," Durocher claims today. "I was still thinking about holding onta second place when we went to Philly for that weekend
series. Hell, the Phils were still closer to us than we were to the
Dodgers. All I was thinking about was tryna make sure we held onta
that second-place money."

Wonder finally rekindled the flames of hope, at least among local
fans, as the New Yorkers extended their streak to sixteen straight victories with successive come-from-behind doubleheader wins over the
Cubs at the Polo Grounds on Sunday and Monday, August 26 and
27, while the Dodgers were splitting a pair of twin bills. When the
festivities were over on Monday night, the Giants were only 5 games
behind.

Sixteen straight! Five games behind! Giant fans were incredulous.
Knowing better, they permitted sweet anticipation to shove aside
mere hope. And as if to stem them from their suicidal course, the
press continued to hoist warnings. "The Giants have won 16 straight
while the Dodgers have been playing .500 ball," wrote Gene Ward
in the *Daily News* of August 28, "but in my view Leo Durocher's
minions have blown their wad. There is no way they can keep up the
pace. They're due for a loss, and with a team like the Giants, playing
high over their heads, all it will take is one reversal to burst the
balloon."

Durocher's charges got their loss that same day, dropping back to
six behind with a 2 to 0 defeat at the hands of the Pirates. All through
the winning streak they had fielded shoddily, but they had compensated with timely hitting. With no hitting however, as in the loss to
the Pirates, their fielding—or lack thereof—came to the fore.

With the exception of Mays and Westrum, the Giants were never a
threat to beat anyone with their fielding—indeed, they were next to
last in the league in that department. And even Mays, for all his instinctive brilliance on tough plays, revealed a tendency to mess up
the easy ones more often than was comfortable. Whitey Lockman, although coming along nicely in his brief tenure at first base, was not

yet completely used to the big claw mitt and was prone to mistakes. Stanky at second, though a wily fielder, had a habit of going on error binges, as did shortstop Alvin Dark, who had committed ten miscues throughout the sixteen-game streak. Bobby Thomson at third was still making more than an ordinary third baseman's share of bobbles. In right field, Don Mueller tended to muff line drives that he had to reach across his body for, and he had no arm to speak of. In left, Irvin was still so busy positioning Mays for various hitters that his concentration on balls hit to him frequently flagged. The Pirates, then, did not so much snap the Giants' winning streak on August 28 as the Giants gave the game away. They made three errors that day, and it seemed as if their defensive incompetence would be the end of all their dreams. To make matters worse, Westrum suffered a fractured right thumb.

But the Durochermen came back the next day and stifled the Pirates 3 to 1 with Jim Hearn pitching magnificently in his last few outings, fashioning a nifty three-hitter. The club, moreover, committed no errors for the first time in 22 games. The day had considerably more significance than that however, although no one could possibly realize it at the time. Bobby Thomson's bat was still sizzling, so Durocher switched him in the order with Mays. It was now Thomson batting sixth behind Lockman, and Mays hitting seventh. It was the batting order the club would take with them through the rest of the season, and on August 29, Thomson's first day in the sixth spot, it looked like this:

1. Stanky	(2B)	– Avg.	.256 and	steady.
2. Dark	(SS)	– Avg.	.318 and	steady.
3. Mueller	(RF)	– Avg.	.278 and	rising.
4. Irvin	(LF)	– Avg.	.310 and	rising.
5. Lockman	(1B)	– Avg.	.283 and	steady.
6. Thomson	(3B)	– Avg.	.260 and	rising.
7. Mays	(CF)	– Avg.	.290 and	steady.
8. Westrum	(C)	– Avg.	.231 and	steady.
9. Pitcher				

From the point of view of batting averages as well as almost every other item of offensive and defensive statistics, the Giant line-up, though respectable, appeared to be no match for the Dodgers, who had shaken out of their .500 slump and won five of their last seven games. A close position-by-position comparison of the two clubs was all the more depressing.

Behind the plate it was Westrum (when he was healthy) versus Campanella. The Giant receiver had a slight edge on defense, but it was no contest in the offensive category, Westrum's sixteen home runs thus far notwithstanding. Campanella was powering along at a .338 pace and was on his way to the league's Most Valuable Player award. At catcher, then, the Dodgers had the clear edge.

At first base it was Lockman versus Gil Hodges. At bat, the higher average belonged to Lockman by fifteen percentage points, but Hodges had more than three times as many home runs and thirty more runs batted in. On defense, Hodges was the nonpareil first baseman of the league. So again, at first base the Dodgers had an edge.

At second it was Stanky versus Robinson. Robinson would end the 1951 season hitting almost a hundred points higher than Stanky, but that only began to tell the story of the Dodger's superiority at second base. Every time Robinson was on base he was a threat to score, not so with Stanky. Defensively, Robinson had more quickness and range than Stanky. The Dodgers excelled at second too.

Alvin Dark at .318 had it over Pee Wee Reese at .286, but Dark's superiority at the plate was at least partially balanced by Reese's defensive superiority. At shortstop one had to give a slight edge to the Giants.

At third base it was Thomson against Billy Cox, who, like Hodges at first base, had no peer fielding the keystone corner. The contest defensively was made even more one-sided by virtue of Thomson's inexperience and awkwardness at his new position. Offensively, Cox was a .280 singles hitter, Thomson a power hitter who would eventually hit .294 with 32 home runs and 101 RBIs. You would have to say the match-up was even, all things considered.

In left field Monte Irvin had it all over Andy Pafko of the Dodgers. Center field was another story. Mays, though sensational, was a rookie and still made the rookie's frequent mental miscues. The Dodgers' Duke Snider was in his fifth big-league campaign. He could run and throw, and hit with power. Offensively he and Mays were even. Defensively, you had to give the edge to Snider on the basis of his experience.

Right field had to go to Carl Furillo of the Dodgers, if only by a whisker. He and Mueller were hitting about the same. Furillo's defensive talent gave him the edge—with his arm and his uncanny knack for playing balls perfectly off the wall, he robbed dozens of enemy hitters of extra-base hits.

So, the Dodgers led at five of eight positions. The Giants led at two, although one—shortstop—might have been arguable. Third base was a toss-up.

By mid-August the pitching staffs were a toss-up as well, with the Giants gaining a possible edge when they acquired Corwin. But even with that slight advantage, the Dodgers still had to be considered uncatchable.

Which is precisely what Bobby Thomson thought when, after recovering from their 2 to 0 streak-breaking loss to Pittsburgh by coming back to beat the Pirates 3 to 1, the Giants went out the next day and blew a seven-run lead to lose again to the Bucs, 10 to 9.

"That was horrendous," says Thomson, thinking back on it. "We all thought that was it. We'd made another dash at the Dodgers with that winning streak, got down to five behind, and were beginning to think . . . maybe. But then the way we blew that game to Pittsburgh we all felt, well, we tried, but it's just not meant to be."

In two weeks the Giants had descended from 13½ to 5 games behind the Dodgers. For the next two weeks they fluctuated between 7 and 5 games behind.

The New Yorkers hosted the Dodgers in a crucial two-game series on Saturday, September 1. It was a cloudy, windy, cold day and 40,000 customers shivered in the stands. The game was another donnybrook, with Maglie and Robinson at it again. In the fourth inning Maglie let one fly at Robinson. The Dodger second baseman ducked, but the ball appeared to glance off his bat for a strike. The fans approved and even Maglie cracked a smile of satisfaction. Robinson, however, spun around to the umpire and angrily claimed the ball had hit his wrist. The umpire agreed and waved him to first base. When

Maglie realized what was happening he slammed down his glove and came stalking off the mound at the umpire. Westrum was already disputing the call and by the time Maglie got to the plate Durocher had materialized to lead the Giant debating team. The argument raged hot and heavy for five minutes, Durocher appealing to the first-base umpire, the third-base umpire, anyone who would listen.

Fortunately for Maglie, putting Robinson on did no damage this time—the next Dodger hitter flied out to end the inning. The Giants were leading 5 to 1 when he hit Robinson and they went on to get three more runs to win the game with ease. It was Maglie's eighteenth victory of the season, but the game was more memorable for the three home runs hit by Don Mueller—two more than he had hit in his combined first two years as a Giant—and a triple play pulled off by Dark and Stanky.

Sunday was another dreary day, especially for the Dodgers, as they bowed again, this time to Jim Hearn, 11 to 2. It was a day of more bean balls, with Dodger pitchers knocking down Thomson and Mays. It was a day of more arguments, with Dodger manager Dressen at one point sending his entire bench into the distant clubhouse to protest umpires' warnings—more fodder for the booing fans. And it was a day that Mueller hit two more home runs, tying the major-league record of five in two games. But most of all, it was a day that reversed the Giants' despair of two days earlier and made believers of them all. Back at five games behind, they looked at one another in the clubhouse after the game and said, "Yeah, we can do it!"

"That two-game sweep did it for me," recalls Monte Irvin. "We not only beat the Dodgers when we had to, we pummeled the hell out of them. The winning streak was great, believe me, but when it was over we were all let down a bit. Then, losing those two to Pittsburgh—but coming back to whip the Brooks the way we did—well, what can I tell you? We knew then we had a very good chance to go all the way."

"It wouldn't be easy, we knew that," says Bill Rigney, picking up the recollection. "We were going to have to keep winning. Even if the Dodgers only played .500 ball, we were still going to have to go at a better than .750 clip to catch them. We couldn't depend on the

Dodgers playing .500, we knew, but we decided we were going to play .750 no matter what.''

It certainly didn't look the next day as though the Dodgers were going to cooperate by playing .500 baseball. They returned to Ebbets Field to sweep a Labor Day doubleheader from the Braves while the Giants split with the Phils, blowing a 3 to 0 lead to lose the first game 6 to 3, winning the second behind Koslo 3 to 1. They slipped back to 6 behind.

The day after Labor Day was an open date for both clubs. Then on Wednesday, September 6, the Giants won two at Boston, getting back half a notch on the Dodgers, who beat the Phils in a single game in Brooklyn.

On Thursday the Giants were rained out, as were the Dodgers. On Friday the New Yorkers wrapped up their stay in Boston by beating the Braves 7 to 3 behind Jansen, with Bobby Thomson going five for five. But the Dodgers whipped the Phils too, so the Giants returned to meet them in the first of another two-game set at Ebbets Field still 5½ games behind. The date was Saturday, September 8.

In the past four weeks the Giants had posted a record of 23 wins and three losses, an incredible performance for any team at any time. Could they keep it up? Could they continue to do the impossible? They would surely have to because Brooklyn, despite its two-game loss to the Polo Grounders the week before, showed no signs of folding. In the same period the Dodgers had won 16 and lost 11. Moreover, they had won their last four in a row and seemed poised to resume their domination of the league. What worried the Giants most as they readied themselves to meet Brooklyn again was that they had beaten them in each of their last five encounters. The law of averages had to catch up with them.

It did, with a vengeance. "Leo Durocher's happy dream of a two-game sweep over the Dodgers that would put the Giants within striking distance of the National League pennant,'' went one newspaper report, "was rudely dispelled yesterday. After losing five straight at the Polo Grounds, the Dodgers reasserted their mastery over the Giants at Ebbets Field by thoroughly thrashing the Manhattanites 9 to 0 before a surprisingly small crowd of 23,000.''

Dressen and the Dodgers were out to completely humiliate their old boss Durocher and put the Giants in their place, even going so far as to have Robinson squeeze home a superfluous run in the bottom of the eighth with the Dodgers ahead 8 to 0. It had to be an immensely satisfying gesture to Robinson, Dressen, and the rest of the Brooklyn team. Its net effect, however, was to arouse and inspire the Giants. Durocher, ever the opportunist when it came to winning and losing, was overjoyed. "That was a pretty bush thing to do," a writer coaxingly said to him after the game, hoping to elicit a nasty quote.

"What's that?" Durocher answered.

"You know, squeezing in an extra run so late in the game with a lead like that. Make you mad?"

"Mad?" Durocher growled. "I'm delighted."

"Delighted? Why delighted?"

"Because I got their motherfuckin' bunt sign, that's why!"

Bill Rigney recalls his own mood that day. "I'd gone up to pinch-hit—oh, in the seventh or eighth inning. Now, the Dodgers weren't too fond of me—I'd become a pretty good bench jockey and used to save my best remarks for them. Trouble was, from their point of view, I wasn't playing too much that year, so they didn't get much opportunity to get back at me. Anyway, here I come up to the plate late in the game and they're coasting along with a big lead. Wouldn't you know, Newcombe's first pitch comes right at my head. I went down, my glasses went flying, and I busted a lens. Well, that had me peeved—late in the game, easy lead, throwing at me like that, then all of them laughing out there because I'd busted my glasses.

"Afterwards, in the clubhouse, we were all steaming over the Robinson squeeze, and I was especially mad about them throwing at me. I started shouting at nobody in particular, 'Gotta rip these guys tomorrow!'

"Seems back there, the day we won the first game of our sixteen-game streak, back when they had the day for Westrum, we were all trying to encourage him every time he went up to the plate. Somebody shouted out—I think it was George Spencer—'Let 'er rip, Wes, let 'er rip.' Somebody else picked it up and pretty soon half a dozen of the guys were shouting 'Let 'er rip, Wes!'

"Well, after that, when we were going through the streak, whenever we came up against a tough situation, had to get a run or two, we'd start calling out to whoever was coming up, 'Let 'er rip, Mule' to Mueller, or 'Hoot Mon, let 'er rip' to Bobby, or whoever was coming up.

"At first it was sort of a casual thing, nobody paid it much mind. But then one day we realized it had started the day we won that first game, and that it was working—I mean, most every time we'd use it something good would happen. By the time we hit the end of the streak it was like a good-luck charm—every time we wanted something good to happen we'd start saying, 'Let 'er rip!'

"So here I am in the clubhouse saying, 'We gotta rip those guys,' and pretty soon some of the others start shouting, 'Yeah, gonna rip 'em tomorrow! Gonna rip 'em!' From there on in, 'Let 'er rip' became sort of our official slogan. We went out there the next day against the Brooks and all you could hear on our side of the field was 'Gonna rip 'em,' or 'let's rip these sonsabitches,' or 'let 'er rip, Sal,' every time Maglie threw a pitch.''

Maglie ripped his way to his twentieth win of the year against five losses, besting Ralph Branca 2 to 1 in a raucous cliffhanger. So overjoyed were the Dodger fans by what they took to be the previous day's humiliation of the Giants that every time Durocher stuck his head out of the dugout the stands would turn white with waving handkerchiefs. It was the ultimate insult in Brooklyn. Boos, jeers, catcalls, broken bottles flying through the air were nothing compared to the handkerchief number. At one point the waving handkerchiefs became such a distraction to the players that the Dodgers' public-address announcer, Tex Rickard, requested that it cease. Naturally, even more handkerchiefs were whipped from pockets. Ebbets Field became an undulating sea of white. Durocher ate it up.

The game was pressurized all the way, and right to the end the Giants looked as though they were destined to lose, despite Maglie's withering stuff. The Dodgers had gotten their run in the first inning. That was Maglie's one big weakness—he tended to give up a run or two in the first or second inning before gaining command of his curve ball. The Giants got two off Branca in the sixth, but Giant fans knew that didn't mean much in Giant-Dodger games. Sure enough the Dodgers rallied in the bottom of the eighth, Jackie Robinson getting to third base with one out, Pafko the next hitter. Giant fans could feel the air go out of them, their stomachs turning queasy, as Robinson pranced off third, baiting Maglie. He was sure to score; he always did, it seemed.

Then there was a small miracle. Pafko hit a one-hop smash down the third-base line. Bobby Thomson, who had been muffing regularly at the still unfamiliar position, streaked to his right, gloved it, tagged the ducking Robinson, and then whirled and threw to first for the double play—so fast that one hardly believed it. Thomson was in the dugout before the Giant fans could recover themselves enough to express their appreciation.

With the victory the Giants inched back to 5½ behind again, but with a long western trip coming up, time seemed to be running out on them. They had only 16 games left to play. At 5½ games behind, their situation was not to be sneered at; however, they were seven behind in the lost column, which meant that they had played three more games than the Dodgers—games they could never get back because they were on the lost side of their won-lost ledger. As of the night of September 9, the standings stood this way:

	Won	Lost	Games Behind
Brooklyn	87	48	—
New York	83	55	5½

So, even if the Giants now won four in a row and the Dodgers lost four in a row, they would be even at 87 wins apiece, but the Dodgers still would have lost three fewer games. With three more games to play than the Giants, they would always have that extra cushion. And they weren't about to lose four in a row. All the Giants could do was keep winning and pray.

Tuesday, September 11, found the Giants in St. Louis where they split a doubleheader with the Cardinals. Brooklyn won a single game in Cincinnati. Thus the Giants went back to 6 games behind, 8 in the loss column. With less than three weeks left, the newspapers began to play the "magic number" game. Any combination of Brooklyn victories and Giant defeats numbering 11 meant the pennant for the

Dodgers. In other words, even if the Giants continued to play super-lative baseball and won 10 of their remaining 14 games, losing only four, the Dodgers had to win only 7 of their remaining 18 to clinch it.

On Friday, September 14, the New Yorkers moved on to Chicago. Jim Hearn and George Spencer combined with Thomson and Mueller to beat the Cubs 7 to 2 in a game that featured a violent argument be-tween Westrum and umpire Al Barlick. Westrum was immediately suspended for three days for shoving Barlick. With the Dodgers win-ning in Pittsburgh, Westrum's suspension seemed to Giant fans the last straw. They were still six games behind and had been perched around that figure, making no progress, for the last three weeks.

"That was a frustrating time for us," remembers Westrum, "and it's probably the reason I got suspended. All through those three weeks we'd been winning but getting nowhere. When we went on that last western trip we knew that even if we kept winning there was no guarantee it would mean anything. Nevertheless, we were deter-mined to keep winning, and when we lost those two games in St. Louis it really made us tight. Up to then, there hadn't been any real pressure on the club—we were all loose and relaxed and enjoying ourselves. But going west that last time the pressure began to build. No one wanted to make any mistakes—so naturally, we started mak-ing mistakes, which cost us the two games against the Cards.

"But what was even more unforgivable was having to lose on an umpire's mistake. So that first game in Chicago, I guess I blew my stack. It was early in the game, Hearn didn't have a hell of a lot of stuff—heck, he was tired, so was everybody—and the score was tied at 1 and 1. The Cubs had a man on third—Frankie Baumholtz, as I recollect—I believe he'd doubled to open the inning and moved up on an infield out. So there's one out and Baumholtz on third, and the next hitter—Hank Sauer, I think it was—hits a fly ball to left, pretty deep. Everybody thinks sacrifice fly, Baumholtz'll tag and score after the catch.

"Well, they didn't figure on Monte Irvin's arm. Monte came in with a clothesline strike. I didn't have to move more than two inches to get the ball. Baumholtz slid and he was dead out, but Al Barlick called him safe. That's when I blew, I mean I usually kept pretty good control of myself, but that time I just went berserk—I wasn't going to lose on any umpire's goof. So I got thrown out, then suspended. We came back and won that game, and I'd say that little incident shook the club up a bit. We all realized, I mean, really realized at last, that nobody was giving us anything, that we had to go out and get it on our own.''

The following day, with Westrum watching from the stands, the Giants downed the Cubs 5 to 2. The Dodgers lost in Pittsburgh, and now the Giants were five games behind again. But so what? They had achieved that three weeks previously, at the conclusion of their sixteen-game streak, only to find themselves unable to penetrate farther. Their chances had been infinitely better then, with 28 games left to play, than they were now with only 11 left to go.

NEW YORK GIANTS 1951 NATIONAL LEAGUE CHAMPIONS

Back row: Sheldon Jones, George Spencer, Monte Irvin, Jack Kramer, Jim Hearn, Spider Jorgensen, Clint Hartung, Allen Gettel, Bobby Thomson, Monte Kennedy, Larry Jansen, Sal Maglie, Bill Rigney, Whitey Lockman.

Center row: Wes Westrum, Roger Bowman, Artie Wilson, Dave Koslo, Leo Durocher (manager), Rafael Noble, Henry Thompson, Don Mueller, Jack Lohrke, Fred Fitzsimmons (coach).

Front row: Frank Shellenback (coach), Herman Franks (coach), William Leonard (bat boy), Jack Maguire, Sal Yvars, Alvin Dark, Eddie Stanky.

Taken during spring training, the picture does not include Willie Mays, who was called up from Minneapolis in May.

(Top left) Willie Mays joins the Giants, May 1951.

(Bottom left) Whitey Lockman ponders what to do with a first baseman's mitt after the opening of the 1951 season, when manager Durocher asked him to switch from the outfield to first base.

(Top) Sal Maglie (right) makes a muscle for the benefit of Larry Jansen. At this point, September 28, the Giants were a half-game out of first, with two games left to play against the Braves.

(Bottom) *The starting pitchers.* The Dodgers' Ralph Branca (left) shakes hands with rival Jim Hearn of the Giants, before the opening game of the playoff series, October 1, 1951. Branca's record was 13 and 10, Hearn's 16 and 10.

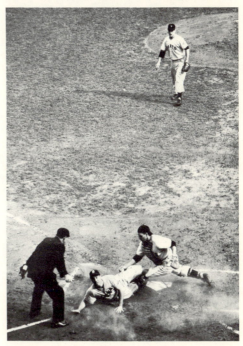

(Top) After getting the force-out, Giants' second baseman Eddie Stanky steps over the sliding Jackie Robinson and fires to first in time to nip Dodger catcher Roy Campanella. The first playoff game ended in a 3 to 1 victory for the Giants.

(Right) An argument erupted during the second playoff game on October 2, when Brooklyn's Duke Snider attempted to score from second on Gil Hodges' slow roller to the mound. Hodges was safe at first after being hit by the throw from Giants' pitcher George Spencer. However, first baseman Whitey Lockman made a fine recovery, and though his throw home seemed to be a trifle late, Wes Westrum blocked off the plate perfectly and umpire Larry Goetz called Snider out.

(Opposite page) In the fourth inning of Game 1 at Ebbets Field, Bobby Thomson smashes a two-run homer into the left-field stands. Giants' outfielder Monte Irvin, here nearing second, hit another home run in the eighth inning to sew up the game for New York.

(Above) New York's Bobby Thomson (right)
pulls a boner in the second inning of the
deciding third game when he goes for second
base, only to find teammate Whitey Lockman
still there. Bobby tried to retreat to first but was
tagged out. Jackie Robinson of the Dodgers
watches the confusion.

(Left) *A piece of the miracle*. Thomson's foul-
up was completely forgotten seven innings
later, however. Here he slugs his historic three-
run homer in the bottom of the ninth to clinch
the game and the pennant for the Giants.

(Above) Giants' players and fans converge on Bobby Thomson (here his head is being rubbed).

(Below) Hero Thomson is hugged by club owner Horace Stoneham (left) and manager Leo Durocher in the Giants' dressing room.

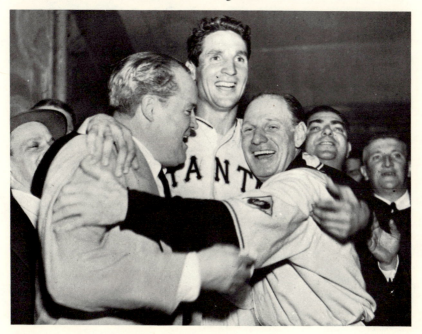

(Above) Thomson and Durocher (extreme left) attempt to enter the dressing room, but the ecstatic fans have other ideas.

(Left) Giants' catcher Wes Westrum: ''It was just meant to be. . . . We were a team of destiny.''

8

"No Day For Weak Hearts"

THE DRAMA WASN'T FINISHED yet. The winning streak of August had only been the first act, the past three weeks the intermission. Now the second-act curtain was about to rise.

On September 16 the Polo Grounders traveled from Chicago to Pittsburgh and won the first game of the twin bill with the Pirates—Irvin and Thomson accounting for all but one of the team's runs. At the end of the game the scoreboard showed that the Dodgers had beaten the Cubs in a single game, so the Giants remained 5 behind. But they had a second game to play.

"Durocher had Sheldon Jones scheduled to start that second game," recalls Sal Maglie. "I'd pitched the last St. Louis game and'd had only two days' rest, but Jones hadn't been going too good, so Durocher came up to me between games and asked me if I was ready to go. It was a chance for us to break that five-games-behind mark we'd been tryin' to get through all that time, so I said sure."

Maglie's arm was half-dead, and the Pirates jumped on him for four runs early in the game. The he pulled himself together and pitched shutout ball into the ninth. Meanwhile the Giants scratched and clawed their way back to a 4 and 4 tie. "It's hard to say that when you're all playing for a common cause you're gonna get base hits and runs just when you need them,'' Alvin Dark philosophizes, ''but in that game we were really together on breaking that five-game stymie. We all felt that if we could do it, we had a real chance. We'd been coming from behind to win games time and time again during those weeks, but it wasn't as if it was something we consciously set out to do. It just kept happening. But there, in that second Pirate game, we knew—and I emphasize that word—we *knew* we were gonna come back and win it. It was like it was predestined, like the good Lord had been sitting up there all that time looking down on us, putting obstacles in our way all season, and observing how we dealt with them, and now He decided He liked what He'd seen and chose to put Himself on our side at last.''

In the top of the ninth Don Mueller led off with a single to right but was thrown out at second on Irvin's bunt, which was intended as a sacrifice. With Irvin on first and one out, Whitey Lockman laced a single into right-center, and the fleet Irvin slid safely into third. The next batter was Hank Thompson, who had been recalled from his minor-league exile a week or so before and who for defensive purposes had been put into the game an inning earlier in place of Bobby Thomson. Thompson lofted a short fly ball to the Pirate rightfielder. After the catch Irvin tagged and sprinted for home, beating the throw by a whisker in a storm of dust. Mays then walked, pushing Lockman to second. And then Ray Noble, subbing for the suspended Westrum, redeemed three months of ineffectiveness at the plate by singling Lockman home.

That was all the scoring, but it was enough. Maglie set the Pirates down in the bottom of the ninth for his twenty-first victory against only six losses. More important, the Giants had finally penetrated the barrier—they were 4½ games behind the Dodgers.

But that meant more pressure, for now they were faced with another obstacle, one they would attack for a full week—the next to last week of the season—without cracking: the three-games-behind barrier. Since that fateful Sunday of August 12 they had won an unbelievable 29 games and lost only 6, and now, even if they were to win *all* their remaining nine games, they were still going to need some help from Brooklyn.

With the Dodgers losing five of their next seven, the Giants got it, but it didn't seem to do much good. On Monday, the day after their twin victory over the Pirates, the Polo Grounders were idle, traveling to Cincinnati. But the Dodgers, with Roy Campanella being beaned, lost in Chicago. The Giants inched up to 4 behind. On Tuesday they again came from behind in a heart-stopper to beat Cincinnati, while the Dodgers lost in St. Louis: 3 behind. But on Wednesday the Dodgers shut out the Cards while rain washed out the Giants and Reds; Brooklyn regained half a game. And on Thursday the Giants lost to the Reds 3 to 1, another ninth-inning rally this time falling short, while the Dodgers bested the Cards 4 to 3. Back to 4½ games behind!

It was the end of the Giant road trip and, many were convinced, the end—finally, finally the end—of the dream. "Giants' Pennant Hopes Sink with End of 5-Game Streak" read the headline in Friday's *Times* as the club, saddened and dejected, arrived at Pennsylvania Station that morning.

"It was a pretty gloomy ride most of the way," recalls Bobby Thomson. "Some of the guys were still 'up,' Rig, Stanky, Leo, but most of us were feeling what the newspapers were saying—sunk. But then somebody remarked that one of the papers said the Dodgers were going to start selling World Series tickets that afternoon. If you ask me, that was a mistake on their part. A lot of us were ready to concede on that train back from Cincinnati, but we were damned if we were going to let the Brooklyn management concede for us. We all got to talking about that, and by the time we got into New York no one was ready to concede any more."

That Friday the Giants weren't scheduled, but the Dodgers had a game at Ebbets Field against the Phils. A few of the Giants, with nothing else to do, journeyed to Brooklyn to have a look, and what they saw heartened them. The Dodgers, suddenly playing uncharacteristically cautious baseball, let the Phils walk all over them 9 to 6. On Saturday, when the Polo Grounders regrouped in their clubhouse for a home game against the Braves, the word was out: the Dodgers are feeling the pressure—they're squabbling among themselves and making stupid mistakes. There's still a chance!

That Giant fans had given up on the club was attested to by the fact that only 11,000 customers showed up at the Polo Grounds that afternoon. I was one of them. Leaving for Indiana and college the next day, it was my last chance to see my men. I wasn't disappointed. Even though they had reverted to shoddy fielding, they pulled another one out of the fire at the last moment.

Larry Jansen was going for his twentieth win. Despite two errors by Bobby Thomson at third and one by Lockman, Jansen managed to hold the Braves to a single run for eight innings. Going into the last of the eighth, the score was tied at one-all.

With one out in the Giants' half of the eighth, Thomson worked Warren Spahn for a walk. Irvin followed with a booming two-strike triple into deep right-center, scoring Thomson. Lockman walked, then Mays lashed a single, scoring Irvin and sending Lockman to third, whence he scored on Mueller's sacrifice fly.

Jansen blanked the Braves in the ninth; the Giants had won the thirty-first of their last thirty-eight games. In Brooklyn the Dodgers were losing the second day in a row to Philadelphia, 7 to 3. The Giants were back to 3 behind.

On Sunday, September 23, I was at Grand Central Station about to entrain for Indiana when that day's scores were announced over the public-address system. The Giants had won again 4 to 1 as Maglie got his twenty-second win. But Brooklyn also won, Preacher Roe getting his twenty-second as well. The Giants were still 3 games behind, unable to get closer since breaking the five-game barrier the week before. Damn! I though as I found a seat. Later, while the train sped north along the Hudson, I was oblivious to the spectacular scenery. Instead I was busy figuring the possibilities and probabilities. The Giants simply *had* to win all their five remaining games; then, assuming they did, the Dodgers had to win only four of their remaining seven to hold on to the pennant. One could reasonably expect the Dodgers to win at least four, especially with the pressure on. To expect the Giants to win all their remaining five was unreasonable, no matter how fantastically they'd been going—indeed, it was downright irrational, absurd. They were not experienced in a pennant-pressure situation, they hadn't gone through one in twenty years, whereas the Dodgers were recent veterans of it. Yet, the irrational cogitator noted, with a record of 32 and 7 since August 12, the Polo Grounders had been winning at a rate of nearly five games for every loss. Was it conceivable? They had just won two, which meant they were due for a loss in their remaining five—the law of averages being what it was. And if they were destined to lose one of their last five, the Dodgers would only have to win three of their seven. I dozed off with the gentle swaying of the train, my dream locked in combat with common sense.

Monday was the day the Giants resolved all doubts: going into the final week of the season, no matter what, they were not going to fold.

"Of all the 'key' games we played in that six- or seven-week stretch, that Monday game was in my opinion the 'keyest,' " says Monte Irvin.

"It was that game that made me begin to think matters had been taken out of our hands, that we were no longer doing it ourselves, but some greater force had taken over," Alvin Dark ruminates.

"It was like living through a dream—that game and everything that happened after," reflects Bill Rigney. "After that game I knew for sure we were going to do it. In fact the decision as to whether we *could* do it or not was no longer in our hands. It was inevitable that we would. I mean, that last week we could have lost half our starting line-up and our two top pitchers, and still it would have happened."

The game represented the New Yorkers' last appearance of the year at the Polo Grounds. The populace was so sure the Giants had made nothing more than a magnificent gesture in their comeback that only 6,000 turned out to watch them.

The Giants were wrapping up their three-game series with the Braves, who were to play a stellar supporting role in the events to come. Behind 3 to 0 by the sixth inning, the Polo Grounders should then and there, by all the rules of logic, have tossed in the towel. Instead they pounded two runs across in the seventh, and then, with the aid of a Boston error in the eighth, milked another score to tie the game at 3 and 3. The few witnesses present collapsed back into their seats with hearts racing.

The Braves came back in the top of the ninth to put men on second and third with only one out. Dave Koslo in relief got the next two Braves to pop up, and the Giants came off the field still tied.

The tension was unbearable. "How many more times were we going to be able to pull this stuff off?" asks Wes Westrum rhetorically. "If we could do it again—well, I mean that was it, we were gonna go all the way. It was the only way you could figure it. I think Don Mueller went up there to lead off our half of the ninth. I remember I was behind him, on deck, and as he stepped in he looked back at me for a second—don't know why. He had this worried look on his face, so I yelled at him. 'Let 'er rip, Mule!' I said."

Mueller let her rip, bouncing a single past Brave first baseman Earl Torgeson. With none out and Mueller on first, it was an obvious sacrifice situation. Durocher called Westrum back to the bench and sent up Rigney, one of the team's best bunters, to pinch-hit. He dropped a beauty along the third-base line, and Mueller went into second standing up as Rigney was thrown out at first, the only play Boston third baseman Bob Elliott had.

With the winning run on second and Koslo due up next, Durocher sent Davey Williams out to run for Mueller and brought catcher Rafael Noble in from the bullpen to hit for Koslo. "Let 'er rip, Ray baby!" Noble, overanxious, swung mightily at the first pitch and lofted a high pop to second base for the Giants' second out.

The next hitter was Stanky, the only Giant regular who hadn't been contributing much in the big push—his average was down to .245. "G'wan back, Eddie," Durocher yelled from third base, scanning his bench for a left-handed pinch hitter. Stanky spun around and glared at Durocher through slit eyes, the back of his neck turning scarlet. "Nah," Durocher said, having second thoughts, "g'wan up there 'n' hit one."

Stanky stalked back to the plate and settled in. He took the first pitch for a strike and stepped out of the box to address a remark at the umpire. The next pitch missed the inside corner for a ball. Stanky looked at Durocher for a sign. The Giant manager was a mime in the third-base coach's box, his hands flying about his uniform like a pair of hummingbirds. Finally Stanky saw the "swing away" sign.

Up and slightly in, the next pitch sped at him. But seeing it come off right-handed reliever Phil Paine's hand, Stanky thought it was a slider and stood his ground. The ball held high but veered away at the last moment. It was a bad pitch. Stanky normally would have taken it in the hopes of working the pitcher for a walk, but he didn't want to be on first base in this situation. That would set up the force play at any base for the third out. So he lashed at the pitch and sent it skittering through the hole between second and first, into right field, for a base hit. At third, as the ball went through, Durocher furiously waved Williams home, and the pinch runner scored easily to give the Giants their twenty-first come-from-behind triumph in the last six weeks. They trotted into their clubhouse 2½ games behind the Dodgers, who were not scheduled that day.

They had broken the three-game barrier, and from that moment the pennant race took on a life of its own. Not just New York but the entire country became interested again. Then as new kinds of pressure began to build, the nation became mesmerized by the doings of the Giants and Dodgers in the last week of September.

Most of the Giant players claim today that whatever pressure they felt only helped them. "Sure there was pressure," says Bobby Thomson, "but we had nothing to lose, so it was a free-wheeling kind of thing. If I came up in a clutch situation, even in that last week, I was just looking for a good pitch, not thinking about other things, like what'd happen if I didn't get a base hit. By then I knew if I didn't come through, someone coming up behind me would. That's the way it'd been going, and everybody in the first eight felt the same way. The only thing that was in the back of our minds was that it was all too good to be true, that the bubble might burst. But not that last week. That last week we knew it was too late for the bubble to burst. Things were just happening, and there was no accounting for them. When we needed a run, we knew the run would come. Either somebody'd make a hit, or the other side would make an error, or one of their pitchers would walk someone, or throw a wild pitch— something. That's the way it was, and there was no accounting for it, no way at all. So we just kind of floated along with it, enjoying every minute of it."

"The only really bad pressure," recalls Jim Hearn, "was on the pitching staff. We were just plain worn out, our arms were hanging dead. That was the real miracle to me. You look it up and you'll see something. You'll see that in those last four games of the season— let's see, the two in Philly and then the last two in Boston—we gave up a total of four runs. Four runs in four games! And us with our arms hanging off, pitching with two, three days' rest. That to me is the miracle at Coogan's Bluff.''

"I'll tell you about the pressure," Larry Jansen says today. "It wasn't so much that our arms were tired. Sure, we were working hard, but it wasn't our arms. It was—well, did you ever try to pitch after three nights of *no* sleep? That's what we were doing. Me, I mean, I'd finish a game and I'd be so exhausted, so drained, I couldn't sleep at all that night. The next night I'd get a few hours, but then the pressure'd begin to build to the next start two days away, and I wouldn't sleep for two nights. By the time I got out on the mound I'd be pitching from memory. But, by God, it must have worked, because that was one of my best years. It was the same with the others—Maglie, Hearn, Koslo, and the rest."

The pressure on the Dodgers was of a different kind. The Giant challenge had begun to take its toll, and although for the past few weeks they had held it off, they were now beginning to sense collapse. Each Dodger player, in his own way, secretly had a foretaste of it. Whereas the pressure on the Giants somehow unified them, perhaps because they discussed it among themselves and accepted it as a positive force, the pressure on the Dodgers began to tear them apart, perhaps because they didn't discuss it but kept it each to himself, refusing to acknowledge it. Just as the Giants couldn't wholly believe until the last week that, in the end, it was possible to catch the Dodgers, the Dodgers were becoming more and more certain that they were doomed to be caught by the Giants.

Roy Campanella recalls the mood on the Brooklyn club. After his beaning in Chicago he was out of action for a few days. "Our lead over the Giants had been cut to four games when I got back into the line-up. There was pressure on us now. A month before we were a free and easy bunch, breezing to an easy pennant. Now we were playing tight and nervous baseball, looking back over our shoulder and watching the scoreboard to see how the Giants were doing.

"During the last week we fought desperately to keep the pennant from slipping through our fingers. Everybody was grim and silent. There was no horseplay on the field. Tempers were short. We stayed out of each other's way."

There was still another kind of pressure building as well—this throughout the country. As the pennant race livened up again after the Giants' victory over the Braves in that final Polo Grounds' game, tension and suspense began to grip the nation at large. Anticipation spread from New York and across the land like a happy virus, and more and more people, even women, were turning first to the sports pages over their morning coffee.

The script of the final week of the race, wherever it was written— whether in the heavens above (according to Alvin Dark) or in the brain of Leo Durocher (according to Durocher)—was to be played out with increasingly deliberate and agonizing suspense. It was to bring New York and environs to a virtual standstill, much the way the city had been in 1927, waiting to hear if Lindbergh had made it.

The schedule helped set the stage for the suspense. Beginning Tuesday, September 25, the Giants had four games left to play and six days in which to play them. They would play Tuesday and Wednesday in Philadelphia, then be off Thursday and Friday, and then finish on Saturday and Sunday with two games in Boston.

The Dodgers had seven games left—which of course was to their advantage, and which made the Giants' prospects, in spite of any favorable heavenly factors operating in their favor, seem all the more hopeless. Brooklyn would play a doubleheader in Boston on Tuesday and a single game on Wednesday. They would play another single match against the Braves on Thursday while the Giants were idle. On Friday, while the Giants were again idle, they would play in Philadelphia, then finish with two more games against the Phils on Saturday and Sunday.

The newspapers were now obsessed with numbers and the myriad possibilities attached thereto. The Dodgers had to win only four of their last seven to assure themselves of the pennant—even if the Giants won all their remaining four. If the Giants lost only one, then Brooklyn needed to win only three. If on the other hand the Dodgers won only two of their remaining seven, the Giants could capture it by winning three of four. And so on. One enterprising reporter got Albert Einstein to analyze the mathematical probabilities of the last six days of the race. His conclusion was that the Dodgers would eliminate the Giants on Friday. Indeed, all the Dodgers had to do was win their Tuesday doubleheader in Boston and the pennant race would be all but over. The standings looked like this as the two teams got ready to play on Tuesday:

	Won	Lost	Games Behind
Brooklyn	93	54	—
New York	92	58	2½

The Dodgers did not win their doubleheader. Instead, while the Giants were winning 5 to 1 in Philadelphia, they floundered their way to two stunning defeats, 6 to 3, and 14 to 2. Their two-and-a-half-game lead had suddenly shrunk to a single game. Just as suddenly, New Yorkers, along with a large portion of the nation, dropped everything to focus on the events in Philadelphia and Boston. The pressure was now squarely on Brooklyn.

"The nearest thing I could liken it to," Ruby Walker says today, "would be to imagine what it must be like when you're expectin' some really bad news, like waitin' for the jury to come in with your verdict in a courtroom. Your stomach muscles are always crampin' up like they was tryin' to make a fist. You've got this feelin' in your groin and your bowels all the time, like you're standin' on the edge of a tall buildin'. Your nerves seem to be danglin' right through your skin. Somebody drops a book or somethin' on the floor and you like to jump straight through the ceilin'. A good steak tastes like cardboard, and your nights come and go without sleep. That's the way it was for all of us that last week in fifty-one."

The sudden reversal of the Dodgers' fortunes worked its way into the innards of every man on the club. The pressure was like a wrench thrown into the gears of a perfectly functioning machine. "Every day was nerve-wrecking," Pee Wee Reese recalls. "Here we were, with the Giants picking away at us, never letting up. Instead of coming closer together, we grew farther apart. Suddenly everybody was deathly afraid of making a mistake. And when a mistake *was* made, everybody else would start shouting blame. We fell apart on mistakes during that doubleheader in Boston. After we lost the first game and knew the Giants had won again, we just came apart in the clubhouse. I still think if we'd been able to pull ourselves together and come out determined to win that second game, we'd have been all right. But we bitched and complained and fought with each other in the clubhouse between the games, and when we came out we were all so tight, there was no way we could have taken the second game. We couldn't have beaten a high-school club that day."

Instead of forcing them apart, the pressure on the Giants pulled them closer together. "I don't think there's ever been a club in the history of baseball that's been closer than the New York Giants were the last week of that season," says Bill Rigney. "I mean, guys were helping each other out so much it was unbelievable. We could taste the flag now, and we saw how Brooklyn was falling apart. We were still making errors, throwing to the wrong base, that kind of thing, but instead of getting on the culprit, or giving him the silent treatment, everyone else would sort of swarm around him and shower him with encouragement and love. I never saw anything like it, before or since. Even the Lion gave up his usual bitching.

"I remember when we won that first Philly game. Jim Hearn started for us and pitched beautifully through seven or eight innings. Then he tired and the Phils began to threaten. Leo brought in Maglie to relieve, and when Hearn came off the field he was crying. We all gathered round him and somebody asked him what the matter was. 'Jesus, I'm so damn mad at myself,' he says. 'Sal's arm's just as dead as mine is. If I coulda hung in there, Sal coulda gotten some rest today. We need him for the big ones.' He wasn't thinking about himself, he was thinking about Maglie and the club. Maglie had just pitched a whole game two days before."

On Wednesday, September 26, the Giants won again at Philadelphia 10 to 1, as Larry Jansen got his twenty-first victory. The Dodgers, however, gave themselves a reprieve, coming out of the previous day's doldrums to blast the Braves 15 to 5.

The magic number was now three: any combination of Brooklyn wins and Giant losses amounting to three would give the Dodgers the pennant. The Polo Grounders were still two games behind in the loss column. The Giants now had two days off before meeting the Braves in their final two games of the season. The Dodgers still had four games to play—one more in Boston, then three in Philadelphia. The odds continued to favor them. If they could win their next two games while the Giants were idle, they would restore their lead to two games, and the worst they could expect would be a tie for the pennant.

"It was that day we all finally knew for certain we had them," recalls Jim Hearn. "We'd come back to New York from Philadelphia and had a day off while the Dodgers were playing their last game up in Boston. That afternoon a few of us were invited over to the big Botany Mills clothing factory in Paterson, New Jersey. The boss of this factory was a great Giant fan, and he offered everyone on the club free suits. He sent limousines to pick us up, take us over, and bring us back. Well, Bobby and Lock and myself and one or two others were in this one limousine going back to the city and we had the Dodger-Boston game on the radio. I think the game was tied in the eighth or ninth inning and the Braves had a man on third. There was a close play at the plate, and the runner was called safe to put the Braves ahead by a run. Campy was the catcher and he went through the roof at the umpire. The ump threw him out of the game, and then cleared the entire Brooklyn bench. The Dodgers lost the game on that play just as the limousine pulled up to the curb to drop us off in Manhattan. We came tumbling out of that car like crazy men. Bobby Thomson was dancing around shouting 'We got 'em, we got 'em!' and people were looking at us like we were a bunch of escapees from an insane asylum.

"But that's when we knew we had them. Listening to Red Barber describe Campy being thrown out, and then the whole bench, we knew they were cracking. You could even hear a tremor in Barber's voice. It sent us up to Boston the next day fully confident that we were going to catch them."

It was Thursday, September 27. According to Campanella, the score was tied 3 and 3 in the eighth inning. The Dodgers were staggering under the pressure, and it was a game they simply had to win to keep their equilibrium.

Bob Addis was on third and Sam Jethroe on first for the Braves. As Earl Torgeson, a left-handed hitter, stepped to the plate, Campanella motioned the infield to play in close to cut off the run.

Preacher Roe, who had already won 22 games, delivered a good curve ball and Torgeson rapped a slow grounder to second base. Jackie Robinson swooped in, grabbed the ball, and fired to Campanella. "Addis came charging into the plate," Campanella relates in his book, *It's Good to Be Alive,* "but I had the ball waiting for him. He slid hard and bowled me over, but I held onto the ball. I had him cold, but Frank Dascoli, the plate umpire, called him safe.

"I exploded. I got in front of him and shouted, 'No, no, Frank, he's out!' But Dascoli turned his back on me. That got me even madder. 'I had him! I had him!' I shouted. 'It wasn't even close. Man, I had him, I tell you.'

" 'He was safe!' Dascoli yelled back, and he turned his back again and began dusting off the plate with his little whisk broom.

"Then I really let him have it. I stormed around him and flung my mitt on the ground. I really told him off. By this time practically the entire Brooklyn team was surrounding Dascoli. Big Frank straightened up, put the whisk broom back in his pocket and raised his right arm.

" 'You're out of the game!' he shouted at me, and I think everybody in the ball park heard him. Then he heaved out coach Cookie Lavagetto. Before the game was resumed, Dascoli had chased the entire Dodger bench, leaving only manager Dressen and coach Jake Pitler in the dugout.

"That was the first time I ever got thrown out of a ball game. I was thrown out two or three times since, but I've never been as mad as I was that day. What made it worse was that I was due to hit in the next inning, with men on first and third and only one out. And a lefthander, Chet Nichols, was pitching too. Instead they put in Wayne Terwilliger to bat for me and he hit into a double play."

The Dodgers lost 4 to 3. Campanella claims he could have gotten at least one run in if he hadn't been ejected by Dascoli. With a .325 batting average at the time, his claim has some merit.

"What happened on the field was mild compared to what took place in the runway outside the umpires' dressing room after the last out," Campanella continues. The umpires' door in Braves Field was right next to the visiting team's clubhouse. As the Dodger players went by, "they banged and kicked that door, shouting names you don't hear in no church. Preacher Roe, still fuming over the defeat, kicked at the door. So did Jackie and one or two others. The next thing I know someone had kicked the panel out of the door.

"Of course, we didn't get away with it. The umpire handed in a report to the president of the league. The upshot was that Jackie and I were fined $100 apiece and the Preacher got smacked for fifty bucks."

Shortly before he died, Jackie Robinson said to me, "Look at the pictures. Addis was clearly out. It wasn't an easy out, but he was out. Dascoli blew it. I felt that way then, I still feel that way. I used to have a pretty short fuse, and I guess you know I had my share of rhubarbs. But I don't think I was ever any madder than I was that day. I mean, the guy was taking the pennant away from us. I don't want it to sound as though I'm denigrating what the Giants did that season, but they had an awful lot of help from Frank Dascoli."

A look at the pictures contradicts Robinson's assertion. When placed in sequence, the first photo shows Campanella, with the plate well blocked, leaning toward second to take Robinson's throw while Addis is in mid-slide two or three feet away from the plate. The next photo, from a different angle, shows Campanella, with the ball, bringing his mitt back to meet Addis, who's now less than a foot away. The third shows the collision, Campanella leaning into Addis as the Braves' runner hooks his left foot across the plate. From this angle it appears the Dodger catcher has not yet tagged Addis. The final picture shows Campanella making the tag as he flips over Addis; the Bostonian's momentum has carried him through Campanella's legs and beyond the plate. It is a fairly close play, but the pictures say safe.

The Dodger loss left them only half a game ahead of the Giants. Suddenly nothing made sense—no amount of careful figuring of the percentages and probabilities helped to fathom what might happen next. By their mass tantrum in Boston the Dodgers revealed their panic for the whole country to see. Disgruntled, despairing, they left Boston for Philadelphia and the first game of their three-game wrap-up series. They had lost three of their last four. Their bettors began to sweat, dipping into reserve accounts to cover their Dodger wagers with fresh bets on the Giants.

By now the Giants were the darlings of the nation. First their amazing comeback from 13½ games behind, then their refusal to quit in the face of the odds against them—it was the ultimate underdog legend. It's safe to say that with the exception of regular Dodger fans, the entire country was praying for the Giants.

The Dodgers arrived in Philadelphia on the morning of Friday, September 28, to learn of the Robinson-Campanella-Roe fines. That afternoon's game with the Phils would be it—the game they had to win not only to keep their slender lead but to maintain their self-respect. What a tragedy it would be to squander those fines by losing the pennant.

They wasted no time in Shibe Park. Angry, aroused, they jumped on the Phillies for three runs early in the game and led 3 to 0, going into the last of the eighth inning. Then they ran out of steam. Philadelphia scored three in the eighth to tie it and put across another in the bottom of the ninth to win 4 to 3. Without lifting a bat that day, the Giants were now tied for first place!

"We went up to Boston that afternoon on the train," recalls Whitey Lockman, "and when we arrived we heard the Dodgers had blown their lead and lost. It was really an inspiration to us, but now that we'd finally caught up to them, we were all of a sudden faced with a big hunk of pressure ourselves. Bobby Thomson was my roommate, and I remember neither of us could sleep that night. We just stayed awake workin' out all the things we had to do, this 'n' that. The Dodgers may have given us a little help in our finally going into a tie with them, but we knew we couldn't depend on them to lose two more. We knew we had to win our last two. All along in those six or seven weeks we were loose and freewheelin', with nothing to lose and everything to gain. Now we had everything to lose, and overnight this great ton of pressure descended on us. When we rode out to Braves Field the next morning we were all bleary-eyed from no sleep, and there wasn't one of us whose hands weren't shakin'."

Each team had two games left. Each had won 94 and lost 54. It was now a two-game season. (The Yankees had just clinched the pennant in an exciting three-club American League race, but hardly a soul took notice.)

On Saturday, September 29, the country came to a virtual stand-still, all ears cocked to Boston and Philadelphia where events were being reported by radio. Throughout the land that afternoon the voices of Russ Hodges and Red Barber dominated the airwaves.

If the Dodgers won both their games and the Giants failed to win both theirs, the pennant would belong to Brooklyn.

If the opposite occurred, the Giants would take the flag—certainly the most remarkable finish in baseball history.

If the Dodgers split and the Giants lost both their games, again the Brooklynites would be the winners; but the Polo Grounders would possess the flag if the contrary happened.

And if they both lost their last two games, or if they both split, or if they both won the last two, the race would remain tied and a post-season playoff would be required.

On Saturday the Giants and Dodgers both won, remaining dead-locked. It all came down to Sunday—sudden death or a playoff!

Sunday dawned clear in Boston, but by noon the weather had turned cold and gray. Sal Maglie, who had pitched a slick 3 to 0 shutout against the Braves the day before to gain his twenty-third victory and keep the Giants going, describes it, "It was chilly, real football weather. It made us all feel like strangers to the game of baseball. The fans were hostile, and so was the climate. Later it got so dark they had to turn the lights on. Even though we had all played at Braves Field dozens of times before, it was like being on a strange planet. We were all paralyzed before that game. Everybody was in some kind of daze. I never thought we'd win the way everybody was moping around the clubhouse up there."

Larry Jansen was the Giants' starter for that final game. He carried a 21 and 11 won-lost record out to the mound, and it was on his weary arm that the Giants' final destiny rested. The Braves scored once in the first inning, but Bobby Thomson, his bat still sizzling, came back with a home run in the second to tie the score. Once past his shaky opening inning, Jansen settled down and seemed to grow stronger as the game progressed. The Giants scored another run in the third and one more in the fifth, Monte Irvin's single driving Alvin Dark home from second. Things kept looking better as the game went into the last of the ninth. The Giants were ahead 3 to 1 and Jansen was still going strong.

Then suddenly the Polo Grounders faltered. With two men down Bob Addis of the Braves—the man who had hurt the Dodgers so grievously two days before—doubled. Sam Jethro followed with a bloop single that moved Addis to third. Ex-Giant Walker Cooper, the favorite Durocher had traded away after taking over the Polo Grounders, was next up. He bounced a Jansen pitch high into the infield air. By the time Eddie Stanky fielded it Addis was across with a run, and the lead-footed Cooper was on first. Jethro, the tying run, held at second.

The Giants, who had proved themselves masters at the art of drawing out suspense and milking it for all it was worth, were at it again. It appeared that they were in the process of deliberately throwing it all away—the game, the pennant, the miraculous comeback. It would have been a cruel irony had they done so after so inspirational a seven weeks, but it would not have been out of character. After all, wasn't this the Giants' style—to repeatedly raise hopes, only to dash them? Hadn't they been doing just that for years?

But Larry Jansen and the weird workings of fate were not to be denied. Jansen, exhausted beyond even his belief, his chronic bad back aching, stood on the mound and gazed haggardly down at Willard Marshall, the Braves' next hitter. Marshall, another former teammate of Jansen's when he was with the Giants, was a power hitter, always dangerous in the clutch. Now he was relaxed and cool—the Braves had nothing to lose, the Giants everything—and he met Jansen's glare with a wry, placid look of his own. Jansen stared in at him and thought about how often it happens in baseball that an ex-teammate, after being traded away, invariably comes back to hurt you at the most crucial time. All it would take would be a single by Marshall. One measly single would get the tying run in from second, and the Giants would be in the hole. Everything—the entire season, the entire incredible comeback to this point—hung on Jansen's throbbing arm.

Suddenly Durocher came out of the Giant dugout. Casting glances toward the bullpen, he marched to the mound. He wanted a new pitcher, someone who hadn't been with the club when Marshall was a member. To Durocher, a man who subsisted on superstition the way others live on meat and potatoes, the ploy would circumvent Marshall's inviting chance to wreak almost certain revenge on his old team. Also, Marshall was a left-handed hitter, Jansen a right-hander. Durocher had Spencer and Koslo (his only reliable left-handed pitcher) warming in the bullpen.

Jansen, an obdurate soul, stalked off the mound and met Durocher halfway. "Leo," he said, "I've come too far. Let me finish, damn it."

Durocher looked up at the scoreboard, which showed the Dodgers trailing 8 to 5 in Philadelphia. He could feel the pennant in his hands. "Ya see the Dodger score?" he said to Jansen.

The pitcher nodded. "Believe me," he said, "I'll get this last out."

Okay, Durocher thought to himself, go with your best when the chips are down. Right now, Jansen was his best. That's what he'd tell the writers if Marshall parked one. He gave Jansen a hard look. "Don't pitch him too fine," he said. Then he turned and strode back to the dugout, taking care to step over the third-base line, his fingers crossed in the pockets of his jacket. He was afraid to look back.

Jansen wearily collected himself and looked in for the sign from Westrum. The bat Willard Marshall held poised in the air looked like a log to the Giant fans in the stands. Many of them clamped their eyes shut as Jansen delivered his first pitch, a slider. Ball one.

The stadium came alive as Braves' fans, eager for their club to be the spoilers, screamed at Marshall to unload. Giant fans sat in foreboding stupor. Marshall ripped Jansen's next pitch—an inside fast ball—down the right-field line. The 13,000 spectators jumped to their feet as the ball left Marshall's bat, then sat down just as abruptly as it curved foul and caromed off the railing in the right-field corner.

Jansen's third pitch was a fast curve that Marshall watched dip across the outside corner of the plate for a strike. A ball and two strikes now. Marshall stepped out of the box. While the chants and rhythmic clapping of the fans thundered over his head, he determinedly rubbed some dirt into his palm. Jansen stuck his glove under his armpit and, still staring in at Marshall, furiously massaged a new baseball. He figured that Marshall, never a good curve-ball hitter and with two strikes on him, would be looking for another bender. That's what most catchers would call on him in this situation. Jansen knew his former teammate well enough to be sure that the heavy-set slugger would be looking for such a pitch, a curve designed to catch the outside of the plate, perhaps a bit off-speed. That's exactly what Westrum called for.

Jansen shook his catcher off, then acknowledged the fast-ball sign. He felt that with a good fast ball, low and out, he could whiff Marshall, who would be hanging back for the curve. With the Boston outfielder settled in again, the lanky Jansen clenched his teeth into his stretch and delivered.

The ball was a blur as it shot toward Westrum's mitt. Marshall was clearly fooled, yet with uncharacteristic alacrity he recovered. He got his bat around at the last split moment and caught a piece of the ball, not a healthy piece, but a piece nevertheless. It lofted into short left-centerfield, and as Monte Irvin drifted over to gather it in for the final out, Jansen marched grimly toward the dugout to be engulfed by his whooping teammates.

The game was over. The Giants momentarily had sole possession of first place and were assured of at least a tie for the pennant. It was all up to the Dodgers, who, the scoreboard indicated, were still trailing the Phillies 8 to 5 in the seventh inning.

There was no sense of celebration yet in the Giants' dressing room at Braves Field. Immediately, a couple of radios were brought in and everyone gathered round to listen to the conclusion of the Dodger-Philadelphia game. The game had gone into the top of the eighth inning with the Phils still leading 8 to 5. Surely this was it, everyone thought—the Dodgers were at the end of their rope. The pressure was all on them—they must have gotten the word by now that the Giants had won. That would be the final straw. There was no way they could come back and beat the Phils. The pennant would belong to the Giants.

Cases of champagne were ignored as players, coaches, reporters, and other visitors listened tensely to the Philadelphia proceedings. The smell of victory lay thick in the steamy air of the clubhouse in Boston, and a cork popped in anticipation of the final celebration. Then a hush settled over the room. Only the sound of a distant shower could be heard as the voice of Red Barber came over the radio from Philadelphia.

Although the Dodgers may have given in, Jackie Robinson hadn't. With Robinson the principal instrument, the Dodgers got three runs in their half of the eighth inning and tied the Phils at 8 and 8. The Giants listened in disbelief as the game went into extra innings. The champagne remained untouched. Showered and dressed, the Giant party left to catch their train back to New York. As the train pulled out of the station, the game in Philadelphia was still tied.

The suspense, already at an incredibly high plateau, rose even higher as the game went through the tenth and eleventh innings. Then, with two out in the last of the twelfth, the Phils got the bases loaded. Eddie Waitkus, the Philadelphia first baseman, that old nemesis of Sal Maglie, was at the plate. A single or a walk was all he needed to put the Dodgers down once and for all. Suddenly every Giant fan listening loved the previously despised Waitkus with a passion that bordered on adoration.

The count went to 3 and 2 on Waitkus. As Don Newcombe, the sixth Dodger pitcher, wound up, the Philadelphia base runners were off and running. Waitkus, a left-handed hitter, swung at Newcombe's pitch and sent a scorching low line drive past Newcombe toward center. It looked like a sure base hit to win the game for the Phils and the pennant for the Giants. But no one figured on Jackie Robinson. Robinson came out of nowhere, leaped, and speared the ball while it was still rising. The impact sent him smashing into the dirt, but he held it. A spectacular, electrifying catch to save the flag for the Dodgers! By now the entire nation was drunk with stunned admiration. The oaths and curses that exploded on the Giants' train when they heard the news need not be described.

Robinson was not finished with his heroics. In the fourteenth inning, with darkness settling over Philadelphia, the indomitable Brooklyn second-sacker dragged himself to the plate. With a last single-minded effort he poled a home run deep into the left-field stands and had hundreds of thousands of radio listeners in bars and taverns all over the country falling off their stools in disbelief.

The Dodgers put away the Phils in the last half of the fourteenth, and the game was over. The Dodgers had won. They had staged their own incredible come-from-behind finish and left millions of baseball fans limp. The pennant race had ended in a tie. Now there would have to be a playoff and a postponement of the World Series.

New York City went mad. Although the Giants had not gotten to splash all that champagne over each other in Boston, they returned to New York that night to find more than 5,000 delirious fans jamming Grand Central Station, awaiting their arrival. The Dodgers had less of a turnout later at Penn Station, but their boosters were no less jubilant.

Even the New York *Times* found it fitting to comment on the day's events in its editorial columns:

> Yesterday was no day for weak hearts. The Giants, with the most tremendous comeback in baseball history, set the stage for an electrifying finish. The Dodgers, who seemed to be whipped, arose at the last moment and saved it. Now the playoff comes. For the next few days, just as in the past weeks, even the grimmest of world-wide news will have an overshadowing rival for attention in the whirl and clash of the great American game. This is as it should be. It is not thoughtless or careless to turn away from time to time to the drama of fine sport, and what we have witnessed and, one hopes, will be privileged to continue witnessing for at least two more days, is the highest and most inspirational drama we could hope for.

In view of what was to come, the *Times'* editorial was a classic of understatement.

9

"The Shot Heard Round the World"

THE FIRST TWO GAMES of the playoff—which was structured on a best two-out-of-three basis—were like a playwright's notes to himself. They were useful for setting the stage, organizing the action, refining and drawing out the suspense, but they were merely pale drafts of the final script. The Giants won the first game, which was played at Ebbets Field, 3 to 1 behind the adept pitching of Jim Hearn—the castoff from the St. Louis Cardinals—and the hitting of Monte Irvin and Bobby Thomson. Ralph Branca was the Dodger starter, and when Thomson connected for a home run off him in the third inning, no one in his wildest dreams imagined that here was yet another foreshadowing of the miracle to come.

The first game was played on Monday, October 1—a beautiful Indian summer afternoon with the temperature in the low 70s. The weather repeated itself the next day at the Polo Grounds for the beginning of the second game, but the Giants' performance did not.

The erratic Sheldon Jones started for the Giants. Although the bone-weary Maglie could have gone that day, Durocher decided to save him for the third game if one was necessary—to be able to go with his best in the event of a rubber match. And if there was no need for a third game, Maglie would be ready to start the World Series.

The Dodgers countered Jones with rookie Clem Labine. As if to purposely drive their fans up the wall one last time, the Giants lost 10 to 0, handcuffed by Labine's clever mix of curves and sliders, all served fast, low, and with exquisite control. The high point of his performance came in the third inning when he struck out Bobby Thomson with the bases loaded to snuff out a Giant rally.

Halfway through Tuesday's second game the weather turned dark and chilly, and in the sixth inning play was suspended for a time by rain. On Wednesday rain again threatened as thousands gathered on Eighth Avenue shortly after dawn to ensure themselves of seats. When the two teams took the field for the conclusive game however, only 35,000 spectators sat in the Polo Grounds—hardly the sellout one would have expected. Commentators suggested that the threat of rain kept many away. More likely, most Giant fans believed their team had exhausted its quota of miracles—wise to the ways of the Giants, they would save themselves from experiencing the ultimate disappointment in person.

It was Maglie versus Don Newcombe. The Saturday before, in shutting out the Braves, Maglie had pitched what was probably his finest game of the year. But now, even with three days' rest, he was still tired and wasn't at all sure he would have anything left for the Dodgers. "I remember when I was warming up," he says today. "I just couldn't get anything on the ball. I usually wouldn't have said it, but this time I told Leo to get me out of there the first sign of trouble."

Maglie was a finesse pitcher. Don Newcombe was an overpowering fireballer with a reputation for invincibility. But he wasn't feeling invincible that day. Pitching with even less rest than Maglie, "I was dead," he says. "My arm felt shriveled, like an old hamhock left out in the sun too long. That's why I was surprised the way things went—up to a point. With Maglie in there, the way he'd been goin' against us all year, I didn't expect I'd last long. Charlie said if we didn't score by the fifth and they was a run or two up, he'd take me out for a pinch hitter. He told me to give my all for five innings, but the way my arm was feelin' I wasn't expectin' I'd last even that long."

One advantage for the Giants—Roy Campanella, the Dodger

catcher, was unable to play. He was suffering from a torn hamstring muscle—an injury incurred the Sunday before in the wild wrap-up game against Philadelphia when he tried to stretch a double into a triple. Dodger manager Dressen watched Campanella try to run before the game, shook his head, and told Rube Walker that he'd be catching for Newcombe.

The Dodgers got to Maglie for a run in the very first inning, Reese, Snider, and Robinson combining to do the damage. It was the old Maglie habit at work—giving up that first-inning score before settling down to pitch brilliantly. Newcombe came out for the Giants' half of the first and set the tense Polo Grounders down in order. It looked as though a pitcher's duel was in the offing.

With one out in the bottom of the second, the score still 1 to 0 Dodgers, Whitey Lockman stroked the first Giant hit, a single, and it looked like the Giants might get the run back. Thomson, next up, looked at two Newcombe fast balls, then lined a slider at the wall in left field. Two-base hit at least, he thought, as he tore away from the plate. He approached first base with his head down, concentrating on cutting down the arc of his turn. But unbeknown to him, Andy Pafko played the carom perfectly. Lockman rounded second and then stopped as Pafko's strong throw whistled in to Bill Cox at third base. Thomson meanwhile, his head still down, was on his way to second.

Once the ball was safely in Cox's glove at third, Lockman retreated to second. As he touched the bag he was astonished to see Thomson bearing down on him. "Get back!" he shouted. Thomson looked up and a similar look of astonishment flashed on his face, then the recognition of his boner. With the idea of trying to make it back to first he thundered to a halt a few yards from second, but by this time Robinson had the throw from Cox and was racing to tag him. Thomson, realizing he was caught, just shrugged in profound chagrin as Robinson tagged him out. His ears were burning as he loped dejectedly back to the Giant dugout. Fred Fitzsimmons, the first-base coach, was cursing him for all he was worth. He had tried to stop Thomson, but the quixotic Scotsman hadn't even heard him. Thomson tumbled into the dugout, flopped onto the corner of the bench, and held his head in his hands. Nobody consoled him.

Newcombe got out of the inning without harm, and he and Maglie dueled across the next five frames without a score. It was still 1 to 0, Dodgers. The screw of tension was turning tighter with each pitch. Maglie and Newcombe were both tiring, but by now pride had conquered common sense and they both claimed to be getting stronger.

In the bottom of the seventh Newcombe gave the Giants another chance to tie the score. This time they successfully exploited it, Thomson scoring Irvin from third with a sacrifice fly. It was a brand-new ball game. Giant fans came alive, hoping against all hope. Naturally, their hopes were short-lived.

With one out in the eighth, Pee Wee Reese slapped a single past Thomson at third. Snider followed with a sharp single to right center, sending Reese to third.

With Dodgers on first and third and only one out, Maglie looked strained as he watched the next Dodger batter—Jackie Robinson— move pigeon-toed up to the plate. The Dodger fans at the Polo Grounds were screaming for blood as Robinson, all business now, settled in and pumped his bat high. Maglie's first pitch was inside, and the usual words flew back and forth.

The Giant infield was playing deep for the possible double play. The stands were a cacophony of noise, and Maglie couldn't hear Eddie Stanky yelling, "Keep it low, Sal, make him hit it on the ground, we'll get 'im outta there!" Maglie's next pitch was high and outside, nearly pulling Westrum off his feet as he lunged for it.

Maglie was rattled, that was for sure. Whether it was Robinson, the noisy Dodger portion of the crowd, or the pressure—it was impossible to tell. But he was rattled. He proved it on his next pitch, a hesitantly thrown curve that bounced in front of the plate and eluded Westrum's diving attempt to block it. The ball skittered to the backstop, and Reese raced home with a run to put the Dodgers ahead. Snider went to second.

In the bullpen, Larry Jansen hurriedly warmed up with Jim Hearn. Now a second run was in scoring position and the potential double play was off. Durocher shouted at Westrum to put Robinson on intentionally to set up a force at the plate, then came out for a conference. Leftfielder Andy Pafko was the next hitter. "Bring Jansen in!" someone pleaded to Durocher from the stands. On the mound, Maglie said, "No, damn it, I still feel strong, leave me in."

Durocher looked down at his bullpen, then at Westrum. "He's still got his stuff," the Giant catcher said. "I shoulda had that pitch to Robinson."

"OK," Durocher said to Maglie. "Pull yerself together and relax. Ya got Pafko. Keep it inside and low, break it sharp, and we'll get outta this with a deuce."

Pafko looked at a strike, then bounced Maglie's next pitch hard at Bobby Thomson, drawn in close at third. Thomson, anxious to make the force on Snider at third, bent low to scoop up the ball. But it bounced faster and higher than he expected, and before he knew it the ball was over his shoulder and on its way into left field. Not only did Snider score, but Robinson thundered into third while Pafko held at first. The official scorer gave him a base hit since the ball hadn't touched Thomson's glove.

Thomson, it appeared was doomed to be the goat of the Giants' fold-up. The impending loss would be an ignominious conclusion to the Giants' heroic season, and the miracle of the comeback would be forgotten in the laughter and ridicule over the Polo Grounder's last-moment bumbling. Thomson's head was down around his knees with shame as Gil Hodges, the next Dodger hitter, struck out.

Dodger fans were still whooping it up as Billy Cox stepped to the plate. With Robinson howling at Maglie from third, and Pafko leading off first, they called for Cox to deliver the coup de grace. He did, again with help from Thomson. Cox swung at Maglie's first pitch and sent a hard grounder slightly to Thomson's left. The Giant third baseman, his concentration gone, his confidence destroyed, let the ball get under his glove. It was through to left field and the Dodgers had another run, Robinson dancing home with a few well-chosen epithets for Maglie.

"I don't think I was very serious about it, though," he told me before his death. "For all the crap between us, I had a great deal of respect for Sal as a pitcher. There wasn't a better pitcher in baseball that season, not even Roe. He hadn't pitched badly those first eight innings and, you know, he was pitching on pure guts. You almost had to feel sorry for him, standing out there while everything collapsed around him."

Maglie got Rube Walker out and the disastrous inning was over.

The Dodgers led 4 to 1, and the Giant fans present sat stunned, crushed. Throughout the city, throughout the country, the millions of Giant rooters listening to Russ Hodges, the Giants' announcer, on radio, or to Ernie Harwell on television, shrank in despair. In the Giant offices over the clubhouse in center field, the guests of Horace Stoneham belted down stiff ones and began to rehearse their condolence speeches to Stoneham.

Due to hit in the bottom of the eighth for the Giants were Westrum, Maglie, and Stanky. Durocher, without much enthusiasm, called on Bill Rigney to pinch-hit for Westrum. "My God," Rigney remembers, "Newcombe was throwing aspirin tablets. Tell you the truth, I was so tight up there I couldn't have swung the bat if I wanted to."

Rigney looked at three Newcombe fast balls, all strikes, and slunk back to the bench. One out.

Durocher called for Hank Thompson to bat for Maglie. Scattered clapping in the stands—Thompson was a left-hander and could hit with power. Maybe he'd get something going.

Not today. Thoroughly intimidated by Newcombe's blinding speed, he swung hesitantly at an 0 and 2 pitch and dribbled it back to the Dodger pitcher for the second out.

Next up was Eddie Stanky. He worked Newcombe to a 2 and 2 count, then whiffed on a pitch that was a blur in the late afternoon's gathering darkness. Three up, three down. The Giants looked thoroughly beaten.

According to Newcombe, "After we got those three runs in the top of the eighth, we were goin' wild in the dugout. I was really charged up when I came out to pitch the bottom of the eighth. All my tiredness left me and I just had so much adrenalin goin' I don't think I ever threw the ball harder in my life. Got those Giants outta there real quick. But when I got back into the dugout I could feel all that energy goin' outta me. While we were hittin' in the top of the ninth I said to somebody—Campy, I think—'Man, I'm shipped, don't think I'm gonna make it for the ninth.' Well, they were all jokin' and hollerin' in there, figuring we got it won easy. They paid me no attention, just told me hang in there, big Newk, it's gonna be a breeze."

As Larry Jansen was setting down the carefree Dodgers in the top of the ninth without a hit, many fans began drifting toward the Polo Grounds' exits to get a head start on the crowd.

A strange tension filled the Polo Grounds as the Dodgers took the field for the bottom of the ninth. Sitting in the press box was Jack Schwarz, who helped run the Giant farm system. He had noticed something a few minutes before and was eager to pass on his observation to someone. A reporter came by. "Whaddya think, Jack?"

"I'll tell you what I think," said Schwarz, a forceful speaker. "Did you notice Newcombe's last inning?"

"Sure, how could I help it? He was throwin' bullets."

"Yeah," said Schwarz, watching Newcombe warm up for the ninth. "But did you notice how, between each pitch, he was throwing his arms up in the air and taking deep breaths—like he was trying to stretch himself out?"

"Yeah, so what?"

"Well, I've seen him do that twice before this year. It's the kind of mannerism you notice. What I'm saying is, each time he did it, the next inning he was blasted out of there."

The newspaperman looked at Schwarz through slit eyes, then laughed. "Aw, c'mon, Jack, just wishful thinking."

"Maybe so," said Schwarz.

Down on the field Newcombe finished his warm-ups. He beckoned Robinson over from second base. "Jackie," he whispered, "I ain't got nothin' left."

"Goddamnit," Robinson shot back, "get up there and pitch those bastards outta there! You come this far, you go all the way!"

Coming up for the Giants were Alvin Dark, Don Mueller, and Monte Irvin. Leo Durocher hung back in the dugout before taking his place in the third-base coach's box. "All right," he rasped, pacing the narrow aisle between the bench and the steps, "we come this far, you guys, we come this motherfuckin' far and it ain't over yet. We still got a motherfuckin' chance, so get out there and do somethin' with it!"

No one in the dugout looked at Durocher. Stanky pounded his glove against the wall in frustrated rage, muttering curses at himself for having gone hitless. Willie Mays, normally ebullient with high-pitched chatter, looked confused in his silence. Westrum, a quietly emotional man, was fighting back tears in a corner. Larry Jansen stared stonily out at Newcombe talking with Robinson. Bobby Thomson stood with his hands gripping the edge of the roof and gazed absently at the initials carved into the back wall of the dugout. He was hoping he wouldn't have to come up this inning. Let's get it over with, he thought.

In the bullpen, Jim Hearn unhappily ground a hole in the dirt with his spikes. "Hey, Hearn!" he heard a voice cry from overhead. "Yer a bum, yer all a buncha fuckin' bums!" A despairing Giant fan? Or a vindictive Dodger rooter? Hearn didn't look up.

Sal Maglie, already in the clubhouse, looked out the window one last time, took an indifferent slug from the beer bottle in his hand, and headed for the shower room. Halfway there he encountered the bulky figure of Horace Stoneham. Stoneham had a queer, solicitous grin on his face. "It's all right, Sal," he said. "Just wanted ya to know. . . I . . . 'preciate the job ya did f'r us this year." Maglie nodded and turned his head away.

Alvin Dark climbed out of the gloom of the Giant dugout, black bat in hand, and walked to the plate. Don Mueller moved to the on-deck circle. "Let 'er rip, Alvin," he said without much conviction. Dark looked back at him with a hint of distaste in his face. He had never cared for Mueller's country-boy cliche-mongering. Coming from him, the phrase rang particularly hollow. Dark blinked away his annoyance and stepped in to face Newcombe. A fierce determination smoldered in him as he set himself in the batter's box. "Be aggressive," he commanded himself, "attack the ball."

Newcombe took the sign from Rube Walker. The book on Dark was to keep the ball low, Newcombe thought to himself. A good high-ball hitter, Dark pulls an inside pitch and goes to right with an outside ball. Pitch him at the knees and he beats the ball into the ground. Got him out that way the last three times. Gotta do it again. But the goddamn arm's gone to rubber. Can I control it?

His first pitch to Dark was a fast ball aimed knee-high and toward the outside corner of the plate. The perfect pitch to Dark, and he took it for a strike. The Brooklyn fans announced their approval with a great roar, many of them edging down the aisles of the stadium to swarm onto the field and mob their heroes once the last out was made.

Newcombe came back with an identical pitch. Dark had waited the whole game for a good pitch to hit, but he resolved to wait no longer. Rather than swing, he simply pushed his bat out in front of him, barely breaking his wrists. Bat struck ball and sent it slicing and bouncing to the right side of the diamond.

Gil Hodges, the Dodgers' master craftsman at first base, leapt to his right to cut it off. As he stretched his glove across his body the ball unaccountably took a quick, low skip. It glanced off the tip of Hodges' glove and angled into short right field, where Jackie Robinson retrieved it. Dark was on first with a scratch single.

What did it all mean? No one knew, but all the fans heading for the exits stopped in their tracks. As for those already outside the ball park, the roar of the crowd had them retracing their steps.

No one out, Dark on first, Mueller coming to the plate—what does Durocher do? Have Mueller bunt? Not when he's three runs behind. Hit and run? What if Mueller misses? Good chance of a double play on Dark. And Newcombe's been zinging the ball past Mueller all afternoon.

What Durocher does, for the first time in his life, is pray.

Mueller, oblivious to the odd rumbling noise all around him—a sound the likes of which he had never heard before in the Polo Grounds—moved placidly to the plate. He looked down to Durocher at third. The manager wiped off all signs and began to clap furiously. "C'mon, ya Mule ya, do it, do it, do it!"

Mueller measured Newcombe as the big pitcher shifted his hulk on the mound. Stroke the bat, he said to himself, just be calm and stroke the bat. Newcombe went into his stretch, checked Dark at first, and a light bulb blinked on in Mueller's brain. He let Newcombe's first pitch go by, studying it like a curator. It was slightly low, a ball. He then stepped out and cast a quick glance down at first base.

Was anyone else aware of it? he thought. They're holding Dark close at first, Hodges is sitting right on the bag. What the heck for? With them ahead by three, Dark doesn't mean a thing.

"Well now," says Rube Walker today, "Charlie Dressen got second-guessed to hell on that, didn't he? As I recall, the idea was to keep Dark tight on first, so if the ball's on the ground we got an easy double play."

Walker's account is unconvincing. It was the last of the ninth and the Dodgers were up by three runs. A small mistake, one that went unnoticed by just about everyone in the ball park until its consequences became apparent. But Mueller says he noticed it right away.

He stepped back in, his mind made up, and readied himself for Newcombe's next pitch. "When Big Newk went into his stretch," Mueller recalls, "I took another look and, sure enough, there was Hodges playing the bag, holding Alvin tight. I never got much credit for it, but what happened next was no accident."

What happened next was that Mueller, manipulating his bat like a magician's wand, picked out Newcombe's belt-high fast ball and sent it skipping sharply to the left of first base. Had Hodges ignored the harmless Dark and been in the normal first baseman's position, the ball would have been right at him for the beginning of a double play. As it was, he had to come off the bag and go a distance to his right. By the time he made the move, the ball was just past his glove and bounding into right field for a base hit. Dark raced to third as Furillo's throw came whistling into second to hold Mueller on first.

After the roar of the revived Giant fans died down, a tense, excited buzzing remained. Men on first and third, none out! And who else coming to the plate but Monte Irvin, the league's leader in RBIs.

In the Dodger dugout the bench players squirmed on the edge of panic. Charlie Dressen finally realized his mistake, and his ferret face screwed into rage. "What the fuck's that dumb Hodges playin' Dark like that, what the fuck's the matter with them out there!" he screamed. " 'Sawright, Newk, keep it low. Let the fuckin' run score 'n' get the double play!"

At third base Durocher was alive with chatter. "We done it before," he shouted to Alvin Dark, "we can do it again, goddamnit." Then he looked at the Dodger third baseman. "Whaddya say now, Cox?"

"Fuck it," said Cox.

Ralph Branca and Clem Labine, sent down to the Dodger bullpen at the beginning of the inning just in case, jumped into action. Newcombe, gazing in at Irvin from the mound, looked bewildered. Robinson came over. "Don't worry about it," he said. "Two cheap hits, you're all right."

"No I ain't. Ain't all right at all."

"Shit, man, we'll get two. Just keep it down."

Irvin, a home-run hitter, represented the tying run at the plate. The country came to a standstill. How could anyone possibly dare to hope? Were the Giants going to pull off another miracle, one that would make the first one pale into insignificance?

Evidently not. Newcombe reared back and put everything he had left in his first pitch to Irvin. It was a ball, coming in high and outside, and with nothing on it. But Irvin, overanxious, went after it. His swing was vicious, a swing for the fences. The ball shot high into the air, only a few yards in front of the plate on the right side of the diamond. With the infield-fly rule on, Hodges drifted under it in foul territory and put it away for the first out. A huge groan issued from the stands. Irvin, who hadn't even bothered to drop his bat, now slammed it into pieces in the dirt in front of the Giant dugout.

Men on first and third, one out. With left-handed Whitey Lockman coming up, Robinson was back at the mound. "Okay," he said to Newcombe, "see how easy it is? This pennant belongs to us, baby, it belonged to us all year. All you gotta do is get Lockman to hit it on the ground and we're outta here."

"Jesus, I dunno, Jack, my arm—"

"Fuck your arm, man. Stop bein' a crybaby and get this man outta there!"

Lockman stepped in. "Hey, Whitey, get a good one, Whitey!" shouted Durocher, wondering if there was any kind of special strategy called for here that he might be overlooking. Now it was Lockman who was the tying run.

"Let 'er rip, Lock!" yelled Mueller from first.

"You can do it," called Bobby Thomson, kneeling into the on-deck circle.

Lockman took a few half-swings with his bat as Newcombe fidgeted on the mound, throwing both arms high over his head and gulping air. "There it is again," exclaimed Jack Schwarz in the press box to the writer sitting next to him.

"Aw, Jack—"

The newsman was cut off by a voice over the press box's loud-speaker. "All accredited writers should pick up their press passes for tomorrow's World Series game at Ebbets Field immediately after this game. Passes will be distributed in the Dodger clubhouse until five P.M."

"This game isn't over yet!" shouted the aroused Schwarz to no one in particular.

Suddenly Dressen popped out of the Dodger dugout and walked slowly to the mound. "Y'all right?" he said to Newcombe.

"He's all right," said Robinson, joining the conference.

Dressen looked at Rube Walker. "Whaddya think?"

Walker shrugged. "Still looks strong to me."

"Maybe I oughta come out," said Newcombe. "My arm's dead after that last pitch."

"Ah, shit!" exclaimed Robinson. "He's been sayin' that all day."

Dressen nodded.

"Hey, ump!" shouted Durocher from third base. "Ya gonna give him all day?"

"Let's go, Charlie," said plate umpire Lou Jorda.

"Up yours, Jorda. I gotta right to visit with my pitcher."

"He's just tryna give his bullpen time to warm up," argued Durocher.

"I know, I know," Jorda retorted. "I don't need you to tell me that."

"Well whaddya gonna do about it?"

"Now, listen you. . . ."

By now Dressen was on his way back to the dugout—slowly, but on his way. Durocher turned his back on Jorda and returned to third, kicking dirt all the way, getting a cheer from the Giant fans. Radio listeners heard Russ Hodges say, "And now action is ready to resume. Dressen is leaving Newcombe in, and he's got Carl Erskine and fireballer Ralph Branca still throwing in the bullpen. Jim Hearn is pumping hard in the Giants' bullpen—just in case. And here's Whitey Lockman stepping back to the plate as the Giants struggle to keep matters alive."

Lockman set himself for Newcombe's first pitch. Would he convert it into a double-play grounder and thereby abruptly crush the gut-twisting hopes of every Giant fan? Or would he simply fly or pop out to extend the agony? Or would he in some miraculous way hit safely to keep the rally, and the impossible dream, faintly breathing?

The odds were overwhelmingly against the last. Even if he flied out and scored Dark it wouldn't mean much. The difference between one out and two out was vast. It would cause the psychology of the game to shift acutely. With one out and men on first and third, the pressure, the chest-crushing pressure, was on the Dodgers. With two out—even if Dark should score on a sacrifice fly—the pressure would be transferred to the Giants. They would be down to their last gasp, needing a home run simply to tie. Bobby Thomson would be the hitter. He had hit 29 so far during the season, but was not known for hitting them on order. Everything depended on what Lockman did here and now.

The blond first baseman swung at Newcombe's first pitch and fouled it on a hard line back into the netting behind home plate. A gasp of relief was expelled from the crowd, revealing what little confidence the Giant fans had in Lockman's ability to stoke their mad wish.

With the next pitch, 20,000 pairs of eyes clenched shut in fearful anticipation. At the crack of the bat they blinked open to see the ball sailing on a low line over third base, hitting the ground a yard inside the foul line in left field. The stands erupted in an unbelieving roar. The ball was in safely and Andy Pafko was chasing it into the left-field corner. Dark was across home plate, Mueller was lunging around second on his way to third, Lockman was making a wide turn around first and was heading for second, and Durocher was leaping up and down like a spastic acrobat in the third-base coach's box.

Pafko pursued the ball to the high green wall of the lower stands, automatically thinking, try to keep the tying run off second! He grabbed the ball with his bare hand and without taking the time to look fired it in the general direction of second base. But it was too late. Lockman had it easily beaten for a double.

Coming into third in a rain of paper and beer cups hurled gleefully from the stands, Don Mueller had started to slide, changed his mind, then changed it again. As a result he neither slid nor came in standing up. Instead he got his feet mixed up, and desperate to keep his momentum from carrying him beyond the base, he jammed his right foot against the bag. His momentum was too much, though, and he heard the sickening sound of tendon snapping in his ankle.

Mueller, writhing on the ground but still clutching third base, was at first overlooked in the frenzy that exploded over the Polo Grounds. Then Durocher noticed him and began waving for the trainer, Doc Bowman. Bowman emerged from the first-base dugout and dashed toward third, passing Charlie Dressen who was on his way from the third-base dugout to the mound. Newcombe was finally getting his wish—he was coming out.

The crowd abruptly fell silent when it noticed Durocher and Bowman bent over the prostrate Mueller. The Giant rightfielder tried to stand up but immediately collapsed with a yowl of pain. Bowman turned back to the Giant dugout and shouted for a stretcher. They were going to have to carry Mueller out of there.

Meanwhile, on the mound, Dressen was signaling to the Dodger bullpen for another pitcher. He had Branca and Labine warming up. Who would it be? "I suggested Labine," says Rube Walker, "even though he'd gone the route the day before. He had the good curve. Bobby Thomson was comin' up, and Thomson was weak against a good spinner. And remember, Labine had struck Thomson out the day before with the bases loaded—Labine was the natural one to come in, in that spot. The rest of them out there on the mound said the same—Robinson, Pee Wee, Gil. But Charlie, he says, 'Nah, Sukeforth says to use Branca.' Labine was bouncin' his curve warmin' up, he says, and he'd probably come in and throw a wild pitch."

Dressen called for Branca as Bill Rigney and three other Giants trotted toward third base with a stretcher.

"So now I say to Dressen," continues Walker, " 'you wanna put Thomson on, Charlie?' Tell you the truth, I had this eerie feelin'. Thomson had a pretty hot bat, you know, and he always hit Ralph pretty good. I don't know if anybody else was thinkin' about it, but I was thinkin' about the ball Thomson'd hit off Ralph in the first game. Charlie thought about it for a second while Ralph was walkin' in from the bullpen. We put Thomson on and we got the bases loaded, but we also got all kinda double-play possibilities—that's what I was figurin'. Mays was up next, and Willie was a green kid then, scared outta his pants, you gotta figure. But Charlie was a step ahead of me. 'We walk Thomson,' he says, 'and we put the winnin' run on first.' No way am I gonna put the winnin' run on first, I could see him thinkin'. So he says we pitch to Thomson.''

"What the hell," says Walker after a pause to think about it, "it didn't seem to me to make that much difference whether the winnin' run was at first or at the plate. If Thomson hits a single, the Giants got us tied with Lockman—he was a fast man—scorin' from second. Then we got Thomson on first, the winnin' run, and still only one out. If we put Thomson on and got Mays up, we have a good chance of getting one out and maybe even two."

Dressen took the ball out of Newcombe's glove and handed it to Branca. "How ya feelin'?" he said to the tall Italian.

"Good, Charlie, feeling good. I'm plenty loose."

"Awright. Throw fast balls, don't fuck around with 'im. Ya know the book, pitch 'im fast 'n' tight. Keep it up on 'im, fast and tight, and then let's go home."

Branca nodded. As he started his warm-up pitches, Rigney and his stretcher crew were slowly bearing the wounded Mueller toward the clubhouse. A polite cheer went up as the group made the long trek across center field, but Mueller was quickly forgotten as the game prepared to resume.

The break in the action reminded one of a rock climber pausing for breath and nerve before hoisting himself the final few feet to the pinnacle. The tense buzz in the stands turned once again into an expanding roar; the suspense was pumping back into the Polo Grounds.

"Your attention, please," said public-address announcer Jim Gorey from his seat next to the Giant dugout. His voice over the loudspeakers was lost in the din. "Now running for Mueller at third base, number 29, Clint Hartung!" Nobody heard him. The tall, ungainly Hartung, nervously kicking the bag at third, had no idea he was about to become a footnote to history, the subject of the trivia fad that would sweep the country 20 years later. He was worried about pulling a base-running boner if the ball was hit to the infield. In his five frustrating years with the Giants he had made more than his share of goofs. With his big protruding ears he was known behind his back as Dumbo.

As Branca threw his last warm-up pitch, utility infielder Jack Lohrke sprang from the dugout and raced toward the Giant bullpen in right field to warm up next to Jim Hearn. In the event the Giants tied the game and forced it into the tenth, Thomson would go into left field and Irvin would move over to right for Mueller. With Hank Thompson and Rigney already used and out of the game, Lohrke would be needed at third base.

Robinson, Reese, and Hodges gathered around Branca at the mound for a final conference. Eddie Stanky, his voice hoarse with profanity, stood on the steps of the Giant dugout and screamed at Branca, trying to rattle him. Then he grasped his neck in an exaggerated pantomime. Branca glanced at him over Hodges' shoulder, then turned away with a muttered curse.

Russ Hodges spoke with surprising calm to the country from his broadcasting booth, although he was practically shouting into his mike to make himself heard over the intensifying roar of the crowd. "Clint Hartung is at third base, Whitey Lockman's at second, the Dodgers lead 4 to 2, and there's one man out for the Giants. And Ralph Branca, who's won thirteen ball games on the year—thirteen and eleven—he's given up eighteen home runs. Bobby Thomson, against the Brooklyn club, has hit a lotta long ones this year—he's had seven homers. So don't go anywhere, will ya fans. . . .

". . . We're gonna stay right with it," Hodges continued after fitting in a plug for Chesterfield cigarettes. "And we'll see how big Ralph Branca will fare against Bobby Thomson, and then Willie Mays to follow. Jim Hearn is warming up in the bullpen—he's not appeared in relief this year. Clem Labine is throwing in the Dodger bullpen along with Carl Erskine. And Bobby Thomson is on the biggest spot of his entire baseball career. Bobby has never been involved in a pennant race as yet. This is the biggest spot of his entire history, and he'll be up there swinging against big Ralph Branca. A home run will win it for the Giants and win the championship. A single to the outfield'll more than likely tie up the ball game and keep the inning going. So Leo Durocher comes over to talk to Bobby. . . ."

Thomson had already had two hits—the single he had nullified into an out back in the second inning when he found himself thundering into second base while Lockman was perched on the bag, and a double later. Had he used up his quota of base hits? Most observers would have thought yes.

The Giant manager and Thomson met halfway down the third-base line. Durocher put his hand on Thomson's shoulder. He could feel it quivering like a harp string. "Fer Jesus' sake," he said to the Scotsman, "if ya've ever hit one, hit one now."

Thomson nodded. Trying to force his concentration through his nervousness, he barely heard Durocher's exhortation. With Branca waiting on the mound, he stepped into the batter's box. Back at third base, Thomson's blank look fresh in his mind's eye, the quivering of his shoulder still hot on his fingers, Durocher despaired.

The crowd was beside itself as Thomson stepped in and set himself for Branca's first pitch. Giant fans were clapping and stamping wildly, and the sharp rhythmic thud reverberated through the Polo Grounds like an artillery barrage. With men on second and third Branca did not need to stretch. He wound up and zipped a perfect strike past the seemingly paralyzed Thomson, who never got his bat off his shoulder. The crowd suddenly quieted, the clapping abruptly ceased. Branca looked fast. Thomson appeared handcuffed. Never! Never in a million years could it happen!

Thomson recalls the moment. "It's true, that first pitch was a blur, not because it was so fast but because I was so nervous my eyeballs were vibrating. I had to step out for a second to get myself oriented. But to tell you the truth I wasn't feeling very much better when I stepped back in."

Branca snorted with satisfaction and looked in with hot Italian dignity at Thomson. The swarthy big-limbed pitcher had been an important part of the Dodgers' staff all summer—no reason to doubt him here. That first pitch had filled him with confidence and he now looked positively menacing as he nodded to Rube Walker after getting the sign.

"Watch the damn ball!" Thomson muttered to himself. The first pitch had been right down the pipe—a shade on the inside portion of the plate, a whisker above the belt, perfect. Suddenly Thomson had a flash: he's so sure out there he's gonna throw it again!

Branca wound up, not even bothering to look at Hartung leading off third, and let fly. In an instant the ball was at the plate—the same pitch all right, but this time an inch or two higher, an inch or two further inside, maybe even too high and in to be a strike.

At the same instant Thomson swung, his broad back with the number 23 on it rotating powerfully. Crack! as bat met ball. And the miracle at Coogan's Bluff happened.

On the radio it was like this. "Branca throws," said Russ Hodges. Then a pause as the crack of the bat was heard. Then a sudden, momentary silence as though all sound in the Polo Grounds had been swallowed in a vacuum. Then Hodges' voice erupted back onto the airwaves, rising, rising, rising, then screaming, rattling the ears. *"There's a long drive . . . it's gonna be . . . I believe—The Giants win the pennant! The Giants win the pennant! The Giants win the pennant! The Giants win the pennant!"*

It was true. The ball leapt off Thomson's bat on a low but rising bullet's line to the right of third base. It seemed to gain momentum as it went, still rising, toward the sixteen-foot-high green wall of the lower left-field grandstand, about forty feet on the fair side of the foul line.

At first it looked as though it was going to slam against the top of the wall, but incredibly, it kept rising as it went. Every person in the Polo Grounds was now on his feet—Giant fans deliriously urging the ball on, Dodger rooters trying to pull it back with the concentrated effort of their collective stunned wills.

Andy Pafko raced back to the wall. Suddenly, almost imperceptibly, his straining body relaxed. He looked tiny and helpless against the majesty of the wall.

Duke Snider, the Dodger centerfielder, was at a right angle to the flight of the ball and had a better perspective on its trajectory. Even before it got to the wall, Snider dropped to his knees and slammed his glove against the grass.

Thomson was speeding around first, unaware of the madness in the stands, wondering whether the ball had gone in or had hit the wall.

Then he saw Snider drop to his knees in center field. His initial impression was that the Dodger centerfielder had tripped over one of the hidden sprinklers buried in the outfield turf. Then he noticed Robinson at second base, his head down, beginning to walk toward center field. It was at this instant he realized what he had done. As he slowed down to a lope, his mind went blank.

The ball cleared the top of the wall by no more than six or seven inches, smashing into the back of an empty seat and cracking it into splinters. The gray-clad figure of Andy Pafko slumped in defeat against the wall. In the Dodger bullpen Clem Labine, before realizing what he was doing, took a bite out of the wooden bench with his teeth. "Well, Clem," said Carl Erskine, "that's the first time I ever saw a big fat wallet flying into a grandstand."

The roar of the crowd gathered in Thomson's ears like a sudden increase of air pressure, then exploded and brought him back to a semblance of reality. It was the loudest noise he had ever heard and it sent his head spinning as he ran leaping toward second base. He had hit the home run to end all home runs.

As the realization of what he had done washed over him he lost all sense of time and place. He seemed to be floating toward third base. He reflexively slowed his pace, trying to hold onto the present by reminding himself to be sure to touch the bag. He did not see Durocher and Stanky, wrapped in each other's arms, engaged in a crazy, joyous wrestling match in the coach's box. The roar in his ears, after the first explosion, grew more intense until he thought his head would come apart and his eyes go completely blank.

Durocher leaped on Thomson as he rounded third. The manager was screeching hysterically, spraying spittle all over Thomson's neck. Thomson grinned but didn't have any words. He dragged Durocher halfway to home plate on his back before the Giant manager slipped off and continued his frantic jigging with Stanky.

When Thomson touched home plate he was engulfed in a sea of pounding arms and white-flanneled bodies—his teammates. The ball game was over. The Giants had won the pennant!

It was, the newspapers agreed the next day, the greatest event in the history of sports. Nothing had ever happened before that could match the bone-chilling emotion of Thomson's home run—the "Shot

Heard Round the World'' as the *Daily News* immediately branded it. It was nothing short of a miracle. True, the Giant comeback in itself had been miraculous, but this—this was *the* Miracle at Coogan's Bluff. How else could it be explained, except in terms of the miraculous?

With a single and, he admits today, not very confident swipe of his bat, Bobby Thomson brought New York City, the entire country, indeed many parts of the world, to a limp and traumatized standstill. The joy of Giant partisans was orgasmic. The stunned grief of Dodger fans was as though the grim reaper had rung their bell. And for millions of nonpartisan baseball fans, for even millions more people who didn't know a rosin bag from a two-bagger, the effect was overwhelming. To this day few have forgotten the grand chill of emotion that froze their beings when Russ Hodges screamed over and over again at the world, *"The Giants win the pennant!"* They may have forgotten the names, the place, the date, but they will never forget the profound, mysterious feelings they experienced.

The prose that issued from journalistic typewriters for publication in the next day's papers was bloated with incredulity. "To be at the Polo Grounds yesterday afternoon was like having an aisle seat for the San Francisco earthquake,'' began one account.

Experienced, hard-bitten newspapermen outdid each other in violating the rules and standards of their profession. Accuracy and objectivity flew away on the wind created by the nationwide paroxysm of emotion. Writers were reaching for descriptive jewels and coming back with all the rusty old cliches they had been trained to avoid like salmonella. But then what could one really say? How could anyone report such a story? One prayed for divine guidance, for surely the nature of the events witnessed was on an order beyond the temporal.

With standing room, the Polo Grounds held just over 52,000 people. It would have had to hold well over a million to accommodate all those who claim to have been there when the astonishing event that constituted the final miracle of Coogan's Bluff occurred.

In one of those human-interest sidebar pieces that spiced the regular newspaper coverage, several spectators were identified and quoted. One was a fellow named Arnold Winick, 21 years old at the time. I recently tracked Winick down. He is now a 45-year-old father of three living in a small two-family house in the Douglaston section of Queens. He works as a cashier in a branch of one of New York's larger banks.

"Man-oh-man," he says today, "I'll never forget it. People were actually foaming at the mouth with joy. It was frightening. I was sitting way down along the right-field line with a couple of other guys. We were hoping and praying and squeezing ourselves dry with concentration, trying to make it happen, when Thomson came up. I remember seeing Durocher come over and say something to Bobby, and Bobby nodding back at him. I wasn't that close to home plate, but I could see Thomson's nerves working. Christ, you could cut the tension in that ball park with a knife. Everyone was nervous, and it wasn't just ordinary nervousness. It was the kind that ate your stomach up, that rang in your head like a Chinese gong without let-up. Then, believe it or not, I just blacked out. I vaguely remember seeing the ball heading for the stands. The next thing I knew I was down on the field trying to get at one of the players, just to touch him. You've never seen such an outpouring of pure hysterical glee. It was like a million people all having a communal orgasm."

Winick brings me into his bedroom and points out the large framed and yellowing blow-up of a newspaper photo of himself, circled, in a mob of people bunched around Bobby Thomson, who was obviously trying to make his way through the sea of humanity to the Giant clubhouse. "There I am," Winick says with pride. "That was in the *Daily News* the next day. My brother spotted me. And that's Thomson. Somebody stole his hat, and other people were trying to rip the shirt off his back. I remember seeing somebody holding up a baseball shoe—I think it was Bobby's. He took quite a pummeling. You wouldn't believe the pandemonium that was going on down on that field. I even saw. . . ."

Here Winick looks towards the door to make sure his wife isn't nearby. "I even saw a man and a girl lying in the dirt along the railing by the first-base boxes, right next to the dugout, and he had his fly open and she was . . . you know. There was a big crowd around them, but nobody was paying a bit of attention to them. I think she was paying off a bet."

Another spectator identified by the papers was Robert O'Brien, a clerk who was 32 at the time and lived on the West Side of Manhattan, hard by Broadway. O'Brien, having come up a bit in the world, now lives a few blocks away on Riverside Drive. He's 56 today and works as a middle-level insurance executive.

O'Brien corroborated Winick's story when I recently visited him at his apartment, where he lives with his second wife. "Yeah, I saw the same thing. I even told the *Times'* reporter I was talking to about it, but they didn't quote me on it. I saw newspaper photographers taking pictures of the two people, but of course they never got published. I'll bet they're still sitting in the morgues of a lot of newspapers, though."

I ask him what his impressions were of the scene when Thomson hit his home run. "You can't imagine it," he replies. "They could have announced that the Russians were about to drop an A-bomb on New York and no one would have cared. Least of all me. I just went apeshit. I mean I was in Paris on V-E Day and I thought that was about as delirious as a mass of people could get. But it was nothing compared to the P.G.s. People were just beating on each other with joy. Nobody cared whether they got hurt or not. The noise was deafening. No one wanted to leave, we just stayed and stayed and stayed. I think I got home at three in the morning. I just stayed up there, hanging around, for hours. There were still thousands of people there when I left. Even after all the players had gone, there were still thousands there. They wouldn't leave. Finally they turned out the lights and still people wouldn't leave. Even today I can't describe it properly. I still can't put it into words. You had to be there to understand it. I was there, but even then I'm not sure I understood it."

10

Interlogue

RED SMITH, a sportswriter more gifted in language and insight than most, was left practically wordless. Suffering from a paucity of words, he nevertheless said it best. "Now it is done," Smith wrote in the next day's New York *Herald Tribune,* "now the story ends. And there is no way to tell it. The art of fiction is dead. Reality has strangled invention. Only the utterly impossible, the inexpressibly fantastic, can ever be plausible again."

At the time Red Smith was right. There was no way to tell the story of that season and its monumental climax. People were too close to it—the players, the writers, the fans, everyone. It unfolded too quickly, too abstractly for human perception. The emotions it generated were like a metaphysical siren that only higher beings— perhaps the gods—could hear.

A Chicago newspaper described the scene in a North Side tavern shortly after Bobby Thomson, the son of a carpenter, smashed the gut-twisting blow that brought the nation to its knees, "Tough men, hardened to most emotions by years of observing the frailties and triumphs of men, were crying. 'I've seen a lot,' one of them said, his cheeks shiny with tears, 'but this is just the greatest. Years from now, when we tell our grandchildren about this, you know what they'll do? They'll sneer and walk away and say that we're nuts. They'll never know how these guys have reached deep inside us and grabbed our hearts with both hands.' ''

And what better way to try to comprehend the mechanisms of the miracle—if they are indeed there to be comprehended—than to rummage in the memories of those who brought it about?

PART II
The Miracle Workers

11

The Say-Hey Kid

WHEN THE GIANTS MOVED to San Francisco in 1957, I vowed once and for all to retire from baseball fandom. The Giants were gone, and with them went a large fraction of my emotional energy. The effect of their move was like a summary disinheritance. For a few years I followed the Giants' fortunes in San Francisco with an instinctive curiosity, the way a man is curious about the activities of his ex-wife. Then, as strange new disembodied names replaced those of my Polo Grounds favorites in the box scores, I gradually lost interest altogether.

But my withdrawal would never be complete until that day when Willie Mays hung up his spikes for good. Only the retirement of Mays, the final relic of the Polo Grounds and my earlier life, would rid my system of it once and for all.

But Mays didn't retire, and when he suddenly came back to New York in the early summer of 1972—aged and sore—and donned the uniform of the New York Mets, I quite unexpectedly found myself transformed into a Mets fan.

Shea Stadium, the Polo Grounds' one and only offspring, bears no resemblance to its forebear. Maybe it's the way all those functionless pink plastic panels adorn its skin like a bad case of acne, replacing potential majesty with cheap visual thrills. The stadium is the product of an assembly-line mentality and is positively Caribbean in its conception, as insubstantial and out of place in New York as a row of coconut trees along Park Avenue. Someday it will disappear as quickly as it materialized, along with its incongruous organ music and its trivial, distracting electronic scoreboard, and no one will know the difference.

Willie Mays delights in the pregame ritual even more today than he did twenty years ago. He drills the first batting-practice pitch against the fence in left, then smashes another straight over the 400-foot mark in dead center. A thin, rising cheer from the early arrivals echoes through the stadium. This is what they came to see.

Mays smacks a third pitch back against the shield that protects the pitcher. Then he sprays some easy grounders around the infield. "Sheet!" he shrieks, stepping out of the cage, a glint of playful anger in his eyes. He lopes out to play some shortstop. A coach beats a few grounders at him and he handles them like the rookie of the year. Then he slides over to first base and gloves some more.

Mays lopes into the dugout and everybody starts bantering, all seeking an edge with him. But he has a serious look on his face now. He goes over to Ed Kranepool. "Hey, man," he says, slurring his words, "the man's puttin' me on first tonight. What is this shit?" The dugout grows quiet, sensing a confrontation. Berra, down at the other end, has heard it. Mays grimaces like a kid caught with his hand in the cookie jar. Then he turns and shouts down at Berra with mock seriousness. "Hey, Yog, you know I cain't play that position." Berra smiles tightly and shrugs.

"Get up there and hit with the regulars, Mays," Tom Seaver says to him.

"Cockseekers!" Mays grumbles as he heads toward the cage again. Here is a different Willie Mays. Penciled in to start as a result of a last-minute change of tactics, there falls upon him in the cage the desperation of a prisoner in his cell. There is no mistaking how old he has grown.

The truth about Willie Mays was that he no longer liked to play baseball. He still liked to suit up and he still came alive in pregame sessions when he was not scheduled to play. But when he knew he was marked down on the manager's line-up card he withdrew into himself. He had spent 23 years in the major leagues and at least 15 of those as the greatest player in the game. He had become used to being the greatest, and when his body began to fail him he grew afraid.

He offered me a lift back to the city and, in a surprising moment of candor to someone he had never laid eyes on before, admitted his fears.

His car, a flamingo-pink Imperial, was parked inside the stadium under the right-field stands. Most of the other players park their cars in an open fenced lot behind the right-field bullpen at Shea Stadium. Mays had special permission to keep his car inside the stadium so that the hundreds of autograph seekers who wait for the players to go to their cars could not get to him.

"How do you feel about playing baseball these days?" I asked.

"Whuddya mean?"

"You know, you seemed to get uptight when you heard Berra had you in there tonight."

"That, you mean?" He laughed. "I hate playin' first base. Make a fuckin' fool of myself out there. Every time, man, every time."

"I don't know," I said, "you seem to handle it pretty well."

"I'm a centerfielder. If I cain't play center field, I don' wanna play at all."

"You can tell me to mind my own business," I said, "but I had the feeling you don't enjoy it any more.

"Sheet, man, don' enjoy what? What you sayin'?"

"Don't enjoy playing baseball."

He looked at me across the dark interior of the car and I could see his face relax. Suddenly he looked old and depressed.

"What else I gonna do?"

The rest of the ride passed in silence, but when he dropped me in front of my apartment, not far from his hotel, he looked across at me and said, "You know, you're right, I don' enjoy it no more."

He made a date to meet me the next morning in his hotel suite for breakfast. When I got there, he was gone.

I next encountered Mays two springs later at the Mets' training camp in St. Petersburg, Florida. Mays had retired and was now a coach with the Mets. It was not without some trepidation that I approached him. In the interim I had heard almost nothing but unfavorable stories about him from people who at one time or another had been close to him.

Jim Gorey, the long-time public-address announcer at the Polo Grounds, had befriended the wide-eyed 19-year-old Mays when he first came to New York in 1951. "He used to call me Judge," Gorey told me. "And since I was sort of New York–wise, a lot of times he'd come around and ask my advice about something or other. He was really the sweetest kid you'd ever want to have around you, and in all those years he was in New York he never let the acclaim he got go to his head.

"When the club moved to San Francisco in 1958 my wife and I (Gorey's wife Doris had worked in the Giant ticket office) decided to stay in New York, so I didn't see Willie for a few years. Then—oh, about four or five years later—we went out to San Francisco on a visit and of course we went down to Candlestick to see the Giants play. Well, I'll tell you, I was shocked by the change in Willie. I mean, he barely knew me. Okay, so it'd been a few years and maybe I wasn't all that important to him any more. He was no longer a carefree kid, he was a man who'd gotten wise to the ways of the world. It was no great tragedy in my life that he sort of gave me the cold shoulder.

"But I'll tell you what really hurt me to see. I was out there at the park and in the clubhouse for four or five days. And you know how it is, people would bring kids in every day after a game to meet the players. Well, Willie would jump on those kids if they approached him. I remember one kid came up to him for an autograph and Willie shouted at him, 'Get the hell outta here, kid, go bother somebody else.' Now that really hurt me to see. The Willie Mays of the old days would never've done something like that. Yeah, Willie Mays changed, all right."

The difficulties Mays had when the Giants moved to San Francisco are no secret. The story has been told hundreds of times—about how he was rejected by the San Francisco fans and writers because he was a New York hero and they needed to develop their own idols. Moreover he was a threat to the myth of Joe DiMaggio, *the* centerfielder San Francisco had sent to New York.

"A lot of that was true," says Al Murray, a Bay Area sportswriter and friend of Mays. "Willie came out with the biggest New York reputation you could imagine, the greatest ballplayer who lived. His first year out here he hit .347—the highest he'd ever hit—and he was at the prime of his skills. But one thing that hurt him was playing in Seals Stadium. Candlestick wasn't ready yet, so those first two years the Giants played all their games in Seals Stadium, which only held about 23,000 and had a very shallow outfield—nothing like the Polo Grounds. It was great for the fans, but lousy for Willie. He was hitting for average that year, a strategy devised by Bill Rigney, the manager. The Giants had so many good hitters, Rigney figured Willie would be more valuable to the club swinging for base hits than home runs. So he led the club in hits, but he only had something like 29 home runs, whereas for the past four years in New York he'd been averaging more than forty a season. So this was one strike against him as far as the San Francisco people were concerned: he wasn't living up to his reputation as the big home-run hitter. And no matter how many times Rig explained that he'd asked Willie to lay off the home-run swing, no one would believe it. They just figured Willie was not all he was cracked up to be.

"But the real disaster was in center field, and here again it was beyond Willie's control. With that shallow outfield at Seals Stadium, balls that would have been easily within his range at the Polo Grounds were home runs at Seals Stadium. So what happened was, there were none of those sensational catches 400 feet from the plate that Willie'd become noted for. Oh, he made plenty of sensational plays—on balls hit in front of him. But anything hit over his head he converted into an easy out, or else it sailed over the fence. And it was those impossible catches going away that he was famous for. So the fans decided that Orlando Cepeda, who was starting his first year in the majors with the Giants, was to be their man—even though he hit

35 points lower than Willie. He at least had no New York reputation.''

Others suggest that the change in Willie Mays from happy-go-lucky boy to mistrusting man was wrought by his marriage at the age of 24 to a woman who had been twice divorced and who was several years his senior. Out of the marriage came, three years later, an adopted son whom Willie and Marghuerite Mays named Michael. Soon thereafter the marriage failed and Willie, confused and embittered, was forced to move from under the roof where lived his only son—a boy who had become precious to him.

Others blame it on the financial fleecings he took, submitting his country-slick naivete to the blandishments of an army of get-rich-quick con artists.

Still others attribute it to the reactions of his neighbors when he first moved into a wealthy all-white neighborhood in San Francisco and had rocks and bottles thrown through his living-room window.

''Oh sure, it was a lot of those things,'' says Garry Schumacher, a man who knew Mays well throughout his tenure with the New York and San Francisco clubs. ''But if you ask me, the big change in Willie's life came when Leo left the club.''

Durocher won his second pennant with the Giants in 1954. It was Mays' first season back at the Polo Grounds after two years in the service. He blasted 41 home runs, hit .345, and was more brilliant than ever in the outfield. By now he and his manager were like proud father and son, and there was nothing Durocher wouldn't say in praise of Willie. Indeed, the more he praised him, the better Mays seemed to play.

In 1955 the Giants, picked as a cinch to repeat as pennant winners, faltered. Durocher was cleaning house again. Jansen and Maglie went. Bobby Thomson was already gone, and Irvin, Dark, and Lockman were on their way.

Durocher's ambitions did not sit well with Horace Stoneham. After winning the 1954 pennant and World Series, Durocher began to talk to newsmen as though he himself owned the team and made the command decisions. Stoneham liked to have as managers men who would drink with him—men who drank together could be friends. But Durocher had grown bored drinking with Stoneham; he preferred the company of the Hollywood stars he'd gotten to know through his marriage to Laraine Day. Compared to them, Stoneham was a buffoon.

"When Leo went," says Schumacher, "it was the end of Willie's carefree youth. Bill Rigney replaced him as manager. Now Rig liked Willie, and of course was just as much in awe of his talents as Leo was. But that last year Leo was there, all he talked about was Mays. The other players began to resent him for it, and resent Willie too a bit, and there was a lot of bad feeling on the club. We finished third that year, about 18 or 19 games behind, and it should never have been if Leo'd been doing the job. But he just gave up on the rest of the club and spent all his time talking up Willie.

"So when Rig came on in 1956 he had a lot of patching and mending to do as far as morale was concerned. He sort of ignored Willie and concentrated on the rest of the players, especially the new boys coming up to replace fellas like Irvin and Lockman and Dark and Maglie and Jansen. Well, without Leo there to give Mays his daily injection of praise, Willie had an off year—I mean, an off year for him. I think he hit only .295, which would be a fine year for most other ballplayers.

"But that's when I saw Willie really change. Without Leo around he had to grow up, and I don't think he liked it. Of course, that was the year he got married too, and a lot of people were on him not to.

"When Rigney was fired and Alvin Dark came on as manager in 1961, Willie was sort of the senior citizen of the club. Dark treated him with deference and Willie responded by doing everything you could possibly want him to do on the field. Off the field he more or less went his own way.

"Then there was that unfortunate business in 1964. Alvin was dropped and Herman Franks brought on to manage. Now remember, Franks was a Durocher man—he'd come to the Giants with Leo in 1948 and was with us in 1951 when Willie came up and through a lot of those following years. Well, he did the same thing with Willie that Leo did—the praise, the banter, the whole shebang. Of course Willie was ten years older.

"But when Franks left the club a couple of years later, that was the end of Willie Mays the ballplayer. He was on the downhill side of

35, he'd lost a step or two, and was beginning to have trouble hitting the fast ball. Pretty soon the papers were on him for hanging on, and it got so he wouldn't talk to reporters or anyone. Then Horace got him back to New York.

Willie Mays came to the New York Mets in May 1972 in a cauldron of favorable publicity. The newspapers ate it up—at the age of 41 Willie Mays, the prodigal son, was coming home where he belonged.

Things went beautifully for a month or so. Mays played more or less regularly and produced a startling on-base average, scoring runs almost at will. But then one began to hear rumblings of dissension from behind the scenes at Shea—arguments with manager Berra about when Willie would play, and where. With the Giants he had been used to writing his own name in the line-up when he was in the mood to play, scratching it out when he was feeling tired. Berra, who had earlier lost a managerial job with the Yankees because his employers believed he could not exercise control over his team, was determined to maintain his managerial authority over the Mets. The clash of wills eventually surfaced in the newspapers when Mays took leave of the team for a few days without informing Berra.

A public forgive-and-forget session was staged, but the bitterness failed to subside. By late August the Mets were out of the race and Mays, suffering from numerous middle-age hurts—real and imagined—was complaining more and more about being misunderstood by his manager. Originally a public-relations bonanza for the Mets' front office, he was rapidly becoming a liability. The fans never knew whether he was going to play, and they began to express their displeasure in letters and phone calls.

"Shit," said one Met player at the end of the season. "This has been a real team the last three years, everybody pulling for everybody else. But now the whole thing revolves around Mays. Like we go out on the field and Willie's not in the line-up, the fans boo us. All they come out for is to see Mays. And if Willie *is* in the line-up, all they care about is him. If he walks, say, then gets sacrificed to second—if the next hitter doesn't get a hit and give Willie a chance to score, he gets booed. It's all Willie Mays, and that's not the way it should be. I wish to hell he'd hang 'em up. He had his day in the sun here, now he should go out gracefully and let us be a baseball team again."

Nineteen hundred seventy-three was a disaster for Mays, and to cover the rapid erosion of his skills he became a full-time malingerer, claiming twisted knees, bruised ribs, etc. Although he was guaranteed $50,000 a year for doing nothing for the next ten years, he simply could not read the handwriting on the wall. He flopped and floundered through the season, impotent at the plate, like a drunk in the outfield. Then, mercifully, came the retirement announcement.

The Mets started their spring workouts at 10 A.M. That morning, with the clubhouse empty at 10:45, Willie Mays strolled in with Dick Young of the New York *Daily News*. The previous season Young was the author of many of the stories detailing the Mets' disenchantment with Mays. Now he was asking him an abrasive question about Hank Aaron.

I had to wonder if Mays would remember me from our brief encounter two years before when I rode into Manhattan with him from Shea Stadium. When Young was finished I walked over and reintroduced myself. There was a flash of recognition, and as he changed into his uniform he agreed to sit down and talk about the miracle at Coogan's Bluff.

Then came a discussion about when. "How long's it goin' to take?"

"Oh, a couple of hours. So how about this afternoon?" I said.

"Playin' golf," Mays muttered.

"Tonight?"

"Got somethin' else."

"Tomorrow morning—at the Hilton?"

"I ain't stayin' there."

"Well, can I come to you?"

"Nope."

But several frustrating days later, Mays did agree to talk.

With the Mets off to Tampa to play an exhibition game, Mays and I sat down in the deserted clubhouse. "You don't mind if I put you on tape, do you?" I asked, pulling out my tape recorder and setting it on an equipment trunk.

"Oh gee," he said, his eyes widening in pretended innocence. "You want to check me for lies, hey?" He eyed the small recorder with the same distrust he had evinced two years before. I thought of the stories I'd heard. His defensiveness told me that he was aware of his reputation.

"It's not a lie detector," I said. "It's just a tape recorder."

"What you need that for?"

"I like to use it so I have things straight when I come to write. You know, facts, quotes."

"You goin' to quote me?"

"I expect so."

"What about?"

"Mostly about fifty-one, I hope."

"Anything I got to say 'bout that you can find in that book of mine." He was referring to his autobiography, which was written by Charles Einstein and published in the mid-sixties.

"Look," I said, indicating the Sony, "if you'd rather I didn't use that. . . ."

"You can use it if you want."

"Nah, I'll put it away." As the recorder went back into my bag I could see him relax a little.

"How much time you want to spend on this?" he said.

"Much as you can give me. By the way, I appreciate your calling me last night."

He shrugged. "I got to be at the golf course by one."

It was already past twelve. He'd been almost an hour late. "Let's get to it then," I said. "The first thing I'd like to know is, how it felt for you coming up to the Giants that May in fifty-one. I mean, I know what you say in the book, but how did you really feel?"

"I was scared shitless."

"Didn't you know how good you were?"

"Oh yeah, I knew I was good. But I didn't think I was good enough for the Giants."

"Do you recall the thing about Artie Wilson?"

"Artie Wilson? What about him?"

"You've given him credit for being the first to recommend you to the big leagues—I think it was to Brooklyn."

"Where I give him credit for that?"

"In your book."

"Oh." Mays fell silent. He still didn't get the meaning of my question.

"To make room for you, they sent Wilson down—I think it was to Ottawa. I just wondered if you recall having had any feelings about it."

"Why should I?"

Mays, I decided, had no sense of irony.

"So who helped you the most when you first came up?"

"Leo sure helped me. And Monte Irvin—he taught me the hitters, taught me how to play the pitches, showed me around the cities."

"When did you feel you were there to stay, were really part of the club?"

"After I started hittin', 'bout the middle of the summer. Leo was always tellin' me I was there to stay, but I didn't begin to believe it till the middle of the summer."

"Even before you started hitting you were making fantastic plays in the outfield. Didn't that give you some hint you were there to stay?"

"They don't pay outfielders for their gloves, they pays for their bats. Besides, I was makin' mistakes out there, too—throwin' to the wrong base, tryin' to catch everythin' in sight instead of playin' some balls safe."

· "Why do you suppose it happened—the comeback from thirteen and a half behind to tie? Then that ninth inning in the last game of the playoffs when the Dodgers looked like they had it wrapped up? Did you ever think about why it happened?"

"I never did think on it much. We just played great baseball."

"I know, but did you ever have the feeling, like some people, that something was operating there that no one on the club had any control over?"

"Well, I guess the Lord was bein' good to us."

"I don't mean so much the Lord, but something else—like destiny or fate."

"I ain't much for that kinda thing," he said, shaking his head and checking his watch.

"Well, was there any time during the comeback when you thought, or you knew, you were going to catch the Dodgers?"

"Don't recall it. We was playin' for our life every day. Never stopped to think 'bout it hardly."

"You personally won a couple of key games."

"Everybody won games, that what made it happen," he said. "But if you ask me, there shouldna been no playoff."

"Oh?"

"I blew a game in that stretch drive. We win that game, and there's no tie and no playoff. Thomson wouldna got to hit his home run, and people wouldn't barely remember that season."

"What game was that?"

"We was playin' the Phillies a doubleheader," Mays said. "It was just after our streak and we was down to 'bout five games behind and we just beat the Dodgers two. So now we up against the Phillies and I hit a ball off Robin Roberts in the first game that goes for an inside-the-park home run. Only I forgot to touch third. I was so busy watchin' Leo wavin' me in I forgot to touch the fuckin' bag. So now I get called out, and we go on and lose the game. We was all in a state of shock after I get called out. Now, I touch third and we got another run and we probably win the game. So we would of caught the Dodgers a day before we did, and instead of tyin' for the pennant we would of won."

"What about Thomson's home run? You were due up next. What if he hadn't hit it? What do you think you would've done?"

"You mean at the plate?"

"Yes."

"Sheet, man, I was shakin' in my shoes. No way I want to go up there. Thomson—he save my life."

"How?"

"Don't know, don't know how it would of gone, but don' think I would of done much against Branca. If Thomson makes out, then I'm the last hope to keep it alive. I use to have dreams 'bout that. The one thing I remember most of all 'bout that season—me out there on deck and thinkin' it was goin' to be all on me at the end there. I was shakin', I can tell you that. I was so busy worryin', I didn't even realize Thomson's ball was a home run till 'bout half a minute after everybody else.''

"You don't think if it'd come down to you that there was one more home run in your bat that season?"

"Yeah, I would of been goin' for the wall, and that's probably why I would of struck out. Or popped out. I wasn't hittin' all that good at the end of the season. Look what I did in the World Series— nothin!''

"Nobody's perfect," I said. "But I just have a sneaking suspicion that if Thomson hadn't done it you would have. I suppose that's because I believe the Giants were fated to win that game."

"Maybe so. But I was sure glad it was Thomson done it, not me."

"How come?"

Mays was at the door now, ready to leave. "'Cause then I'd only be remembered for hittin' the so-called miracle home run. Nobody remembers Thomson except for the home run. It's like nobody remembers Branca but for that one pitch. Thomson was a pretty good ballplayer, so was Branca."

Watching him the morning before in his role as "special instructor" with the Mets, I had been astonished to see how fit and youthful he appeared. For probably the last time in my life I had seen Willie Mays track a ball hit far beyond an ordinary outfielder's range, float after it with just the required speed, and smoothly, casually, flick it into his glove as he ran from underneath his cap. He may have lost a step or two at the age of 43. But he had lost none of his amazing grace.

12

The Cricket

HE WAS KNOWN in the newspapers as the Cricket, and I had always assumed the nickname referred to his tall, spindly figure. "That wasn't it at all," Bill Rigney told me when I visited him. "The Cricket moniker came from the chatter I used to serve up out there behind the pitcher. Let's face it, my baseball talents were never going to be immortalized in stone monuments. To make up for my limitations, I did a lot of talking-it-up. Pretty soon people started saying I chattered more than a cricket. The newspapers picked it up and then I was stuck with it. I never really liked the name—it conjured up an image of, I don't know, call it inconsequentiality. And nobody likes to feel inconsequential. Thank God, no one on the club called me Cricket. Except when they were ragging me."

Six members of the 1951 New York Giants seem to have two things in common. One is that they all went on to become major-league managers—as far as I know a record representation from any single club in baseball history. The other is that at least four of them live today alongside the fairways of a golf course, and the other two live close by a course. Whether there is some correlation between managing a baseball team and going around a golf course must remain a matter of speculation, but three of the six I talked to insisted that the challenges and strategies were similar. Both baseball managing and golf are languorous activities punctuated by periodic moments of excitement and decision-making, and success in each is based on how well one plays the percentages and probabilities.

Bill Rigney's home adjoins the top handicap hole of a golf course carved out of what was once a gorgeous rural valley a few miles south of Walnut Creek, California. The valley is being swallowed by creeping urbanization and all the sleaze that accompanies it, and one fears for the still pristine and breathtaking ranchland further east, where the valley rises to meet the slopes of Mount Diablo.

Rigney was much as I had remembered him—tall, thin, bespectacled. His voice had a soft-edged rasp and he takes delight in reminiscing. There was only one marked change in him: at the age of 55 his hair had turned completely white. Yet he still had a ruddy Irish complexion, and the spring of youth remained in his step.

Old ballplayers tend to set aside one room in their homes to display their trophies, treasured bats, prized autographed baseballs, and laminated newspaper headlines attesting to the exploits of their heyday. Rigney's house was devoid of such trappings and I remarked on it at once. He grinned slyly and took me into an old bedroom he was in the process of changing into a den. "This might interest you," he said, looking up at the wall over the door. There, framed, hung a single-team picture of the 1951 Giants, each player standing with a bat in his hand, the team arranged in a fan-shaped curve on the grass of the outfield.

"That's the only memento I keep," said Rigney. "My whole playing career is wrapped up in that club, and that picture says it all for me. Just the fact that I'm in it—well, what more could a man ask for?"

Rigney is as proud of an athletic career wrought of limited talents as a man can be, yet his reminiscences about himself as a player are laced with self-deprecation. He signed with Oakland of the Pacific Coast League in 1938 as a shortstop and knocked about the minors for five years. "You know the phrase 'good field, no hit?' " he said. "Well, it might've been invented to describe me."

After three years in the Navy during the war, he was invited to the Giants' first postwar spring training camp in 1946. "That was some camp. It seemed like every baseball player in creation was there. I hustled my tail off just to get attention. After five years in the minors, then the war, I was already going on 27. I figured it was now or never if I was going to make the big leagues. And I'll tell you, nobody ever wanted to make the big leagues more passionately than I did."

Rigney had an outstanding spring. He hit the ball with uncharacteristic authority and temporarily won the shortstop job from longtime regular Buddy Kerr. He was amazed with his success and ecstatic to find himself opening the season in a Giant uniform.

"But I had trouble making the double play. I was hitting something like .390 those first few weeks and, oh boy, I was the first one in the ball park every day. I worked on that double play relentlessly, but I just couldn't master it. So Mel Ott finally asked me to move over to third. I'd never played there before, and learning that new position—well, my hitting plummeted. Not that I ever had any illusions about myself as a hitter—I mean, I figure that spring I was having the luck of the Irish. But it sure hurt to see that old average go down."

He had made the club, and if he had played only one year it would have been achievement enough. But he was back in 1947. "This time Mel moved me to second base and I played a lot there. I think I hit .267 that year, but the big thrill was the home runs. That was the year the club set the National League record with 221 homers. I roomed with John Mize that year. He hit 51 of the big ones, and I remember a lot of them. As a matter of fact, I think it was catching—because I hit 17 myself. Leading off. Now do I look like a home-run hitter?"

Durocher arrived the next year. "The Lion had me playing all over the infield in '48 and '49. One day I'd start at second, the next at third, the next at short, then back at second. I had a pretty good year in '49, hit .278. But then he traded for Alvin Dark and Eddie Stanky, and had Hank Thompson, a good power hitter, primed for third base, so I knew I wasn't going to be playing as much as I'd like to in 1950. That's when I became a utility infielder and occasional pinch hitter. It was hard to swallow at first. You know, there comes a time in every ballplayer's career when he gets to the point where he says, 'I really know how to play this game.' Well, I was just at that point when I found myself not playing much any more.''

''Did you harbor any resentment against Durocher?''

''Aw no, how could I? He did what a manager had to do—went with his best. If anything, I had to be grateful to Leo. Once I became a bench player my whole perspective began to change. Watching the Lion work, I began to get interested in managing, and I couldn't have had a better teacher.''

''Was he the best manager you ever saw?''

''Well, the only other manager I'd had in the majors was Mel Ott. Now Mel was a supreme gentleman and everybody loved him. But if they were to start a Hall of Fame just for managers, the Lion would have to be one of the first three to go in.''

''A lot of people connected with the Giants resented the fact that Durocher was coming over from the Dodgers to be the new manager,'' I said. ''He seemed to represent everything that was anathema to the traditional Giant philosophy. How did you feel about it?''

''I was in awe of Leo. None of us knew him at all. All we knew about him was what we'd seen when he managed against us. I know his choice was unpopular with the fans at the time, but after all, we were ballplayers. Here was a man who could really affect our careers. We were all comfortable with Mel Ott. I think you can say there was a good deal of apprehension when Leo came over, but I don't recall any resentment on my part. There was some resentment on the part of a few of the guys, though. Walker Cooper, I remember. Leo had said some uncomplimentary things about Coop's catching abilities, and I don't think he was too happy about Leo coming over. Of course he was the first to be traded when Leo started cleaning house.''

''When do you think all Durocher's pronouncements about 'my kind of team' began to shape up?''

Rigney thought about it for a moment. ''Well, starting out in 1950 we thought we had a really top-notch ball club. We had Dark and Stanky, we had Monte Irvin and Hank Thompson, plus Whitey and Bobby and Mueller left over from previous years, and Wes behind the plate. You could feel the club was jelling and we were going to be right up there in contention. But for all of Leo's crafty trading and moving new people in, even though he got the club he said he wanted—you know, speed, defense, daring—we started off in fifty real badly. And when you think back on it, it was only a couple of accidents, things the Lion hadn't counted on, that really brought the club together.''

''What were they?''

''One was when the big Italian, Sal Maglie, came out of nowhere and started winning game after game. Now that was one thing Leo never dreamed of. The other was getting Jim Hearn. I mean, Hearn was like a gift from heaven. Here's this kid who couldn't win for losing over three or four years with St. Louis. The Cards were about to send him down, except we were so hungry for pitching bodies they sell him to us for junk, figuring that's all he's worth. And all of a sudden he becomes a big winner for us. You explain it.''

''So the Giants finally came together more by accident than through any design of Durocher's.''

''You can't help but think that, can you? But that was Leo too, that was his particular genius. Now other managers may have had it too, but the difference was that Leo always recognized it right off and exploited it. Maglie had been pitching relief. Out of desperation Leo gives him a start and he wins. Another manager would think, 'Oh, lucky game,' and throw him back in the bullpen. Not Leo. He sends him out again four days later and he wins again. And he keeps winning. The same with Hearn. Coming over to us, Jimmy had the worst reputation a pitcher could carry with him—sore arm, no confidence, cheap price. So what does Leo do but put him right to work and he wins one, then two, then three. And suddenly, out of the blue, we've got a dependable, top-notch pitching staff where before we only had Larry Jansen. It was our pitching that really hurt us in the first half of the fifty season. Once we found a pitching staff the team finally jelled and we almost snuck away with the pennant. And you've got to say that was Leo's doing. The man would try anything. He was a man who always figured he had nothing to lose. And he had enough luck, and insight into his own luck, to come out ahead more often than not.''

''So what about 1951?''

''Well, in my mind what I just said sort of tips off what 1951 was all about. Again, a bunch of fortunate accidents that came about because Leo took the desperate gamble and won out almost every time.''

"Like what?''

"Oh, the Irvin-Lockman switch. Now who would take an outfielder who'd never played first before in his life and put him on first after the season began and you were supposed to be a definite contender? Only Leo would do it. And it paid off in a dozen ways. Irvin started hitting a ton. Lockman turned out to be pretty stylish around first. It perked up the club after that horrendous losing streak at the beginning. And then, there was Willie. Leo insisted on bringing Willie up, then stuck with him through his poor start. Any other manager would have benched him, or even sent him back down, after going—what was it—one for 26? Of course Willie came out of it, but only because Leo gave him a chance to.

"And how about moving Bobby Thomson into third base?'' Rigney went on. "I mean what else can you say about that? Pure instinctive genius on Leo's part. Then there was Al Corwin. We bring him up from Ottawa where he's 2 and 4, Leo puts him right to work and he wins five key games for us down the stretch. I could go on all day about the moves Leo made that year, but I think you see what I mean.''

"You think the so-called miracle at Coogan's Bluff was all his doing, then?''

"An awful big part of it was. Not conscious doing, more instinctive.''

"Do you mean to say Durocher was responsible for Thomson's home run?''

"I'd say this—that in some mysterious, instinctive way, yes, he was.''

Bill Rigney was obviously not going to be the reluctant witness Willie Mays was. But he was racing ahead of me. "Let's go back to the beginning of the season. A lot of knowledgeable people were picking you guys for the '51 pennant. In spring training Durocher was doing nothing to discourage the talk. How did you feel about your chances in spring training?''

"Well, to tell you the truth, I wasn't thinking very much about that. About all I was thinking of was Bill Rigney. You see, I hardly got to play at all that spring. Dark, Thompson, and Stanky were set in the infield. I went down to Florida thinking I'd be the club's first utility man, but then I found out we'd made a deal with Oakland for a little infielder by the name of Artie Wilson, who'd torn up the Pacific Coast League the year before. Leo was really high on him and on another kid by the name of Davey Williams, a second baseman. And still another, Bobby Hofman.

"Now, where normally I'd be playing a lot in the spring, these two were doing all the playing. So I was just worried sick about whether or not I would be able to stay with the big club. I was pretty down that spring, had my wife and kids with me, and was dreading getting the message that I was being sent down or released. So I didn't pay much attention to all the talk."

"But you stayed."

"I stayed. And believe me, next to making the club for the first time back in forty-six, that was the happiest moment of my baseball career up to then. Leo told me later he was never thinking of getting rid of me, but the son of a gun made me sweat it for six weeks. Turns out he was using Wilson and Hofman and Williams to put a scare into Stanky. That was his way of handling Eddie, to get him mad. Leo spent the whole spring telling the writers that Eddie'd be lucky to even make the club with fellows like Artie and Davey in camp."

"Are you aware that Wilson was sent down to make room for Mays?"

"Is that right? I'd forgotten. By the time Willie came up, Wilson was really in a bad way."

"How so?"

"Well, I think it was during the long losing streak. Leo was mad at Stanky for some reason, so he sat him down and put Artie at second base for a few days. We're playing the Dodgers at the Polo Grounds and we have a chance to beat them. So up comes Artie Wilson with the bases full and one out. Now the Dodgers had never seen him before, but they must have had some kind of book on him because he was in their organization before he ended up with us. I forget who was pitching for the Dodgers—probably Newcombe or the Preacher. Anyway, Wilson comes up and here's Charlie Dressen running out of the Dodger dugout. With great disdain he motions Jackie Robinson to move over and stand in front of second base. Then he calls Carl Furillo in from right field and puts him in the normal second baseman's position. Then, with that all set, he rubs his hands together like he's just done a nice piece of work, looks over to Wilson with this exaggerated look of pity, and marches back to his dugout.

"Well, this was a real put down of Wilson, and our dandy little fellow, the Lion, was climbing the wall, screaming his head off at Dressen, calling him every name in the book. Remember, Wilson is a left-handed hitter. If he hits the ball over the infield into right, it's a sure triple, maybe an inside-the-park home run—three, four runs score.

"Newcombe, or whoever it was, pitches, and sure enough Artie bounces one right back at him for a force at home. Ever since that day Artie Wilson was practically helpless at the plate. It was the biggest public humiliation of a baseball player I'd ever seen, and Artie never got over it. So I think that's the real reason he was sent down when Willie came up. Anyway, we were back to .500 by the first week in June."

"How do you account for the sudden turnaround?"

"Well first, we were a solid ball club. Then, Leo trading off Lockman and Irvin. And then, our pitching (which was what was really hurting us during the losing streak) settled down. The Italian started to win regularly. Larry was his same old sharp self. Hearn. And we were getting good help from George Spencer in the bullpen."

"It's about the middle of June, and you've come back to a point where you're in second place and you're five games behind the Dodgers. Were you thinking pennant?"

"We certainly felt we had a good chance. I did, I know that. And I know Leo did. Of course I remember that well because it was about then I started playing regularly for a while.

"Whereabouts? I don't recall that."

"Well," Rigney laughed, "you might say I was responsible for Bobby Thomson going to third base. Hank Thompson had been in one long continual slump. Besides that, he was having personal problems."

"What kind?"

"Oh, he was drinking pretty good."

"So what happened?"

"So Leo finally decides to bench Hank, and he puts me in at third. I played there for a few weeks, and although I could handle the glove I had no bat. I couldn't buy a base hit. Meantime Whitey Lockman had hurt his ankle in a big doubleheader against the Dodgers just before the All-Star Game. I'll never forget that series. We were all set to make our move on the Dodgers—could've gotten down to 1½ games behind. Instead we went out and lost all three games and ended up sitting 7½ out when the fireworks were over. Anyway, Whitey goes out with a sprained ankle, so Monte has to come in and play first base for a while. So Leo puts Bobby Thomson, who's been sitting on the bench most of the time since Willie came up—he puts Bobby in left. Now Bobby starts to hit—I think he hit five or six home runs in the course of one week. Then Lockman gets healthy and goes back to first base. Monte goes back to left. So what to do with Bobby and his hot bat?

"Leo looks around and sees third base," continued Rigney. "There's Hank Thompson, who can't buy a hit and suffering from personal problems. There's me with my—I think I was hitting about .205 at the time. So Leo says, aha, that's where the Hawk goes. Well, what can I tell you? That was the move of moves. It just turned everything around for us as far as the pennant race was concerned. I think when Bobby went in at third base he hit close to .400 the rest of the season."

"But things didn't turn around right away, did they?" I said. "I mean, even with Thomson in there and everybody healthy, the Giants kept falling further and further behind the Dodgers."

"Well, we played pretty good ball. It's just that the Dodgers played fantastic ball after the All-Star break. They went on a ten- or eleven-game winning streak somewhere in there."

Rigney's playing career came to an end in 1953. "In 1952 Willie went into the Army, and Monte Irvin broke his leg in spring training. We were really hurting, so Bobby went back to the outfield and I got to play a lot more than I did in fifty-one. Curiously enough, it was the only season of my career I hit .300. An even .300.''

He played in only 19 games in 1953 and then was offered a job managing in the Giant farm system. ''I jumped at it. I was going on 35 years old, and by then I was hot to be a manager.''

When Durocher and Horace Stoneham parted in 1955, Rigney was awarded the job. ''It was the fulfillment of a dream,'' Rigney recalls.

Alas, the dream did not last. He managed the Polo Grounders into two consecutive sixth-place finishes and then traveled with them to San Francisco to finish third for two years in a row. In June of 1960, with the San Francisco Giants in second place, he was summarily fired.

''Was it true, though? I mean, all the stories back then about Mays being your downfall. A feud with Willie, and it was either you or him?''

''Read his book?'' Rigney answered. ''The stuff about him and me, it's pretty much on target.''

Later I looked it up. Here's what Willie Mays had to say through his collaborator, Charles Einstein, about Bill Rigney:

> Temperamentally, he was a lot different than Leo. Whatever might be bothering Leo, he'd let you know about it, but Rig instead was the kind of guy who'd bottle a lot up inside himself—he's got a prize ulcer to show for it too. He had one thing, though—a lot more patience than Leo, and he'd work a lot with the youngsters and steady them and bring them along.

''How about you leaving the Giants?'' I asked Rigney. ''As I recall it was a bit messy?''

''How do you mean?''

''Well,'' I said, ''I seem to recall stories about bad feelings.''

''Look, I happen to believe that what goes on between a man and his employer is between them. You've heard the old line, baseball managers get hired to get fired. Sure, I was bitter at the time, but it wasn't the end of my life. Horace Stoneham had a lot of problems and pressures. Candlestick had turned out to be a disaster. Because of all the complaints about the ball park—well, a lot of them were spilling over onto the Giants themselves. You know the story. It's always the manager who's the first to go. I've got no quarrel with that, mind you. It's the nature of the business, and if I couldn't take it I wouldn't be in it."

In 1961 Rigney was hired to manage the freshly minted Los Angeles Angels, an expansion team whose roster was made up of the dregs of eight American League clubs. In 1962 the Angels, which were by now called Rigney's Ragamuffins, astonished the baseball world by finishing third in the American League.

"Anyone who doubted I knew how to manage sure got their heads turned around that year," Rigney told me. "I've never had a more satisfying year in my life."

The following year the Angels slipped back to ninth place. But by now Rigney was an established manager.

Rigney's next stop was Minneapolis, where he took over the helm of the Minnesota Twins, formerly the Washington Senators. There he had middling success for several seasons and once again went out the revolving door.

"After you lost to the Phillies you went 13½ behind. Then you beat them a doubleheader on Wes Westrum Day."

"That's right. Then we won again the next day and we had another series with the Dodgers coming up—three games. That's when the feeling started to take hold. Not that we were going to make a determined effort to catch them. But that we no longer respected them. Somehow those feelings began to percolate over that weekend we were beating the Phils. And when it came time to meet the Dodgers again, our lack of respect was now foremost in our minds. We were loose and ready to do them damage."

"And you did."

"I'll say. We beat them three straight. We'd lost six or seven in a row to them, and now we beat them three straight—all easy wins. And they didn't lose for lack of trying. I like to think we won because of our changed attitude toward them. Of course they didn't know it, but they were the ones responsible for it. I guess we didn't know it either, but that day they carried on in the clubhouse really sealed their doom."

"So now you've won six in a row and you're back to 9½ behind. Is that when you began to feel you might catch them?"

"Well, I don't know. I don't think so. I know I *personally* began to think they could be caught and I started talking about it. But not too many of the others were thinking it. It seemed an impossible task."

"You kept on winning."

"Oh yes, did we! That was when we put together that sixteen-game streak."

"Anything in particular you remember about that?"

"What I remember most is the way my socks grew stiff and crusty. Wore the same socks every day, most of us did. The clubhouse began to smell like a chicken coop. I think we were all happy when the streak came to an end. Eddie Logan especially. He was the clubhouse man."

"So now we're into September," I said, picking up the thread. "You've won 16 and you're six behind and everyone begins to think you can catch the Dodgers. What was the mood around the club. Tense? Loose?"

"I'll tell you what it was. Even though I wasn't playing much, only pinch-hitting once in a while, I never enjoyed more being a part of a baseball club. Everybody grew closer and closer. We were loose as a goose and enjoying ourselves immensely. You had to see it just in the way we played. Everything else was forgotten. Whatever personal animosities or resentments that existed between one fellow and the next—and there weren't very many to begin with—all disappeared. It was everybody for everybody else all the way down that stretch, and it was a beautiful thing to see and be part of."

"All right then," I said, "we've decided when you thought you *could* catch the Dodgers. Now when did you begin to believe you *would?*"

"Just after our winning streak came to an end we met the Dodgers again. I think it was a two-game series at the Polo Grounds over the Labor Day weekend. We destroyed them! I'll never forget it. We went out there with the intention of beating the pants off them. And we destroyed them!"

"That's when Mueller hit five home runs."

"That's it. We won the first game—I think it was 8 to 1. The Missouri Mule hit three out. The next day he came back and hit two more and we won again. That's the way it was with that club. Every day somebody else would come along and be the hero. Gee whiz, the magic even rubbed off on me. I won a couple of games with pinch hits down the stretch. Every man on the club had a chance to shine."

Rigney went on to tell the story of the train ride back from Cincinnati, of reading the item in the paper about the Dodgers selling World Series tickets. "There it was again. The Dodgers doing the wrong thing at the wrong time. It was like every time we got down, they would do something to get us up again. We weren't yet sure the World Series belonged to us. But we were damned sure it didn't belong to them. And that's what kept us going.

"And that last week," Rigney said, "well, that was proof we were in the hands of destiny. We couldn't lose a game if we wanted to, and most of the time we played as though we did want to."

"What do you mean?"

"Oh!" he exclaimed, "I'll never forget that last week. In some ways it's a bigger memory than the playoff. The suspense! We open against the Braves at the Polo Grounds. Larry was pitching. We must have made three or four errors in the field. Still we win. The next day we win again, despite the fact Sal gives up 13 or 14 hits. What is this? we say. There was—there still is—no rational explanation for it."

"Before, you said you thought Durocher had a lot to do with it."

"Oh, he had a lot to do with us, what we did. But the entire picture—that was something else again. It was like one of those number paintings you see advertised. We painted in some of the numbers. The Dodgers painted in others. But the picture wasn't finished, there were a few numbers in the design still showing. We all woke up the next day and found them filled in. We didn't fill them in. The Dodgers didn't. But somehow they were filled in."

"Sounds like a good explanation," I said.

"How else are you going to explain it?"

I shrugged. "Then how do you feel about the miracle business, Bill? Do you think it was some kind of miracle?"

"Miracle? I don't know. I suppose you could say there were a whole bunch of miracles. Our catching the Dodgers, and even going past them. Then Jackie making that catch and hitting that home run in Philadelphia. And then the big one—Bobby's home run. I don't know if they were genuine miracles or not, but they were as close to what I imagine a miracle to be as anything can be. Especially Bobby's shot." He laughed.

"What is it?" I said.

"I was just thinking—what if that last game had been played at Ebbets Field and Bobby hit it there? You'd have to call your book *The Miracle of Flatbush Avenue.*"

13

The Barber

AT 57 HE STILL LOOKS like the grim reaper. I asked him if he isn't fed up with the way writers describe him. "What the hell," Sal Maglie said, "I never expected writers to be kind to me."

"What about Jim Bouton?" I asked. Bouton, the ex-pitcher, wrote a popular book in which Maglie, among others, came off looking like a jerk. Maglie was the pitching coach of the Seattle Pilots the year Bouton was attempting a comeback.

"Bouton, huh? You want to know about Bouton? I don't think you could print what I can say about him." Maglie's normally dour expression became edged with anger. I could see him cogitating Jim Bouton.

"Well," I offered, "he told some pretty snide stories about you. Painted kind of an unpleasant picture, I thought."

"It was bullshit. I'll tell you about Bouton. He was like a spoiled little brat, always had to have things his own way. I had nine or ten other pitchers to worry about and he was forever comin' around botherin' me about his knuckleball. Look, I'll say this, if he'd still been useful as a pitcher he wouldn't be writin' books, would he? I mean, events speak for themselves, don't they? Bouton was washed up—if it hadn't been for the expansion he'd of been in the minors. And even then he wouldn't't've made it."

182

"Did you read the book?"

"Yeah, I read it. Anybody who read that book and couldn't see Bouton for what he really is has got to be blind."

"Well, you know," I said, "Bouton says you had always been one of his boyhood idols and that he was disillusioned with you."

"That's his problem, not mine."

"I liked to watch you work, too."

"So you gonna try and make me look like an ass too?"

Sal Maglie lives in Grand Island, New York, between Buffalo and his home town of Niagara Falls. He had grown up, the son of poor immigrants, in the large lower-class Italian community of Niagara Falls, a community dominated by a powerful Mafia ethic and presence. I had heard that Grand Island was the place where successful escapees from Niagara Falls' and Buffalo's Italian ghettos settled to shield themselves from their roots, and I was interested to see how Maglie had fared.

I knew he was now a wholesale liquor salesman in upstate New York. It is a long, tiring all-day drive to Grand Island, and I was please when Maglie said he'd meet me in New York City one Sunday.

A high-school and semi-pro star with a precocious curve ball, Maglie first entered professional baseball with the Buffalo Bills of the Class AAA International League in 1938. It was a local-boy-makes-good story, but soon it tarnished: in three years at Buffalo he won three games and lost 15. What's more, his earned run average, the true indicator of a pitcher's effectiveness, soared to 7.17 in 1940.

He was sent down to Elmira in 1941 and against lesser competition showed the first flashes of his brilliance, winning 20 games and compiling an ERA of 2.67. The next year the Giants picked him up and returned him to the International League wars at Jersey City. There he had a good year. But now it was wartime. Maglie was adjudged unfit for the armed forces, but only on the condition that he not engage in professional baseball. "There was always something getting in the way of my career."

He spent the rest of the war working in factories and pitching for semi-pro teams around Buffalo and in Canada. He rejoined Jersey

City in 1945 and "it was like starting all over again. I was rusty."
But he was brought up to the Polo Grounds in midseason and impressed everyone with an ERA of 2.36 in 13 outings. It was not bad for a rookie, and the Giants were eager to see him back in spring training for the 1946 season.

"After all the talk they gave me I get down to spring training and they barely use me." It was the year the rich Mexican raiders were buzzing about the camps. During the winter, Maglie had decided to pick up some extra money pitching in Cuba for the Cienfuegos team, which was managed by Adolphe Luque, a Giant coach. Cienfuegos won the pennant and Maglie became a local celebrity by beating the runner-up Havana club seven times during the short season. In January 1946 Bernardo Pasquel, the younger brother of multimillionaire Mexican Jorge Pasquel, asked Maglie to meet him at the Sevilla-Biltmore Hotel in Havana. He told Maglie that his brother wanted to upgrade the Mexican League and offered him a job in Mexico.

"I told Bernardo I wasn't interested. I had a contract with the Giants for $8,000 and I thought it was fair enough, considering my record in the minors wasn't so hot."

"How much were they offering?" I asked.

"They were offering to double my contract. I think that's what they were offering to everybody. It would've been $16,000. That was a lot of money in those days. Anyway, as I left the hotel, Pasquel gave me his card and asked me to get in touch with him if I changed my mind. Now that was the last I saw of him until I landed in Mexico City a few months later."

"So what was it that finally got you there?"

"Well, I was feelin' pretty good about my chances with the Giants that year. I was in great shape from pitchin' in Cuba, and when I arrived at the camp in Florida, Mel Ott gave me a big hello and said, 'We're dependin' on you, boy.' Ott worked me six, seven innings in an early exhibition game against the Boston club in Miami, then acted like he didn't know I was alive."

"That was the year the Giants had that huge camp, wasn't it?" I said.

"Yeah, but still, they give me the big build-up and then they ignore me. That burned me up, but I never gave a thought to Mexico until a couple of other guys on the club came up to me. They'd heard I'd had an offer. They weren't gettin' any attention in camp, so they asked me if I knew how they could get in touch with the Pasquel brothers. I remembered I had Bernardo's card, had it up in my hotel room, so I told them. And they said, well, can we use it? So we went up to my room and I fished out the card. One of the guys wanted to call right away, reverse the charges. So I said, okay, use my phone.

"That's what fucked me up with Stoneham and Ott. I suppose the switchboard operator told somebody about the call, and since it came from my room the club figured it was me who made it. You know how word gets around a ball club.

"Well, the two guys—George Hausmann and Roy Zimmerman they were—they got a warm reception from Pasquel. So now a couple of other guys come around asking me for his number—Ace Adams, Danny Gardella, Van Mungo. A day or so later I walk into the clubhouse and I know something's up because you can hear a pin drop. Ott calls me into his office and chews me out for supposedly helping the Mexicans steal his players. I don't know, I think in the end they got about 12 players from the Giants. A lot of other clubs got hit, but the Giants got hit the most. But it was their fault, the way they ran that camp. Half the guys weren't gettin' the look they thought they deserved.''

"You still felt the same way?'' I asked.

"Yeah, but that's not what did it for me. Ott ate me out. He wouldn't listen when I tried to explain about the phone call. He accused me of settin' up the whole deal, of actin' as the Pasquels' recruitin' agent. Then later he came out into the clubhouse and went down the line askin' each player, 'Have you been contacted by the Mexicans? Are you gonna jump?' ''

"I honestly didn't know what I was goin' to say when he came to me. All I knew was, I was sore about the brushoff I'd been gettin' all spring. And now I was really mad about Ott accusin' me of somethin' that wasn't true and refusin' to listen. I knew I was marked lousy for sure. I could get twice as much money in Mexico as the Giants were payin' me. I was already 29, and I was thinkin' I only had a few years left to build up a little nest egg for me and my wife. I was thinkin' all these things, and thinkin', now the Giants wouldn't give me a shot. So when Ott got to me I told him I was goin' to Mexico. And that's the true story.''

"In retrospect, do you think it was worth it? Going to Mexico? Being banned from American baseball for five years?''

"I was never sorry," Maglie said. "I not only made good money for two years, but I learned how to pitch.''

"What team did you play for?''

"The Puebla club.''

"Puebla—that's a mountain town south of Mexico City.''

"Yeah. Pitchin' in that thin air really improved my curve ball. You really had to break it off to get any action on it. When I came back to sea level I could bend it like a hoop.''

Puebla was not exactly a glittering metropolis, but Maglie, unaccustomed to glittering refinements, was willing to endure indifferent plumbing, cold showers, strange food, language difficulties, and quaint native customs—like riots at the ball park—for the $16,000 salary he was getting. The only thing that disturbed him were the overnight bus trips through the mountains on bus seats that seemed sprung with cast iron.

Those bus rides must have been soul-searing experiences, for he resorted to a measure no other ballplayer in the history of the world had taken. He began to make all the trips by plane, at his own expense. He estimated he spent $1,500 in two years on air transportation. "What the hell, in those days the planes were safer than the buses.''

He flew high in more ways than one. He turned into the best pitcher in the Mexican League, winning 20 games and losing 12 in a 90-game schedule in 1946. The next year he again won 20, despite a broken pitching hand suffered in a basketball game at home the week before he left for Puebla. But 1948 saw the end of the Mexican adventure. Promoter Pasquel had put the league into the Mexican form of bankruptcy and Sal Maglie was without a job. Unable to play professionally in the United States, he was a pitcher with a wicked curve and no place to throw it.

"What did you do?" I inquired.

"Oh," he said, his deep, monotonic voice growing softer, "I

knocked around. I got by. I pitched a little semi-pro again. I pitched in Canada, Cuba, all over.''

"Couldn't have been much money in it.''

"Like I say, I got by.''

"How did you feel when you found out the suspension was lifted one year early?''

"I was ready to go.''

Maglie returned to the Giants in 1950 at the age of 33. There were no "welcome back'' festivities. Indeed, the reception he received was downright cool. "Did you have any idea that you still had a major-league career ahead of you?''

"I knew I had a couple of good years left,'' he said. "If only Durocher would give me a chance. If he didn't, I was goin' to ask to be traded.''

"I didn't think guys asked to be traded in those days. I thought that was a recent fad.''

"I would of been the first.''

"How did you find Durocher?''

"When a man lets me do my job, I like him. When he doesn't, I don't.''

"He didn't use you much there in the beginning.''

"You got it.''

"So how did it come about that he gave you a shot?''

"After he got to know me a little bit, I think he saw what I was made of. I played his kind of game. I was a competitor.''

Maglie stayed with the Giants through the middle of the 1955 season. His greatest year of course was 1951 when he won 23. After that he became less and less effective. When the Giants won a second pennant—this was an easy one—in 1954, he had a 14 and 6 won-lost record. In 1955, with the Giants out of contention, he was sold to the Cleveland Indians. The Indians were in the thick of the American League race and they bought Maglie for pennant insurance.

"How did it feel to leave the Giants?'' I asked him.

"I didn't mind. Hell, nobody minds bein' sent to a place where there's a chance of gettin' some World Series money.''

He failed to help Cleveland, though: the Indians finished second and Maglie had no wins and two losses. At the beginning of the next season Cleveland sent him, of all places, to Brooklyn.

"I remember that," I said. "It really came as a shock. I mean, you pitching for Brooklyn, your old arch-enemies."

Maglie shrugged. "Tell you one thing. I got treated a hell of a lot better by the Dodgers than I did by the Giants. That was a top-flight organization. And it meant another World Series for me in fifty-six."

"Also that year—didn't you pitch a no-hitter?"

"Yes sir, right at the end of the season, against Philadelphia."

"That must've been a thrill. Here you are, coming to the end of your career, and you pitch a no-hitter."

"Oldest pitcher to do it, they tell me. I was 39."

"Well, look," I said, "how do you explain it? You hadn't been going so good, had you?"

"When I came over to the Dodgers I did real well. Won 13 games that year. That was the way I was. I always pitched better when I was on a good club."

"What was it like to play with Robinson, Campanella, that crew?"

"Robinson was all right. Hell, we got to be good friends. Same with Campy and the rest of them. They were competitors. So was I."

"Those were some battles you and he used to have when you were with the Giants. Did you ever intentionally try to hurt him?"

"You mean skull him?"

I nodded.

"Hell no. He knew that. I'd hit a guy, make him sting a little. But I never put it on his head. I knew where the ball was goin'."

"I've heard stories that you were responsible for ending Davey Williams' career," I said with some trepidation. Maglie's beaked face darkened.

Davey Williams had succeeded Stanky as the Giants' regular second baseman in 1952. In 1955, in a game against the Dodgers, Maglie was up to his old tricks against Robinson. Robinson responded with a bunt down the first-base line, tempting Maglie over. Maglie refused to budge from the mound. Lockman was forced to rush in, field the ball, and throw back to Williams covering first. Robinson, in his frustration at being unable to confront Maglie on the base path, slammed into the unsuspecting Williams. The collision so

severely damaged Williams' back that he was forced to give up baseball at the age of 26. Shortly after the incident, Maglie was sent to
Cleveland.

"You know what I'm talking about, don't you?" I said.

Maglie did, but he obviously didn't want to talk about it.
"Where'd you hear those stories?" he asked gloomily.

After ending his playing career in 1959 as a journeyman pitcher
with the St. Louis Cardinals, he came back to baseball as a pitching
coach. He worked for the Boston Red Sox for several years until dif-
ferences with manager Dick Williams sent him looking for another
job. That brought him to the Seattle Pilots and Jim Bouton. After that
he gave it up for good.

Finally we focused on the fifty-one pennant race. "You pitched
and won the first game of that 16-game streak. Do you remember? I
was there that day. It was Westrum Day. A doubleheader with the
Phils. You'd just dropped 13½ back the day before. You pitched the
first and won it 3 to 2."

Maglie remembered it well. He told me the story of him and
Waitkus in the ninth inning. "Then we came back and beat the
Dodgers three in a row a few days later. It was the last game of that
series. Pitched a four-hitter. Funny thing was, during that winnin'
streak I had trouble winnin' myself. I think I started five games, but I
got knocked out a few times. I think I only won two. Of course the
club would always come from behind."

"What about this business of you always starting slowly? You
know, you'd be a little shaky in the first inning or two, then you'd
settle down and pitch brilliantly."

"Yeah, sometimes I'd have trouble getting my curve ball going.
Warmin' up, I'd have no stuff. I never could get my curve to really
snap until I got my juices going. Sometimes it'd take an inning or
two."

"When did you begin to think you could catch the Dodgers?"

Maglie mused for a moment. "Oh, I seem to remember feelin' it
about a week before the end of the season."

"That late? Most of the other guys seemed to believe it much earlier."

"Well, you know, it's different for a pitcher. It was a Sunday, I believe. We were about three behind and I started against the Braves at the Polo Grounds. They were hittin' me—I think I gave up 13 hits—but they could only get a run. We won it 4 to 1, I think. As I recall the Dodgers won that day too. But that's when I began to believe. You know, like what that McGraw said last year, 'Ya gotta believe.' '' Maglie was referring to the Mets' pennant victory of the previous September—1973—when relief pitcher Tug McGraw's slogan became part of the everyday slanguage of New York.

"I'm trying to get under the surface of things—like what was it, if anything, that made fifty-one happen the way it did?"

I could see Maglie shrug. "It just happened. We were a good ball club those last few weeks, the Dodgers weren't so good."

"But they still had you beat. The last playoff game. They still had you beat, and then out of nowhere, for no apparent reason, you come back at the last instant and take it away from them. You don't think that happened just because it happened, do you?"

"I don't know why it happened. Baseball's a game of funny twists."

"Maybe it was a sort of leftover energy from the pennant race," I suggested. "Maybe after coming all that way from behind in September to catch them, there was some energy left that wouldn't let you lose it."

"Could be, but I doubt it. We were just lucky. We had good talent and we finally got luck on our side."

"You were always a pragmatist, weren't you?"

"What does that mean?"

"You know—you were a practical pitcher. You had a job to do and you went out and did it. You didn't think about it, wonder about it, speculate about it. You just did it."

"I suppose you can say that. I never went much for that philosophy stuff. I just wondered whether I'd get good fielding or not. I remember writers used to ask me what my 'pitchin' philosophy' was. I'd just laugh at 'em. My philosophy was to shave the corners, that's all, I'd say."

"How did you like being called the Barber?"

"I didn't mind. Better than bein' called the Shoeshine Boy."

"How did you get the name?"

"Jin McCully hung it on me. He covered us for the *News*. One day in St. Louis in fifty, when I first started pitching regular, I was really nickin' the corners. Curve was real sharp. It was the first time anybody really noticed I had the good curve ball. That's where it started. McCully wrote I was shavin' the corners like a good Italian barber, somethin' like that. So it caught on."

"In the last game of the playoff it was you against Newcombe. How did you feel about that? Were you tired?"

"No more than he was. I heard he was beggin' to be taken out as early as the fifth, but he seemed to be gettin' stronger as he went. They got that run off me early in the game, but then I began to put 'em away."

"Was it the same old thing of yours?" I said. "Giving up that early run?"

"I didn't have my good stuff warming up. My arm was tight."

"Were you nervous?"

"Not particularly."

"You pitched strong up until the eighth. You got the run back and were tied at one each. And then they got those three runs off you."

"That wasn't altogether my fault. I still had my stuff, and it wasn't exactly as if they shelled me. It was a couple of bad plays on Thomson's part, plus a ball in the dirt, plus a couple of singles. What're you goin' to do when somethin' like that happens? You just bear down and do the best you can. When Leo took me out for the hitter, I figured I did the best I could of. I didn't get much help."

"What were you feeling when you went to the clubhouse?"

"I was sore. Mostly about havin' to be in the playoff to begin with. I'd worked hard for that pennant, and now it was bein' taken away. After we went down in the eighth, I figured we'd lost it."

"You didn't expect the ninth."

"No way. In fact I wasn't even payin' attention until they brought Mueller into the clubhouse. I was talkin' to Stoneham, then I went into the shower. All of a sudden—bing, bing, bing, and here they're draggin' Mueller in. Now Branca's in there and Thomson's up. But I still wasn't thinkin' about it."

"You weren't expecting it?"

"I wasn't expecting it. Hell, we were still two runs behind."

"Then it happened."

"Then it happened."

"What did you do?"

"Cracked another bottle of beer. Then it was just bedlam when everybody finally got in."

"You didn't go out?"

"Are you kidding? Go out there and get my arm broken off? Oh, I went out later. Stood on the steps and took a bow."

"Just one more question. In all the years since then, have you ever wondered about it?"

"About the home run?"

"About the whole thing."

"Can't say I have. Like I said, nothin' to wonder about."

"It just happened."

"Right."

"Do you miss baseball?"

"Nope, not a bit. I miss pitchin', though. I sure loved to pitch."

14

The Captain

When Bill Rigney succeeded Durocher in 1956, the Giants stunned their fans by trading Alvin Dark to the St. Louis Cardinals. He remained with St. Louis until 1958. Then he spent two years with the Chicago Cubs, a few weeks with the Philadelphia Phils, and wound up his playing career in 1960, at the age of 37, with the Milwaukee Braves. That same year Rigney was fired as manager of the Giants. Dark called Horace Stoneham and let him know that nothing would please him more than to start his managerial career with the club that had always meant the most to him. At the start of the 1961 season the job was his.

He inherited a demoralized ball club, and an undisciplined one as well. According to Willie Mays, the Giants of 1960 were a card-playing, hard-drinking, after-hours bunch whose team motto was "Shut up and deal!" Dark rapidly turned them around. A nondrinker, an early-to-bed man by lifetime habit, and still an intense competitor, he led the Giants in 1962 to their first pennant since their move to San Francisco. He did it in a playoff against the Los Angeles Dodgers that almost duplicated, in excitement and tension, the events of 1951.

As the 1963 season began, Dark was one of the most popular men in San Francisco. Not only had he proved himself a good manager, he was a clean-liver and a family man. He refused to drink or social-ize with the newspaper people who covered the Giants, and curried favor with no one. He did his job with competence and sought to be nothing else than what he was—a hard-working baseball tactician. The very qualities in Dark that made him seem straight-laced, self-disciplined, and aloof were the qualities San Francisco admired most.

Dark ran the Giants as a tight ship, and his authority was re-spected. He led by example. He applied the same rules to himself as he imposed on his players, and more than once he fined himself for self-admitted managerial goofs—just as he would fine a player for a performance boner. Off the field he was just as strict with himself, and because he went to bed early—and alone—when the club was on the road, he expected the same of his players.

Dark, the father of four children, had been married for years. Both he and his wife were deeply religious, and there was not a person who knew the Darks who didn't think their marriage, though perhaps a bit dull, was anything short of ideal. "If you serve the Lord, the Lord will serve you," Dark was fond of saying privately to explain his contented domesticity. It was a marriage made in the heaven of Billy Graham.

With his success of 1962, Dark, who had become a lay preacher in the Baptist faith, started to speak out more and more on religious matters. By 1964 he had achieved a kind of piety that began to rankle both the sportswriters and Horace Stoneham, who could still not get his manager to drink with him.

The Giants had fallen back to third place in 1963, and in 1964, after a fast start, they were struggling. No one knew it, but Dark was having personal problems. Then rumors of an incident in Milwaukee began drifting back to San Francisco.

Then followed an interview he gave to sportswriter Stan Isaacs. When Isaacs asked Dark what his club's principal problem was, Dark responded, according to Isaacs' published report, by say-ing, "We have trouble because we have so many Negro and Spanish-speaking players on this team. They are just not able to perform up to the white players when it comes to mental alertness. You can't make most Negro and Spanish-speaking players have the pride in their team that you get from white players. And they just aren't as sharp mentally. They aren't able to adjust to situations because they don't have that mental alertness.''

When the predictable storm broke over Dark's remarks in early August, he did not deny he'd made them; he simply asserted that his words had been taken out of context. When he was fired at the end of the season, most observers assumed that it was because of his racial views. Such was not the case. Stoneham had decided to get rid of his manager early in July after the Milwaukee incident. Speaking as he allegedly had to Isaacs actually saved Dark's job, at least for two months. Stoneham could not fire him so close on the heels of the racial controversy.

In a year when the word racism was becoming part of the everyday rhetoric of America, Dark was immediately branded a racist. The allegation was supported in a book that had just come out about the progress black players were making in baseball. Called *Baseball Has Done It,** it was a collection of interviews ostensibly organized by Jackie Robinson with various baseball figures. Dark's contribution was a rambling, patronizing, largely traditional view of integration in the South.

Curiously enough, though, his ill-considered racial views never became an issue in his future. Out of baseball for a year, he was hired by Finley in 1966 to manage the Kansas City A's. They had finished last or next to last nine times in the preceding 10 years. But the nucleus of a winning team was being gathered and under Dark they finished seventh in a 10-team league. As a bonus, the impulsive Finley gave Dark a Cadillac.

In 1967, though, he fired Dark in a dispute over the fining of a player for off-field misbehavior. Dark had sided with the player. When he left Kansas City, Dark declared that the material was there to have a winner by 1971.

The prediction proved accurate. In 1971 the A's by then transferred to Oakland, finished first in their division under their newest manager, Dick Williams. In the next two years they won everything.

Dark meanwhile moved on to Cleveland in 1968 and soon became embroiled in an executive power struggle as manager of the Indians.

* Jackie Robinson, *Baseball Has Done It,* edited by Charles Dexter (Philadelphia, J. B. Lippincott Company, 1964).

Vernon Stouffer, the club's owner, gave Dark general-manager authority, downgrading regular general manager Gabe Paul. But two years later, the club having made no progress, Paul was restored to power and Dark was dismissed.

During all this, Dark was divorced. He then married the airline stewardess he had fallen in love with during his last days as the Giants' manager. After his dismissal from the Indians he settled into a comfortable home hard by the eighth green of the east course of the Country Club of Miami. Still being paid about $50,000 a year not to manage the Indians, Dark was living a leisurely life of golf and bible lessons with his second wife, Jackie, when Dick Williams quit the A's after the 1973 World Series. Soon thereafter he was on his way to Oakland to see Charlie Finley and begin his second tenure as manager of the A's.

When Dark greeted me at the door of his room at the Mezona Motor Inn in Mesa, Arizona, where the A's were training in the spring of 1974, he carried a small bible in his hand, his name imprinted in gold on its soft brown leather cover. His hair was still mostly dark brown, and except for the slightly bloated look that often afflicts ex-athletes he appeared as though he could still go a full game at shortstop. His smile was warm, showing white, even teeth, and his handsome, faintly Indian features were still smoothly intact.

I admired the personalized bible. "Are you familiar with it?" he said.

"Oh, I used to know it fairly well. Not the way I hear you know it, though. I used to be more of an Old Testament fan."

"Are you Jewish?"

"You might say."

"You don't look it."

Aha, I thought, so he does think in racial terms. "I understand you're a Baptist."

"Yeah."

"You don't look it," I said.

He got the point—I think—and laughed.

"Since we've started on this note," I said, "what about all this

business of religion? Are you aware of all the flak you've been getting in the papers since you've come back?''

''To tell you the truth, I haven't had much chance to read the
papers. But that's all right. People can say what they want about me.
Most of them are probably talking about the old Alvin Dark.''

''You've changed?''

''Somewhat.''

''I know you've probably been asked about this a thousand times,
but what about that business back in sixty-four? The Isaacs article?
Does that still haunt you?''

Dark's eyes sparkled. As we sat down he carefully placed his bible
on the lamp table next to his bed, leaving it open to the page he'd
been reading. ''Well,'' he said, ''I suppose that article—which was
taken out of context, you know—I suppose it'll always haunt me. A
lot of people have asked me that question and about how I think the
black and Spanish ballplayers on the A's would take to me. You
know, they're a pretty outspoken bunch of fellows. Well, all I can
say is that each individual on this club will have to determine for
himself how I treat him. My actions will speak louder than any words
I can possibly use. I'll bet you anything that at the end of this year
each guy on this club will say I treated him fairly. But next year it'll
come up all over again. It's unfair and untrue. Jackie Robinson made
a public statement defending me at the time, you know. But until the
day I die, nothing I can say will lift it off me. So be it. All I can do is
let my actions speak for themselves.''

''Could you help me get one thing straight?'' I asked.

''I'm happy to try,'' he said.

''Did you or did you not say what Isaacs quoted you as saying?
I've heard eighty-five different stories on that.''

''You know, it's been so long ago that I'm not even sure what I
said. It was one of hundreds of interviews you give, and it's hard to
remember what you said to who. Now I know I didn't say it in the
way he had me saying it. I mean he took a sentence here and a sentence there, things I might have said fifteen minutes apart, and strung
them all together to make it look as if I said it all in one breath. It just
wasn't that way, and I was as surprised as everyone else to see this

picture of me speaking that way. Anybody who knew me knew that wasn't the way I talked."

"Well, what about the thoughts behind the words? You may not have talked that way, but was it possible you thought that way?"

"Who knows what a man thinks at a given time? It was possible. I was angry with a few of the guys on the club, the way they were playing, and I could have been thinking that way out of my own frustration at not being able to understand them. But that's all changed. I don't do that any more."

"How do you account for the change you say you've gone through? I'd heard you were always a pretty religious fellow."

Dark smiled a private smile. "Well, you see, I always thought I was a good Christian, but I found out I wasn't. When I first started managing in sixty-one and I'd make a decision, I'd never worry about that decision at all. Then, after we won the pennant in sixty-two, I started to think too much about what *I'd* achieved, instead of giving God credit. And in sixty-three I started doing things I knew were not right, sinful things. As a manager I was losing inner confidence in the decisions I was making. But instead of recognizing where the real fault lay, I began blaming other people. It was the sin of pride.

"Then I had a problem with my wife, met another woman, you know how it goes. It was all wrong, what I was doing, but I just couldn't help myself at the time."

He picked up the bible. "I don't like to talk about this too often because people tend to think, oh, there he goes, being sanctimonious again. But it's just the opposite. I have learned to feel humble and unworthy before God. It's the only sensible way I know how to live. I'm a born-again Christian. For more than two years my present wife and I have been taking instruction in the bible back in Miami. Three years ago, when I got fired by the Indians in midseason, I hit rock-bottom. I thought about where the downfall was. I hadn't been living a Christian life, and God was bringing me back to my knees. There's no feeling in the world like discovering God again. Or having God discover you."

"What would you say is the most important thing in this change?" I asked, fascinated by Dark's intense sincerity.

"Love," he said. "I've learned to love. I've learned the difference between head knowledge and heart knowledge. Now, I'm not as advanced as I'd like to be, believe me. I've still got a long way to go. But I'm learning to live by the bible, and I work hard at it. People may laugh at me. But people laughed at Jesus, didn't they?"

"One of the things I'm trying to do is get a handle on what happened in 1951. To what do you attribute the things that happened?"

"Bobby's homer, you mean?"

"Yes, but more than that. The whole season, the last six or seven weeks, then the Robinson home run after you all thought you'd won it, then the playoffs, the last game, the last inning—and then Thomson's home run. You see, I kind of perceive a scheme in the whole thing. I don't know what the scheme was, but I have a strong feeling there was one. And I'm trying to see if I can discover what it was."

"You don't believe it was the Lord's plan?" Dark asked, his voice pained with disappointment.

"You do," I said.

"Of course. How could it have been otherwise?"

"That's what I'm trying to find out," I said, backing off. "If it was otherwise."

"Why would you want to do that?"

"Well, let's just say for argument's sake that it might have been something else."

"What, for instance?" Dark was disturbed by the suggestion.

"Well, could it have been simply the result of chance?" I said.

He shrugged. "I doubt it."

"You were there. You were part of it. What do you think?"

"You've got to know what I think."

"But did you have any sense of it? For instance, did you know when you came up to lead off that last inning that you were going to get a hit? Did you feel it? Anything like that?"

"I felt something, I did. I remember Leo standing up on the step of the dugout, and he said something like, 'Okay, boys, we've been having to come from behind all blankety-blank year, so now's the time we gotta do it again.' Then he said to me, 'It's up to you, Alvin, you gotta start it.' "

"How did you feel going up there?"

"Well, it was a responsibility, I'll tell you. After all we'd been through, to lose it without a fight then would've been shameful."

"So you went up there with base hit in mind."

"I always went up with base hit in mind. It was just that this time it was filling my head."

"You were three runs behind. Newcombe had just struck out two of three the inning before. Wasn't that pretty discouraging?"

"Oh, sure. But in baseball you forget what happened in the last inning. Everything is now."

"So you went up there with Durocher's words in your head."

"Right. And then I looked at two strikes. He had me 0 and 2. To this day I don't know why I took those strikes. I can only figure it was God guiding me."

"Why?"

"Because they were good pitches. The likelihood is, if I'd swung at them, I would have gone out."

"Were you fooled?"

"No, not fooled. There was just something that kept me from going after them."

"God, you say."

"It had to be Him. He had everything arranged."

"For instance?"

"Well, there I am at 0 and 2. I can't take another good pitch. But I can be sure he's not going to give me a good pitch."

"He's going to waste one?"

"Not waste one, that wasn't Newcombe's style. I mean, he wasn't a cute pitcher. He had you 0 and 2, he'd give you a pitch to hit, but it wouldn't be a good one. It'd be inside corner, outside corner. So I knew I'd have to be swinging on the next one. I wouldn't have time to choose. I figured he'd go for the outside corner. I was going to have to protect the plate, so I knew I'd have to go after it. I was thinking, Alvin, you've got to get your bat on the ball!"

"And you did."

"Yes sir. It came at the outside corner. I was always able to handle that pitch pretty good. I got my bat out there and pushed the ball down the right side."

"It wasn't a clean hit."

"Well, no. I mean, I hit it fairly sharp and it got just in between Hodges and Robinson, but it wasn't the cleanest hit I ever made. I was plenty happy to have it, though."

"So," I said, "you're on first and nobody's out. Mueller's up. What were you thinking then?"

"Well, I wasn't thinking a great deal about what was going to happen, if that's what you mean?"

"But you were aware of the moment, no? Were you thinking you might be able to get back in the ball game?"

"I suppose I was thinking, hey, here's a potential rally going. I was also thinking, gotta break up the double play. That's when I realized Hodges was holding me close. I figured they were holding me so's I wouldn't be able to beat a double-play ball. Then as I took my lead I looked out and saw this huge hole between Hodges and Robinson. And I thought, gee whiz, there's our chance. If Mueller could only put it through there."

"Did you hear anyone telling Hodges to hold you on?"

"Don't recall it. He was playing behind me and just off. I don't recall hearing anybody tell him to play there, though."

"Do you think there was anything divinely inspired about that?"

"What do you mean?"

"Well, in effect, with the Dodgers three runs ahead, Hodges shouldn't't've been worried about you, right? I mean you could have stolen second base and it wouldn't have made any difference to the game. So do you think God had a hand in putting Hodges out of position?"

"He had to have," Dark said. "The Dodgers were playing for the double play. They had a lot of pride in themselves. They had it all season, you know, perhaps too much of it. It's quite possible the Lord felt they had lost sight of their place in the world. Their pride made them think they could get the double play and wrap up the game as fast as that. So maybe God wanted to teach them something about false pride."

Then came Mueller's fateful single which sent Dark to third. "Did Durocher say anything to you when you got into third?"

"He was excited. The whole ball park was coming alive. 'We're gonna get 'em,' he kept shouting. I'm not sure he believed it, but he sure was shouting it. Then he had a few words with Billy Cox.''

"Monte Irvin was up."

"Right. Monte fouled out to the right side."

"Any doubts?"

"I guess so. Whitey was up. My run meant nothing. There was one out now. If Whitey hits a ground ball that doesn't get through, the Dodgers probably have a double play and it's all over."

"How were you feeling? Were you thinking about that?"

"I was numb, I suppose. But I was praying."

"Your prayers were answered?"

"Whitey brought me home with a double. But it was only a run. We still needed two to tie, three to win."

"What was the mood in the dugout when you came in?"

"To tell you the truth, it was pretty subdued. Mueller was down at third base with what we all thought was a broken ankle. Things got pretty quiet. Everything stopped. We had to wait for Mueller to get taken off, then Branca to warm up. Bobby Thomson, I remember, came back and sat down. He was just sort of gazing out at the field. I went over and told him to concentrate. I don't think he heard me."

"So when Thomson finally came up, what were you praying for?"

"I'll tell you, I never expected it. The most I was hoping for was a single to keep us alive. A single would've scored two and we'd be tied. That's all I wanted, was to be tied."

"So then," I said, "you think it was all a gift from God."

"I sure thanked Him, I know that."

The next day I drove back to Mesa to talk to some of the A's players and watch Dark in action with his team. Already some of them were complaining in the press about him. The main complaint was that he was incommunicative—that he was nothing more than a pawn of owner Finley in the latter's perpetual wrangle with his players. Of course the more the A's had to complain about, the better they always seemed to play. So far, no one had thought to give Finley credit for being a master psychologist.

I watched Dark stand stone-faced through a two-hour drill in the hot sun. He was trying to lose weight and was wearing a heavy warm-up jacket. While activity swirled around him he remained aloof. None of the players approached him; he addressed none of them. He was a man apart; a lonely soul.

15

Muscle Memory, the Half-Inch,
This 'n' That

IN THE PAPERS he was known as Whitey, but around the club he was called Lock. This was in honor of the ballplayer's custom of inking his name on the inside of the tongues of his shoes so that when the flaps were turned back over the laces his name would be visible. Whitey Lockman printed LOCK on his left shoe and MAN on his right.

Carroll Walter Lockman was among the most popular Giants, not only with the fans but with the front office as well. By 1951 he was one of the oldest players in point of service, having joined the club in 1945 at the age of 19. He missed a year in 1946 while fulfilling an obligation to Uncle Sam, and again in 1947 when he fractured his leg, but thereafter he became a club fixture, first as an outfielder, then as the regular first baseman. He was so well liked by Horace Stoneham that when he was traded to the Cardinals midway during the 1956 season, the Giants, like penitants confessing their error, traded again to get him back prior to the start of the 1957 season.

The reason the front office liked him so much was because he was the perfect organization man. "Whitey could get along with anybody," Garry Schumacher told me. "He had a beautiful disposition, would happily do whatever you asked him, and never wrangled over money. He always had a pleasant word for everybody, and he always ended up making *you* feel grateful for any favor *you* did him."

Lockman's organizational nature did not go unappreciated after he ended his playing career in 1960. He joined Alvin Dark as a coach when Dark took over the San Francisco Giants. When Dark was fired in 1964, Lockman joined the Chicago Cubs' organization as a minor-league manager. In 1965 he was named Manager of the Year while piloting the Cubs' Dallas–Fort Worth farm club in the Texas League. Thereafter he distinguished himself for four years as a manager in the Pacific Coast League. In 1970 he was named Director of Player Development for the Cubs and in the winter of 1971 was elevated to an assistant vice presidency. During this time he also worked as a coach under his old mentor, Leo Durocher, who was then the manager of the Cubs. When Durocher was fired during the 1972 season, Lockman succeeded him and had been the Cubs' manager ever since. In addition, he is now a full vice president of the club, and is almost as busy in the administrative end of the baseball business as he is on the field.*

Lockman lives on the northern outskirts of Scottsdale, Arizona, and since the Cubs do their spring training at Scottsdale Stadium, his daily routine doesn't change much come the first of March. His house is set in a development whose architecture is Arizona *moderne* and whose flat, austere surroundings—except for the golf course—never let its residents forget that the land was only recently reclaimed from the desert. Each house has a fenced corral for a back yard, and in front a layer of green-dyed gravel substitutes for lawn.

Scottsdale considers itself to be the Beverly Hills of Phoenix, although it's hard to imagine why. Except for displaying a bit more in the way of conspicuous consumption, it's hardly distinguishable from Mesa. The day after my last talk with Alvin Dark, I arranged to meet Whitey Lockman at Scottsdale Stadium. Before we talked, I watched Lockman at work. Where the A's park was as grim as a commando training camp, the Cubs' park was as cheery as a boy-scout rally.

Lockman set the pace. He wandered all over the field, talking to this player here, that coach there, pausing to chat with newsmen, trotting off to work the catchers at the pop-foul machine, jumping into a pepper game, showing veteran outfielder Billy Williams, who

---

* During the 1974 season Lockman resigned his managership of the faltering Cubs, but stayed on as vice president.

was trying to make a switch to first base, how to scissor his feet on pegs in the dirt. Lockman, obviously, was enormously popular and you could slice the good cheer in the air with a knife.

"Let's get right into it," I said to Lockman later. "It's the ninth inning. Dark's on third, Mueller's on first. Monte Irvin's just popped out, and now you're coming up. One out, you're three behind. By now the tension's getting unbearable. Nothing's really happened yet, but all sorts of possibilities are there. Then you hit the double to score Dark and send Mueller to third. The place erupts. But what I want to know is this. A lot of people I've talked to are willing to swear on their mothers' graves that your ball just barely hit in fair territory. I've heard everything from 'it kicked up a puff of lime' to 'it was two inches fair.' What about it? Is that your recollection?"

Lockman chuckled. "My recollection's 'bout a yard, just to be honest with you. Although it sounds better when you say a couple of inches, I suppose. But I can't honestly say it was that. More like a yard would be the truth."

Lockman obviously had a respect for the truth. His white-blond hair was now graying and his leanness had filled out, but without a suggestion of fat. His manner was earnest and sincere behind the soft Carolina drawl, and I liked him immediately.

"What kind of pitch was it?" I asked.

"It was a fast ball. My thinking at the plate was—well, I knew I was the tyin' run, and my thinking was: home run. I didn't think that way very often of course, I wasn't that type of hitter. But in the Polo Grounds you could get away with it a little more than in some other parks—you know, down the line was short, and stuff. So I was thinkin' home run, and it was a fast ball on the outside part of the plate, and muscle memory took over. You know, the actual mechanics of the swing, the timing and everything. It was a ball that obviously I was not the type of hitter to pull to right field, so naturally you go with it. It was an automatic natural thing, and I went to left field."

"Did you take a good cut at it?"

"Oh yeah, it was a full swing. It was just the adjustment the body makes, a hitter makes—when the ball's away from him he goes ahead and goes after it good, you know. I was a left-handed hitter and it's not the type pitch I'm gonna hit far to right field. I had a chance to hit it farther to left field, and it just happened to hit on the bat solid, so it was a line drive. But how far fair it was I really don't know—I was thinkin' about a yard. There was no question in my mind as it left the bat that it was gonna be fair. If it was only an inch or two, there'd be a question, right?''

"How did you feel when you came up to the plate? You already had a hit off Newcombe, but he was smokin' it pretty good by then. He'd set down the side one, two, three in the eighth. Were you tight? Nervous? What?''

"No, I was not. No, I never had any nervousness at all. But later on, I don't know when or where, but I began to think about it. About the fact there were men on first and third and I could've hit into a double play. That gave me the willies for a while, but I wasn't thinkin' about that then. I went up there thinkin' home run, and then just to get the ball out of the infield.''

I told Lockman about the key I was seeking. "Well sure," he said, "I've thought about that a lot, about the reasons for it all happenin' the way it did. I've thought about the religious angle, the coincidence angle, the luck factor, this 'n' that. But really, it came down to those half-inches.''

"How do you mean?''

"Well, all through that streak in August and September, we'd get a key base hit here, a key one there, a key pitch here, a key pitch there. Now, a lotta people'd say our luck had changed, that we were getting the breaks. And that's true. But luck doesn't just happen, I don't believe. Something makes it happen.''

"An outside force?''

"Well, maybe, maybe not. I'm thinkin' it's more those half-inches. Every ball club has its own half-inches. Take your hitters, for example. You've got eight hitters in your line-up, and each of those hitters has his good pitch and his bad pitch. The difference between the two, day in and day out, is half an inch. Now if you have three or four of them getting the good half-inch every day you know you're gonna do well. Same with your pitching. On a day-in, day-out basis, if you've got your good half-inches goin' for you, you're gonna win.''

I thought this was a pretty intriguing, if esoteric, analysis of base-ball's essence. But somehow it seemed to not quite explain what occurred in 1951. "So you attribute what you guys did to the fact that you were getting the half-inches?"

"Most of it," Lockman said. "The other thing was, well, muscle memory. You see, I've got this theory about muscle memory. Let's go back to that last inning in the playoff. I think that entire inning came about through a combination of half-inches and muscle memory. Take Alvin's hit, for instance. It was a lot like mine. Newcombe was pitching fast balls, and he still had a lot of smoke. He pitched Alvin outside. Now that happened to be a pitch Alvin handled pretty well when the half-inch factor was right. You get it? Half-inch up, half-inch down, he doesn't handle it so well. Now this pitch wasn't in Alvin's best half-inch zone, but he knew he had to swing at it because it wasn't that far out either. I believe he had two strikes, so he had to swing."

"He told me he was sort of looking for the outside pitch."

"Well sure, he would be there. I mean, with two strikes New-combe *would* give him the out pitch. But remember, the Dodgers had a book on all of us. Newcombe knew Alvin hit a certain kind of outside pitch well. So he was going to *his* good half-inch, trying to keep it out of Alvin's good one but still lookin' for the strike. What happened was, he didn't quite get his good half-inch, but he didn't quite put it in Alvin's good half-inch either. That's where muscle memory entered the picture.

"When Alvin got a look at the ball his muscle memory took over. I do believe muscle memory comes into play the most when you're really in a last-ditch situation, when you're sort of numb, when you're not thinkin' about how you're goin' to do something but just know you *have* to do something. That's how it was with Alvin, with all of us that inning. Alvin swung at what was for him not his best pitch. Muscle memory took over and he got a better piece of the ball than he ordinarily would have, nine times out of ten. Without the pressure he probably would've gotten a sliver less of the bat on the ball. It would've gone down there a bit slower, would've been fielded, he would've been out. But his muscle memory got his bat closer to the difference between his half-inch and Newcombe's half-inch. He managed to hit the ball just sharp enough to get it through. You follow me?''

"I think so," I said.

The material extension of the thesis for Lockman was that Mueller's single was a combination of the good half-inch and muscle memory.

"What about Irvin, then?" I said, wondering how Lockman would explain the leftfielder's pop-out. "I mean, he was your big hitter."

"Well, I've never talked to Monte about this, but I expect it was a case of the bad half-inch."

"Yes, but shouldn't his muscle memory have overcome it?"

"Not necessarily. The closer a pitch comes to bein' your bad pitch, the less chance muscle memory has of workin'. You get your good pitch, the one that's right smack into your good half-inch zone, and you see it comin' up there fat and ripe for pickin'. It comes up a little off and you still see it, but it doesn't look so ripe. The more off it gets, the less comfortable you feel with it. If it's just off, say a quarter- to a half-inch off the sweet spot and you go after it, muscle memory will help you. You'll make that slight adjustment you need to make to get a good piece of the ball. But if it's more than half an inch off, say an inch or even more, but not close enough to another one of your good half-inches, muscle memory isn't goin' to help you all that much."

"You mean a hitter has more than one good half-inch zone?"

"Oh yeah," said Lockman. "Within the strike zone he can have half a dozen, even a dozen good half-inch spots. He could have one on the inside of the plate, one on the outside, one up, one down, one or two about the middle, this 'n' that, and so on. But in between and all around each good half-inch spot, he has his bad ones."

"So you think Irvin went after a pitch in one of his bad ones," I said.

"It makes sense. It was a case of Newcombe getting his good half-inch and keeping it out of Monte's."

"Irvin had been the big clutch hitter all year," I said. "Bill Rigney says he was the best two-strike, two-out, two-on hitter he'd ever seen that year."

"Oh yeah, I agree with that. And it could be that the more Monte was pressed, the more muscle memory took over. But you see, he had two men on, but he didn't have the two strikes and there was nobody out. Maybe he should've waited for those two strikes. Maybe he was overanxious and went after a bad pitch. That's the way it looked to me. I was kneelin' in the on-deck circle. I remember tellin' Monte to look for the good pitch.''

"You mean the one in his half-inch zone.''

"No, I wasn't thinkin' about half-inches in those days. But I guess I meant more or less the same thing. I meant, you know, he should look for his pitch. It was beginnin' to appear that something was comin' off Newcombe's ball, he was slowin' up just a mite.''

"So Irvin popped out.''

"Yes sir, and I'd be willin' to bet it was because it was Newcombe's pitch, not his. So I'd say that pitch got into one of Monte's bad half-inches.''

"You mean a hitter can tell, or see, the difference between a good half-inch and a bad one?'' I said.

Lockman chuckled. "Hell, if that was possible, baseball would be easy. No, I don't mean that. But I will say a really great hitter has a feel for it. Someone like Ted Williams for instance. You remember how he used to break down the strike zone into little circles? Each circle represented a batting average, what he thought he'd hit if every pitch he got was in a particular circle. Now each circle was maybe two, three inches in diameter. Each of them had their sweet half-inch, and the closer they got to the middle of his strike zone the more half-inches there were in each circle. I suppose that's as close as a really great hitter can come to analyzin' the strike zone, but I'm not saying he can differentiate between his good half-inches and his bad ones within each circle. Not even Williams could do that. All a great hitter has is a feel that a pitch is comin' into one of his good spots.''

"Irvin wouldn't go down as a great hitter,'' I said.

"Well now, I don't think Monte ever thought of himself as a great hitter. But he wasn't an ordinary hitter either, as you well know. I'd call Monte a good solid hitter.''

"Was he a thinking hitter, like Williams?''

"I wouldn't say so. He wouldn't often wait on a pitch. He was an aggressive hitter. If it looked good, he'd go after it. And he had such strength he could get the bat around when he did wait on a pitch. He hated to take.''

"Well anyway," I said, "he popped out. Then it was up to you."

"Right. And I know for a fact it was muscle memory with me. I could hit a certain kind of outside pitch, but I'd most times go to left with it. If you can remember back that far, you might recall I hit a lot of my doubles down the left-field line.''

"I do remember.''

"Well, I always tried to hit the pitch where it was. And when it was in my good half-inch, wherever it was in relation to the plate, I'd hit it pretty good.''

"But you didn't know as it came up there that it was a good pitch for you?''

"Oh no, all I knew was that it was a pitch I could hit—you know, that's a split-second decision. The rest was just muscle memory.''

"Did the crowd bother you? Help you?''

"Once I was up there I didn't hear the crowd. I didn't hear the crowd until I was standin' on second.''

"It must have been quite a feeling, coming through like that.''

"I wasn't feelin' much in the way of feelin's yet," Lockman answered.

"It was really the team's first clean hit of the inning.''

"Yeah, but we were still behind by two.''

"You know," I said, "if your ball had really been fair by only a half-inch or so, it would work into your theory very nicely.''

That amused Lockman.

"Were you thinking home run when you were down there on second?''

"Well yes, I must've been. I'll tell you why. During the time-out that ensued on Mueller's injury goin' into third on my hit, Freddy Fitzsimmons, our first-base coach, came down to second and we discussed the situation. I remember we talked about the possibility of a home run winnin' the game for us. So that was what I was pullin' for, to tell you the truth. I would've been grateful for anything that got me around to tie the score of course, but I was really tryin' to wish a home run onto Bobby's bat. That was why I got so anxious when he took that first pitch right down Broadway—you know? But yeah, I was lookin' for a home run.''

"Do you recall your feelings when the ball took off? Did you know it was going to go in?''

Lockman searched his memory. "Yeah, it was just complete relaxation. You know, I knew it was gone. I knew we'd won the pennant the moment it left the bat. The angle of the ball, you know, from where it was up in the strike zone, the way it left the bat, the sound of the bat, it was a home run, just one of those instant things—you know it's a home run.''

"There wasn't anything tentative about his swing, was there?''

"Oh no, he hit it pretty good. It looked plenty all right to me.'' Lockman smiled at the memory. "So it was just a completely relaxed feeling. Of happiness. Can't really describe it, it was just all kinds of happiness washing over me, like jumpin' into a pool of—well, happiness.''

"I made a big mistake at home plate, though,'' Lockman said after a few moments.

"You didn't touch it?''

"Oh, I touched it, all right, I jumped right on top of it. However, I felt that this man, Thomson, deserved to be carried off the field on somebody's shoulders, right? Well, I elected myself to do that.'' Lockman went on to tell of how he injured his shoulder and neck in the melee around home plate while trying to lift Thomson. "It sure screwed me up for the World Series. It wasn't enough that Mueller was out; I could hardly throw or swing a bat the whole Series.''

"They called it a miracle.''

"Yeah, but when you think about it, it wasn't really a miracle. We'd been doin' that sort of thing pretty regularly since August, comin' from behind with a big inning. It was really the timing and the circumstances that got people talkin' about a miracle.''

"You don't think it was a miracle?''

"Who's to say? I mean, what's a miracle anyway?''

"So tell me,'' I went on, "I gather you attribute Thomson's homer to the same thing.''

"I think you can but, mind you, this is all just a theory of mine. I mean, there could've been other things involved. Bobby'd been hittin' the ball real well all that last part of the season."

"But a home run—snapping victory from the jaws of defeat like that—just when you needed it."

"You mean you think there was something bigger?" he said.

16

Wes

THE FIRST THING THAT COMES to mind upon meeting Wes Westrum in his St. Petersburg motel room is Willie Loman, the pathetic hero of Arthur Miller's *Death of a Salesman*. Willie Loman, the archetypical fugitive from loneliness, forever on the road selling his wares—yet the man by whom American loneliness is best defined.

Westrum lives in Phoenix, but from February to October his life beats to the song of four strong tires on the pavement and is filled with the musty, antiseptic smells of motel rooms. I found him in St. Petersburg, where he'd stationed himself for two weeks in his capacity as the San Francisco Giants' chief major-league scout. Subsequent to our talk, he was made manager of the Giants in July 1974.

Instead of frocks or baubles, his cases were filled with charts and forms. "It's the toughest work I've ever done," he said proudly, handing me a thick sheaf of papers to inspect. "I've got to write a long, detailed report on every member of every major-league club down here, plus reports on all the kids in each club's minor-league camp. Read one, you'll see how much detail I go into."

I hadn't realized it was all done with such exhaustive thoroughness. "What's it all for?" I said, surprised.

"Two things, really. One is for the big club back in San Francisco, so the manager'll be able to keep a book on each opponent and their personnel. But the most important thing is for trades, so when the front office is talking trade with somebody, they'll be able to instantly refer to my report on him."

I was impressed. "It looks like there's everything in here except an FBI report. You'd think this kid was being appointed Secretary of State."

Westrum was pleased. "Well, I believe in doing a job right. A job's not worth doing unless you're willing to put your all into it."

"That must have been your philosophy when you were catching," I said. "You sure put your all into that."

"It's the only way I know how to go at life," he replied.

Once into a conversation with Westrum, all thoughts of Willie Loman faded. His expenses with the Giants must be chary, though, I thought. Outside the room there stood a big comfortable high-priced sand-colored automobile with Arizona plates. Inside, all was linoleum, Formica, and plasterboard, turning our voices hollow. The motel was situated on Tampa Bay, but his room was in the "Annex," which stretched like an old Army barracks toward downtown St. Pete. Once the season starts, he told me, he travels the major-league cities doing and redoing his audits. I wondered what kind of accommodations he entitles himself to—tacky motels on the outskirts? I was tempted to say something about it being a comedown from the old days, when as a member of the Giants or manager of the Mets he went first class all the way. But I didn't. I remembered that Horace Stoneham takes care of his own. And Westrum was probably grateful for the work.

Westrum had just come back from an all-day scouting session at the Reds' camp in Tampa, he said, and wanted to take a quick shower before we got down to the interview. I was astonished by his physique. I had remembered him as a squat, stocky man who seemed to run to fat. Now at 51 his thickly muscled body was trim and his roundish face, though lined, was bright with rosy-cheeked good health. When I remarked on his condition he held up an ever present cigarette. "I try to watch my weight. I love to eat, but these damn things help keep it down."

After finishing his playing career with the Giants in 1957, Westrum signed on with the club as a coach when it moved to San Francisco, working under both Bill Rigney and Alvin Dark. He then went to the New York Mets in 1965 as Casey Stengel's pitching coach. When Stengel broke his hip and had to retire as manager of the Mets, Westrum succeeded him. He lasted two and a half years in New York, and when the Mets refused to give him the three-year contract he wanted, he resigned. "Mr. Stoneham took me back with the Giants. I coached for two more years. Then they decided to put me out to pasture. I've been scouting ever since. This is my third year."

"I'm told by most of the other ballplayers I've talked to that you played a very large part in the comeback," I opened. "Rigney, Jim Hearn, Sal Maglie, they all say it wouldn't have happened without you."

Westrum was nothing if not a modest man. He actually blushed. "Well," he said, "I wouldn't want to take too much credit. I like to think it was a great team effort. Everybody contributed something important each day."

"But you were the Rock of Gibraltar, they say. Especially playing with all those injuries."

Westrum gazed at his hands. His right was as gnarled as a Monterey cypress. "Gee, I don't know. Sometimes I feel I was out of there more than I was in during that stretch. Let's see, the game we lost that ended our winning streak—I broke my thumb. I was out a few days. Then no sooner do I get back than I get suspended for three days."

"Now," I said, "here's the really interesting thing about the broken-thumb business. You're playing the Pirates—I believe it was August 28—and you lose 2 to 0 to end your 16-game winning streak. But here's what I want to ask you. As a result of that loss, Durocher decided to fiddle with his batting order. Do you recall being aware of it at the time?"

"Gee, I don't know."

"You see, Mays was batting sixth, then Thomson, then you. Against left-handers the order stayed the same, except Thomson would go up to third and Mueller would come down between Mays and you. But after you lost that game to the Pirates, Durocher moved Mays back permanently to seventh and would juggle Thomson and

Mueller between third and sixth, depending on the pitcher. That's the way the order stayed, unless somebody was hurt, right into the playoffs. You see my point?"

"Sure. You're saying that's why Bobby came up when he did in the last inning, instead of Willie."

"Right."

"Well, you know, in the clubhouse after the game, after Bobby hit his home run, I remember—"

"It was chaos."

"Oh yes, but I remember, someone walked in, I forget who it was, it could've been Toots Shor—you know, he was one of the great Giant fans of all time, certainly the loudest—it was either him or Jim Farley, the politician. Well anyway, whoever it was, he came storming in and boomed out in this great loud voice, 'I don't know what you were all worried about. You had Mays on deck, you know. If Bobby hadn't've done it, Willie would've!' "

"You remember what I said to you on the phone—about one of my points in this book being to see if I can't find the key to what made it all happen the way it did."

"Yeah, I remember."

"Well, what do you think?" I said.

"You mean, do I think that was the key?"

"Yes."

"Gee, it sure sounds interesting. But you know, there were a lot of key things that happened during the season that led up to the playoff, to the last inning."

"Oh, I know," I said. "You're talking about things like the Lockman-Irvin switch, calling up Willie Mays, moving Thomson into third."

"Yes," said Westrum. "Then there was Al Corwin. I mean who would've thought that Al Corwin would come up and win, what, I think it was five games for us. I mean there were probably a dozen or so big key events, and most likely hundreds of minor ones that all sort of mixed together to produce that ninth inning."

"To produce it," I asked, "or just to make it possible?"

"Well, to make it possible," Westrum agreed. "You're right, producing it was something different. But if you want to write about a miracle, write about that last week. Up to then we'd been kind of joyriding along. But that last week was something. We had to win every game and we won every game. That was when I knew for sure we were going to catch the Dodgers. I think we beat the Phillies 10 to 1 about the middle of that week. That's when I knew—when we did that. Everything was adding up, and I knew we were a team of destiny."

"You were in there most of the way," I said. "In spite of all your injuries you were in there. It was always amazing to me how you were able to hit all those home runs, the kind of shape you were in."

"Well, I was lucky enough to win some big ball games for us with the long ball."

"When you came up, did you think of yourself as a home-run hitter?"

"Oh sure," Westrum said, checking his hand again. "I *was* a power hitter until—you see, I'd had eight broken fingers. And most of those games Leo Durocher made me catch in, he said, 'Wes, I don't care what you hit, as long as you handle the pitching staff.' And Maglie—Maglie always wanted me to catch him. That was a must, because I was a low-ball catcher and Maglie was a low-ball pitcher, et cetera."

"Everybody says one of the most important things was the way you handled the pitchers down the stretch."

"All I had to worry about was, oh, scooping that ball out of the dirt once in a while and throwing people out. We always kept a book on every hitter in the National League. Leo, he forced me to do this—first-ball hitters, et cetera, where they hit—it was the basics of baseball, as simple as that. To catch the pitching staff wasn't hard at all. It was just the everyday grind you went through—I loved to hit, and I couldn't hit too well there towards the end because of my hands."

"Did you have to, say, goose one pitcher and shout at another?"

"All the time, but this was standard on any team. Frank Shellenback, he helped me a whole lot on that score. He'd say, 'Wes, there're certain times you're gonna have to get on this fella, now, when he starts to get a little lazy,' and so on. Some of them you had to talk tough to, and others you soft-soaped a little bit."

"So you think a catcher really can have an effect on a pitcher aside from the actual playing aspects of the game."

"Well, I think there was a lot of psychology going on between me and most of the pitchers that year, especially toward the end. A pitcher is like a race horse when he's out there on the mound. I mean, just like a horse, you put him on a track, all he knows is to run. He's primed to run. All that specialized training. Well, a pitcher's the same way. All that training and he's primed to pitch. And he gets spooked just as easy as a racehorse. So his catcher's got to be a kind of jockey, he's got to keep a rein on him. A catcher can do a lot of things well, but if he can't understand and handle a pitcher's idiosyncrasies he's not going to be much of a catcher."

"In that last game of the regular season at Boston," I said. "Willard Marshall's up, and he's in a position to beat you. Durocher comes out. Do you remember what was said?"

"Well, I think Leo came out to change pitchers, but Larry kind of gave him a fierce look. By the time I got out there, it was settled. Then, as I recall, we discussed what kind of pitch we were going to make Marshall hit. I think we decided on a breaking pitch. So I went back behind the plate and flashed the sign for the curve. Larry, well, he shook me off. Had a change of mind, I guess. So I flashed the fast ball and he nodded. Uh oh, I thought, if Marshall hits it out of there, Leo's going to have both our heads. So I just stuck my glove out there on the outside corner and said a quick prayer. Of course you know what happened. Marshall popped it out to Irvin."

"Did Durocher know Jansen had changed his mind?"

"Nothing was ever said. To tell you the truth, I don't think Leo was looking. I remember somebody telling me he had his hands over his eyes, there in the dugout. To this day I don't think he knows."

"Let's get back to the playoff."

"Yeah," said Westrum. "That game that Jim Hearn pitched—that first game at Ebbets Field. He and I rode together over to Brooklyn that day, going over our signs and so on. He was pretty nervous about the whole thing, and I said, 'There's nothing to worry about.' And he said, 'Wes, you just lead me,' and I said, 'I'll do my best.' And we did. I don't think I ever caught a game in my entire career when I was so in tune with a pitcher."

"Was Hearn a worrier?" I asked.

"A bit of one. With him, it was all a matter of confidence. If he was feeling confident, there wasn't a better pitcher in baseball."

"He didn't feel confident often enough?"

"If he had, he'd be in the Hall of Fame right now."

"I think that was his best year," I said. "He won 17 games."

"When you think of what he could've done, though, you could cry. He was only, what, 27 or 28 that year. He had six, seven brilliant years ahead of him. But he could never get that consistent confidence."

"So then," I said, "how did you feel going into that last playoff game?"

"I think everybody had some positive thinking going. 'Well, Jesus, we've come from 13½ games back, now we're down to the last one, but we *should* be able to win it.' That's how I felt. I think that's how everybody felt. Of course then we got down four to one, and I don't suppose we were thinking so positive any more. At least I wasn't."

"How come?"

"Well, you know, I was taken out for a pinch hitter in the eighth, and I guess I was sort of feeling out of the game. There was nothing else I could do to help, that was the feeling. When you're out of there, you get this helpless feeling—I suppose just like the fans must have felt sitting up in the stands."

"How about the inning the Dodgers got the three runs? Had Maglie lost his stuff?"

"To tell you the truth, he didn't have a great deal of stuff that day. He was tired and he was getting by on his wits right up there into the top of the eighth. The best thing he had was the inside pitch."

"You mean he was throwing at the Dodgers?"

"No, not throwing at them. But he was throwing the curve in on them, all those right-handed hitters. He wouldn't let them dig in. Now, you know he had this reputation for letting an occasional ball get away from him. He was really just trying to keep that in the front of their minds when they came up there. He had good control, but not much stuff, so he kept trying to work that inside corner with the curve. You're standing up there against a pitcher who you know likes to throw at hitters, and you see these pitches coming at your head and then breaking away at the last second, you're not liable to dig in.''

"Was that the way you and he planned to work the game?''

"He came up to me after I finished warming him up, just before the game started, and said, 'What do you think, Wes? It don't look like it's moving.' Well, it wasn't breaking very much, but we decided to give it a try, hoping he'd get it going once he was under game conditions.''

"They got a run in the first,'' I said.

"Right. He tried to catch Robinson on an outside curve and Robby got a good piece of it, knocked in Reese. So from there on in he started going inside, and it worked pretty well until the eighth. I mean he shut them out through six innings. We scored in the bottom of the seventh, and it was a new ball game going into the eighth.''

"Did he lose all his stuff then?''

"No, I'll tell you what happened. He got cautious. And of course it was the eighth now, and the Dodgers knew it was too late in the game—there was too much at stake—for him to start throwing at them. They lost their anxiousness about that and started to dig in, waiting for those inside pitches to break. At the same time Sal was trying to get too fine, you know, move the ball around on them. Well, they teed off, got four or five base hits and three runs.''

"With some help by Bobby Thomson at third,'' I said.

"Well yeah, but those balls were hit pretty hard. Those Dodgers, they were loose up there, they were going up to swing those bats. I could tell, sitting back there behind home plate. You could see it, the way they stood up there. All during the game they'd been coming up and standing in there sort of tentative. Now they were setting up with authority. It was like they'd made a pact among themselves in the dugout. They were no longer afraid of Maglie.''

"Were you surprised to be taken out for a pinch hitter?''

"No, not at all. There wasn't much I could do with a bat those last few games. I had my bad hand and a bad leg.''

"How about the last of the ninth? You're a spectator now. Did you stay in the dugout?''

"Oh yeah, I remember, I was sitting right there next to George Spencer, kind of away from everyone else. To tell you the truth, as

Dark went up, there I was thinking about whether I should go into the Dodger clubhouse after the game to congratulate them. Then Alvin got his base hit, and all of a sudden I was thinking, hey, something's going to happen. I remember turning to George and saying that 'we're going to do it again,' I said. What I meant was, come from behind. We'd been doing it so often, I just suddenly knew that was how it was going to work out."

"Then there was Mueller's hit."

"Right. Then Monte popped out and Lockman doubled, scoring Alvin."

"Wes, how do you account for it?"

"Well, I've got to figure we were doing the same thing the Dodgers did in the eighth. It was our last chance, the last chance we'd ever have. It was do something or face a long winter. So those fellows who were coming up that inning, well, they just shed all their fear or anxiety or whatever they had about Newcombe. They just said to themselves, no more excuses, gonna stand in there and hit that ball no matter what. It was like they were all on a suicide mission. Any risk was worth the gamble. There was nothing to lose."

"Of course you got that life from the Hodges business."

"I don't buy that particularly. Everybody says if Gil had played his normal position Mueller's ball would have been a double play. But they don't give any credit to Mueller's ability with the bat.

"I'd be willing to bet that if Hodges had been off the bag Don would have tried to go elsewhere with the ball. And he may well have gotten it through. He had a pretty hot bat those last few weeks. I think the Dodgers have been given too much credit for helping us prolong that inning. I think Mueller would've gotten a base hit anyway."

"That's interesting," I said. "You're the first person I've heard say that."

"Well, you know, the second guess can go two ways."

"You're right. It goes back to one event leading to another. You really can't change one thing without changing everything else that comes after it."

"That's my thinking," said Westrum.

"So what about Thomson's home run?"

"Again, I attribute it—I mean, why he was able to hit it—to what I said before. *How* he was able to hit it was maybe because of your thing—the batting-order change. But *why?* Because he went up there with no fear. My feeling is that he went up there to hit a home run, and he hit it. Remember, he'd had a lot of time to think about it during that long time-out when Mueller hurt himself. Then Dressen brought Branca in. Now Bobby had to know that Branca was going to have to pitch to him. If you ask me, there was a lot more pressure on Branca than Bobby. Branca was coming in with the tying run on second. He couldn't fool around out there, he couldn't be too fine, he had to give Thomson something to hit. It was a perfect set-up for Bobby. I don't know if he thought about that, but I know he went up there loose, figuring Ralph had to give him something good."

"Do you think Dressen should have had Branca walk Thomson? Get to Mays, the rookie?"

"No, that's another second guess that's not worth a plugged nickel. With Thomson on first, Branca's got to be doubly cautious with Mays. Branca was never a top control pitcher, so you know he's got to be worrying about walking across another man. No, he had to pitch to Thomson. But I'll tell you, by that time I was sure we had it. I knew either Bobby would hit one or else Willie would. Not a home run especially, but with Whitey out there on second I just knew one or the other would get him around to at least tie the game."

"How did you feel when Thomson looked at that first pitch?"

"I wasn't worried, if that's what you mean. It was like I said, Branca was grooving it. That's when I started thinking home run. In fact I turned to Spencer again and said, 'One of these guys,'—meaning Thomson or Mays—'one of these guys is going to hit a home run, George, you just watch.' And sure enough, the next pitch and there it was.''

"Did you know it was going out right away?"

"No, I didn't. Not many people hit home runs into that lower deck. Sitting in the dugout, the ball was going away from me, toward that high wall. At first I figured it would hit off the top of the wall and we've got a tie ball game with Bobby maybe on third with a triple. Then, I don't know, I guess I was so stunned when I saw it sail over the wall that my mind went blank. To tell you the truth, I don't really remember seeing it go over. I must have been distracted by Eddie Stanky. He exploded off the bench and raced onto the field, straight for Durocher. That's when I realized what'd happened. Then everything became pure madness."

Westrum's eyes closed for a moment and a barely perceptible shiver ran through his body. "It was just meant to be," he said. "Just meant to be."

17

The Bargain Basement Beauty

To FIND JIM HEARN you take the Northeast Expressway out of downtown Atlanta, get off at the Chamblee exit, and work your way west to the Buford Highway—a typical suburban thoroughfare lined with discount furniture barns, hamburger-and-shake shops, and used-car lots. You come over a hill and there on the right, a large patch of green on the otherwise concretized landscape, is the Jim Hearn Golf Center—a driving range, miniature golf, and a battery of baseball pitching-machines.

I had arranged to meet Hearn there on a sunny Georgia-spring morning. He wanted me to see it so that I could get a sense of what his life was like today. "Sounds to me like you're doing something similar to what Roger Kahn did in his book," he said over the phone.

"I'm sure the comparisons will be made," I said.

"Well, I expect you'll want to see how I live. I want to make sure you get your facts straight. Too many of these baseball books I've been reading—seems to me nobody gets their facts straight." There was a trace of anxiety in Hearn's voice, and I thought of what Wes Westrum had said about him being a worrier. "So why don't you come out and meet me at my golf place? After that, we'll go and have some lunch at my club, and then I'll take you over to my house and you can meet the wife and children."

"See you there," I said.

Westrum was right. Hearn *was* a worrier, at least he was worried about me and my intentions. Constantly throughout the day we spent together he would wrinkle his smooth, handsome face into a frown and say something like, "Well, look, are you sure you're not out to make this book of yours something sensational? I mean, I see how some of these writers can hurt a man, make him look bad, like Kahn did to Billy Cox, like this Bouton did to Maglie. You're not out to do that to me, are you?"

I was constantly reassuring him. I could see that one part of him wanted to trust me and be helpful—call it the Southern tradition of graciousness. But the other part was profoundly suspicious, perhaps out of his long-ago experiences with New York sportswriters. In any event he would speak volubly for a while, then draw himself up with a disclaimer. "Now maybe you better forget I said that. I don't want to make any enemies. Is that thing on or off?" There was still a lot of young-boy wonder in Jim Hearn.

The Jim Hearn Golf Center is a one-man operation, a family business, and Hearn worries after it like a mother hen. "My two older sons help me out after school," he explained, "and I've got a woman who comes in during the peak hours to run the refreshment stand, but I'm here just about all the time, ten in the morning to ten at night, seven days a week." When I arrived, the parking lot was empty. "Don't go by this," he said. "It's still a bit early in the season, but come four o'clock we'll have twenty, thirty cars in here right up to closing time. It's a nice little business, and the land's worth something too."

I hit a bucket of balls while he attended to some telephone business. Midway through the bucket he came out and watched me. "That's a good swing you've got there," he said. "But you lifted your head on that last one."

Hearn took the driver. I recalled that when he was a member of the Giants he'd been a top-notch golfer—he and Alvin Dark. Now, tall and powerful, he settled himself in front of the ball, took a smooth, fluid swing, and drove it 250 yards.

"Not bad for a driving-range ball," I said.

"What do you mean?" he said, teeing up another.

"You know—lead centers."

"Ah no," he exclaimed, his gentle Georgia drawl sharpening. "We don't cheat our customers." He hit another drive, straight as a die. "These are good balls."

"You make it look easy." I said. "Do you still play a lot?"

He shook his head. "Maybe once a week if I'm lucky. Don't get the time. Come on, we'll go over to my club and get some lunch."

Once you get off the Buford Highway you discover that Chamblee is a comfortable, recent-vintage suburb. An occasional truck farm is still in operation amidst the neat, spaciously lawned residential developments. Hearn took a home towner's pride in the area.

"Tell me something," I said. "I find it interesting about baseball players, the way most of them always seem to go back to where they came from when their careers are over. Take you fellows, for instance. With the exception of maybe Dark, Lockman, and Westrum, you've all returned to settle in your home towns. Jansen's out in Oregon, Stanky's down in Mobile. Rigney's right there outside of Oakland. Maglie went back to Niagara Falls. You're back in Atlanta. I would've thought, after spending all that time in New York, it would've spoiled you for small-town living. Don't you miss it?"

"Not at all," Hearn answered. "I mean, you can't ask for better than what we've got right here."

"I know, but this could just as easily be a suburb of New York. It doesn't look much different than some place in Westchester, or New Jersey."

"Well," he said, "we've tried New York. After I retired in 1959 we went back there to live, spent eight years up there. I was working for the Van Heusen shirt people, but it just got to the point where we missed the old home town so much we decided to pack it all up and come back here. I got so I didn't like the pace in New York any more. Down here—well, you know, like the song says, the livin' is easy."

Hearn's country club was like every golf club I had ever seen, only newer. That day the main dining room was raucous with the chatter of a ladies' luncheon, so we retired to eat in the bar. Hearn was anxious to hear news about some of his old friends on the Giants that I'd seen. After I told him about Dark, Lockman, Westrum, and the others, he said, without disguising his curiosity, ''Tell me now, did any of them say anything about me?'' The apprehensive look was back on his face.

''A couple of them talked about you,'' I replied.

''Nothing bad, I hope.''

I decided to change the subject. ''How did you get started in baseball?''

He told me he came out of Georgia Tech just before the war and signed with the St. Louis Cardinals' organization as an outfielder and third baseman. In his first year in the Cardinal farm system the team to which he was assigned ran short of pitchers, so he volunteered to pitch a game. He not only won it but pitched a shutout. From then on he was a hurler.

After three years in the service he returned to make the Cardinal club and had a very promising rookie year with twelve wins and seven losses. He never fulfilled his potential however, and by mid-1950 the Cards gave up on him. He was about to go back to the minor leagues when the Giants, desperate for pitching, made a low-price bid for him. The Cardinals accepted it and Hearn was a Giant.

Giant pitching coach Frank Shellenback immediately went to work on him. He transformed Hearn's ordinary straight fast ball into a sinker, and soon the Atlantan was winning game after game for the Giants. During the second half of the season he won eleven, lost only two, and ended up leading the league with his earned run average. Along with Maglie he was the man most responsible for the Giants' late-season run at the pennant in 1950. Because of the low price the Giants had paid to obtain him, he became known in the papers as the Bargain Basement Beauty.

''So you give all the credit to Shellenback?'' I asked.

''Well, Frank really helped me an awful lot. He had faith in me. As far as my being a pitcher, I guess he did more than anyone to enable me to keep going in baseball. He taught me my best pitch—the sinker. That's what turned me around. Yes, I've got to give him the lion's share of the credit.'' He thought for a moment. ''And then there was Westrum. Old Wes, he was a big help too.''

''There was one thing Westrum told me,'' I said. ''It might interest you. He said you sort of had a confidence problem.''

"He said that?" There was a hint of hurt in Hearn's voice.

"He didn't say it as a criticism," I hastened to add. "But he thought that with all your raw ability, if you'd only been able to really have confidence in it you'd be in the Hall of Fame right now."

"Well that sounds like a bit of a criticism to me."

"No, no," I said, "he didn't mean it that way at all. In fact, he also told me that first playoff game you pitched—he said you've never gotten the credit you should have for that game. He said it was one of the most beautiful pitching jobs he'd ever seen."

Hearn seemed still to be worrying about how I might interpret Westrum's observation. "There's only one thing about myself personally," he said. "I don't know if I can capsule my career in baseball, but it's true, I *was* blessed with a lot of ability. My trouble was that I always sort of downgraded my ability, personally, within. I didn't realize or give significance too much to what I had going for me."

"You mean you didn't push yourself?" I said, trying to zero in on what Hearn was attempting to get across.

"Oh no, I pushed myself, I worked hard."

"I don't mean for yourself, but with other people."

"Oh, I see," he said. "No, uh-uh."

"You didn't say to other people, 'I'm the best,' right?"

"Oh, gosh no, I'm just the opposite way. I've never been a pushy individual. I'd have to say that I've been—well, I'm not a meek person, by any manner of means. I guess that's because you learn different lessons from life—you know, so that if you start out meek you overcome it somewhere along the line . . . if you get stepped on enough. No, I just had a lot of ability, but my problem was that I was—well, I guess naive would be a fair word. I was naive about a lot of things. You see, when you have a product, you exploit that product and do the best you can with it. I worked hard at the game, but I look back in retrospect and I know that some of the work I did was not fruitful. I mean I was working hard, but I wasn't utilizing myself the right way to gain. . . ." He paused.

"I had all that physical ability, but my head wasn't caught up with my body. I found myself up in the big leagues as a pitcher before I'd had a chance to really learn how to pitch. I had one good year doing nothing but rearing back and throwing the ball. So I thought that was all there was to pitching. And when I began to have all those bad years with the Cardinals I found that rearing back and throwing wasn't enough. I was gonna have to learn to pitch. But there was no one there really to teach me, you know what I mean? So I just bumbled along until I'd—well, I suppose Wes is right in a way. I lost all my confidence in St. Louis. By the time I went over to the Giants I had no confidence at all. I guess I leaned on Frank a lot when I realized he was taking the trouble to teach me to pitch. On Wes too. Yeah, Wes is right, I didn't have much confidence in myself. All my confidence was in my catcher.''

"So what about that first playoff game?'' I said. "What was it like for you?''

"That was some ball game.'' Hearn leaned across the table conspiratorially. "Would you like me to tell you something about me that day that nobody's ever known before? When I was warming up I didn't think I'd get past the first inning.''

"No stuff?''

"No, no, it wasn't that. You see, I'd been bothered most of the year with this strained ligament in my side. My arm was strong all season, but this damn ligament kept coming back. Usually it'd hit me about the fourth inning. I'd come into the dugout between innings and rub some of that hot stuff on my side. I'd do that every inning and I could usually get through a ball game that way. Well, the day I was warming up to pitch the playoff game—no, let me backtrack a second. The day before, up in Boston, our final regular-season game—''

"The game Jansen pitched?''

"Right, that's the one. Larry was scheduled to pitch that day, but he was suffering from back problems, so before the game Leo says to me, 'You and Jansen *both* warm up. If he can't go, you're the pitcher.' Now I knew that if we ended up tied with the Dodgers at the end of that day we were going to have to start the playoffs the day after. And I was going to be the pitcher—that is, if Jansen was able to go in Boston. So he was warming up down in the bullpen and I warmed up out there in front of our dugout. I didn't know what to do. If Jansen can't start, I'm in there, so I have to throw hard enough to be ready. If Jansen does start and we tie Brooklyn, I can't throw too hard because I've got to save myself for the next day. So what I tried to do was to throw just hard enough to get my arm loose in case Larry can't go, but not too hard in case I have to pitch the next day. While I was trying to do this I got my rhythm all messed up and could feel that damn ligament go again.''

"And Jansen was able to pitch."

"Jansen was able to pitch. He hung in there and beat down a Braves rally in the ninth and won it. So we were assured of a tie. Now I started thinking about the next day, except when we left Boston to come back to New York, Brooklyn was losing by three or four runs to the Phils late in their game. So I felt pretty good about it, figuring they'd go on to lose and there wouldn't be any playoff and I'd get a couple of days for that ligament to heal before the World Series began. I think the World Series was due to start on Wednesday, and this was Sunday. I figured Leo would open with Maglie, then Jansen, then me in the third game, which meant I wouldn't be needed till Friday. Plenty of time to get that bum ligament quieted down.''

"Then you heard the Dodgers won it," I prompted.

"That's right, we heard it on the train. So there went my idea of getting any healing time. I was sitting in the dining car having dinner with my wife, Bill Rigney, and his wife. Most of the wives made that final trip to Boston. And Leo comes marching in to me and says, 'You ready to go tomorrow, Jimbo?' I guess I sort of gulped as I began to realize the seriousness of it all.''

"Bill Rigney told me the story pretty much the same way. He says that you began to get nervous and that your wife said to his wife something about how you hated to pitch in Ebbets Field with all those fans hanging so close.''

"Well, I don't know if she said that," Hearn protested. "I don't ever remember minding to pitch in Ebbets Field. It's true I got a little anxious, but that was because of this damn ligament.''

"I presume you didn't tell Durocher about it," I said.

"Oh, gosh no. That's not something you do. When a man wants you to go out and pitch for him you don't complain about your aches and pains, you just go out and do the best you can. But I'll say this, that pain in my side began to prey on my mind. My wife kept having to give me little boosts of confidence all night, and you can believe I didn't get much sleep.''

"Did you tell Westrum?''

"Nope, I didn't tell anybody. Except Doc Bowman, the trainer—I think he knew. What happened was, I started warming up and sure enough, just as I feared, I felt this sharp pain up here along my side every time I threw. So just before the game started I went into the dugout and asked Doc Bowman for the jar of the hot stuff. Then I ducked down in the passageway, lifted my shirt, and smacked a big blob of this stuff on me. I rubbed it in pretty good, but the trouble was I'd used so much and it got so hot that it began to burn my skin. In the first inning the burning sensation was so strong that I couldn't feel the pain from the ligament each time I threw. I thought, hey, this is the answer, I rub a lot of this stuff on between innings and the ligament won't bother me. So while we're batting in the top of the second I get in that passageway again and throw another glob of the hot stuff on my side. I forget the name of it, but you know the stuff I'm talking about.''

"It was a salve.''

"Right, a salve, and when you rubbed it into your skin it was supposed to work the heat down to the sore spot.''

"Like Ben-Gay is supposed to do but never does,'' I said.

"Yes, but it wasn't Ben-Gay, it was much stronger. Anyway, I went out to pitch the second inning and found out I didn't use enough of the stuff. It began to wear off, and this really sharp pain started coming out of my ligament again with every pitch I threw. I threw a pitch to Pafko and it came off a jerky delivery as I reacted to the sudden stab of pain. It was supposed to be a slider, but I wasn't able to get my wrist over, so it didn't move, it just hung there like a clay pigeon. Next thing I knew the ball was in the left-field seats.''

"That was the only run you gave up.''

"Yeah, but you see, I went back to the dugout after the inning and this time I got Doc Bowman to lay that stuff on me himself. 'Put it on heavy, Doc,' I said, 'more, more.' And he said 'Jesus, kid, you're gonna burn your hide right off.' And I said, 'Never mind, more.' Well, it worked. I did that between each inning right through the rest of the game, and I felt no more pain from that ligament. My skin hurt so much I couldn't feel anything else. And I pitched a pretty good ball game. Bobby Thomson and Monte Irvin hit home runs, and I won it three to one.''

''A tribute to the magic qualities of the hot stuff, whatever it was called,'' I said.

''Yeah, but you should have seen my side. The skin must have stayed red for three months.''

''Well, you did your bit for the playoffs,'' I said. ''But now we're down to the last game, the last inning. Did you figure on anything like that happening?''

''Well,'' Hearn started to say. An enigmatic smile creased his mouth. ''Gee whiz,'' he said, ''that was something, wasn't it?''

''Were you there when it happened?''

''I was in the bullpen. When Whitey hit his double, Leo sent the word in for me to start warming up. I was warming up all through that time Mueller was being taken off the field and Branca came in. You can start a new one of those trivia questions. 'Who was in the Giant bullpen when Bobby Thomson hit his home run?' Like, 'Who was in the on-deck circle?' ''

''What were you thinking when Thomson came up?'' I said.

''I wasn't really thinking about the situation at all. I mean I had it in the back of my mind that if he or Willie got a clean hit we'd probably tie the game. That meant I'd be coming in to pitch the tenth. Jansen had got the side out in the ninth, but his back was killing him. So I knew if we tied it I'd be in there. And I was concentrating on my warm-up pitches. I didn't even know what the count was on Bobby. Then—I'd just thrown a pitch when I heard the crack of the bat. I came out of my follow-through and looked in to see what was happening. To tell you the truth, I didn't see the ball. Standing out in right field there—you remember where our bullpen was—all I could see was Bobby coming down toward first base. And then—well, I'll tell you, it was something to see. I noticed Jackie Robinson turn away from second base and start walking toward center field. There was a big hush when everybody in the stands was motionless, like they were all frozen. When you were out in the bullpen and looking in toward the diamond, the thing you always noticed first was the big double tier of the stands. And on a crowded day the thing that always caught your eye was this huge patch of colors—shirts, coats, dresses, faces. From a distance it always looked like some crazy-quilt check-erboard. Well, there was this hush, and then the checkerboard just erupted into a frenzy of movement. And the roar! There must have been a hundred tons of paper flying through the air. I turned to Sal Yvars, who was warming me up, to ask him what happened. I was confused for a second, I wasn't sure whether there were one or two outs. For all I knew, Thomson might've flied out or lined into a dou-ble play to end the game. For all I knew, the game was over and those were Dodger fans screaming their heads off. But Yvars was gone. He was racing in toward home plate. Then I saw Duke Snider on his knees in center, pounding his glove on the grass. That's when I took off for home plate. And you know what? I was so stunned I can't recall a step of that dash I made. It was just the greatest thrill of my life.''

It was time for me to turn our talk toward the Question. ''Why do you suppose it happened the way it did?'' I asked. ''Not just the home run, but that and everything that led up to it. I mean, did you feel there was anything operating there in that last part of the season that took control of the club and made it perform the way it did?''

''Now that's a good question, but I can't answer it. You can say we got some momentum going, you can say the Lord was being good to us, you can say we were just so darn lucky, and I suppose it was all of those things. But beyond that, I don't know how to explain it. We weren't a great club, I don't think. I never considered that club one of the great ones in baseball from a purely talent point of view. We had a lot of weaknesses. I don't even think we were as good talent-wise as the Dodgers. But we had something that year. Maybe it was a sense of team. I know it sounds old-fashioned these days to talk about teamwork.''

''You mean it was a close-knit team?''

''Yeah, everybody pulled for everybody else. It was really some-thing. Once we started on that comeback, it was just day after day of pulling for each other.''

''Would you say that sense of team might have become trans-formed into some kind of—well, I don't want to sound too arcane—

but some kind of extraterrestrial energy that sort of took over the club and made it perform feats that were beyond its ordinary human capabilities?''

"Do you mean," Hearn said, "like that business you learn in school about the whole being greater than the sum of its parts?''

"Yes," I said, "that's a very good way of putting it.''

"Well, now, you've got me," he said. "There could've been something like that going on—do you want to know if we realized it? Is that what you're after?''

"No, not especially. I mean, not that you had to realize it while it was happening. I just thought perhaps in retrospect, thinking back on it, you might have recalled that something extraordinary was going on during those last few weeks.''

"But let me ask you something," Hearn said. "Are you a religious man?''

"No, not in the conventional sense.''

"Well, do you know anything about religion?''

"I like to think I know as much as the next man.''

"Well I'll tell you. In religion, as I understand it, they teach you that any mystery, any miracle, contains its own answer. What I mean to say is that the miracle *is* the answer. You don't really try to understand or explain it. You just accept it or you don't.''

18

Mandrake

FROM ATLANTA I TRAVELED to St. Louis to see if Don Mueller had any ideas. During the trip I found Jim Hearn's utterance constantly drifting back to me: *a miracle is that which contains its own answer.* Like the definitive answer I was seeking, success eluded me.

Of all the claims to fame Donald Frederick Mueller might have, he is most proud of the fact that he is the second generation of his family to play in the major leagues. His father, Walter Mueller, was a part-time outfielder for the Pittsburgh Pirates during the 1920s. But that's not the end of it, he informed me when we met. He himself is the father of a 23-year-old son—the child born the very same day Mueller hit his record-tying fifth home run in two days against the Dodgers on September 2, 1951—who is a shortstop in the New York Mets farm system. "If the boy can sharpen up his hittin' a bit," Mueller said, "he has a shot at the major-league career. As far's I know, we'd be the only family where the father, son, and grandson all played in the majors. So you can see why I'm rootin' for Mark."

At 48 Don Mueller has the stolid demeanor of an ex–farm boy, which is partially what he was. The fruit farm and tree nursery on which he was raised, just west of St. Louis, is where he still lives, although the land has been gradually whittled down to only a few acres by creeping suburbanization.

I had always thought that as a ballplayer Mueller approached the game—especially the art of hitting—with the guile of a street-wise pickpocket. The image was nurtured by the nickname hung on him by the newspapers: Mandrake. But meeting him for the first time muddied the image. There is still a lot of country in Mueller; he's not exactly a bumpkin, but neither is he a city slicker. Whatever guile he had must have been of the sort learned on farms, where one is in a never-ending struggle with nature and discovers how to solve the mysteries of life and machinery without any extensive formal schooling.

Mueller was a prodigy of a kind. Playing baseball as an early teenager around the hay meadows of rural Eastern Missouri, on a par with boys and men several years older than himself, he early on displayed a knack for hitting. Since he was so much younger than his fellows, his only drawback was that he could not run as fast as they could. So he was assigned to first base, where foot speed was least required.

By the time Mueller was seventeen he had amassed a reputation as a natural hitter on the local baseball scene, and while he was still a junior in high school the scouts began waving contracts at him. Because he had switched from first base to right field a year or two earlier and had become an admirer of that most celebrated of all rightfielders, Mel Ott, he chose the Giants. He could not yet begin his baseball career, however. The war, though drawing to a close, was still on, and Mueller was a first-rate physical specimen. So he went into the merchant marine.

When he was discharged in mid-1946 the Giants immediately assigned him to their Triple A Jersey City farm, where he hit .359 during the tail end of the season. The next year found him at Jacksonville, where he hit .348 for the full season. He made his first appearance at the Polo Grounds in 1948 at the age of 21 and hit .358 in 36 games. After a brief stay at Minneapolis in 1949, he was brought back to New York. In 1950 he became the Giants' regular rightfielder, a position he held onto until 1957, when he was traded to the Chicago White Sox of the American League.

He played for two years at Chicago. Then, his legs no longer able to respond to the demands of baseball, he retired and returned to St.

Louis. He was only 32. He worked for a while as a baseball scout, then went into the insurance business. Today he works as an adjustor and inspector for a large fire-insurance company in St. Louis. It is a modest but secure job. And Mueller lives a modest but secure life.

His tenure with the Polo Grounders is another source of pride to Mueller. "Do you know," he told me, "that with the exception of Mel Ott I played more games in right field for the Giants than any other ballplayer?"

With New York he had four .300-plus seasons, and in 1954 he came within a whisker of winning the National League batting title with an average of .342. The only man higher was Willie Mays, his teammate, who hit .345.

"Yes," said Mueller, "I remember that season well." We were sitting in a restaurant a few miles from his home, having dinner. "Willie and I were in a race right down to the wire. Duke Snider was in it too. We were all tied at .342 goin' into the final day. Well, I think Willie went three for four that day. We were playin' the Phillies down in Philadelphia. Robin Roberts was pitchin'. I went two for six, so Willie took the title."

Mueller's brow was naturally pinched, deep creases lining the space between his eyebrows and running down along the side of his upper nose. Now it pinched even more. "The thing was, I had 17 more base hits than Mays did that year."

I thought I detected a bit of resentment in his voice, as though he thought that Mays had stolen his thunder. Later I looked it up. It was true, Mueller did have 17 more base hits. But Mays had 54 fewer times at bat. And then of course Mays had 41 home runs to Mueller's 4, 110 runs batted in to Mueller's 71.

Earlier in our conversation though, he *had* shown traces of resentment. We were talking about his son and about how Mueller *père* had tried to get several major-league clubs to take a look at him a year or two before. When a club visited St. Louis to play the Cardinals, Mueller would drive in to Busch Stadium to see the manager and request that his son be allowed to work out with the team before the ball game. "Leo Durocher came in once when he was managin' the Cubs and I asked him, and he said the permission would have to come from his front office. Several other guys I'd known from the old days came in with other clubs, and it was always the same runaround. I couldn't understand it, these guys were supposed to be friends, and they were passin' the buck. I mean I wouldn't't've minded if they'd just come out and said, 'No, we're too busy' or somethin'. But instead they passed the buck, sayin' things like oh, gotta call the general manager back in such-'n'-such, or 'Gee, Don, I'd love to do it but it's against club policy.' Then one day the Mets come to town and I go see Yogi and ask him. Yogi, he says, 'Sure, bring your kid down, we'll give him a uniform.' And I hardly knew Berra—I mean, not the way I knew some of those other guys. So how do you figure who your friends are?''

"How did you get along with Durocher when you played for him?'' I asked, wondering at the disparateness of their personalities.

"Oh, at first, when I came up, I was scared of him. Sort of stayed away from him. But later on I figured him out and we got along fine. I remember one year, I think it was 1950, down in Arizona in spring trainin'. Durocher used to like to bet, he had bets goin' all over the place. He had a bet goin' with Al Rosen of Cleveland. Rosen was boastin' about how Mitchell, Dale Mitchell of the Indians, was gonna hit .300 that year. So Leo said, 'Yeah, well I got a guy who'll outhit Mitchell,' meanin' me. So they made a bet on who would hit higher, Mitchell or me. As I recall, it was for $500. Well, I got a good start that year, got me a handful of base hits, and I was Leo's big pal. Down toward the end of the season I think I was hittin' about .315 or so, while Mitchell was hittin' about .305. Then one day with about ten days, two weeks left, Leo come up to me and reminded me to keep it up, said he'd split the winnin's with me. Wouldn't you know, I get to thinkin' about that and I drop into a terrible slump, go somethin' like 0 for 36 and end up the season below .300. Mitchell, he ends up at .308, and Leo's out five big ones. He didn't let me forget that for a long time.''

More and more, as we talked, I could see that Mueller had a high pride hidden behind his rustic exterior. There was also a meekness about him that, combined with his pride, lent his character a patina of vulnerability. Of all the former Giants he had the best recall of the details of his own accomplishments—for instance, he remembered down to the last hundredth of a percentage point his batting average of each year, the number of hits he had, and so on—yet he was the haziest in memory about the team itself. And although he described himself as having been tremendously affected by the miracle at Coogan's Bluff, he stoically disclaimed any power to see into the magic of it. "Remember," he said, "I was in the clubhouse when Thomson hit his home run. And I was in a lot of pain, really hurtin', my ankle was the size of a melon. So I guess it didn't hit me like it did the others. I mean I was happy and everything, but I was un-happy too because I knew I'd be out of the Series. You might say I had mixed emotions."

"Well, how about that last inning?" I asked him. "Have you ever been able to think of anything that might explain why it happened the way it did?"

"Never thought about it much. Just one of those things."

"But you played a key role. Do you think it was just an accident that it developed the way it did? It seemed that everything just fell into place for all of you at that last moment. Did you have any idea when you went up to hit that something was starting?"

"Well, I knew we were down to our last chance, that it was now or never. But I frankly didn't think that we'd be able to come from three behind. Of course I always went up there lookin' to get a base hit."

"So Dark had scratch-singled," I said. "Now you're up and you're looking for a base hit."

"That's what I was doin'."

"And you got one. But you know, a lot of people claim your ball would've been a double play if Hodges hadn't been holding Dark on. They say that made the difference between a three-out inning and the so-called miracle. How do you feel about that?"

"Now there your talkin' about somethin' I've been hearin' a lot about lately. I just read an article in the *Sportin' News* about two months ago that had somethin' about that. And I'll tell you, it just isn't true." Here Mueller's pride surfaced again. He told me about how he'd noticed Hodges playing Dark tight. "I saw that hole sittin' out there like a deer in huntin' season. And I went for it. I was a hole hitter, always tried to hit the ball where the biggest hole was. If

Hodges was playin' off the bag instead of tight behind Dark, I would've tried to go up the middle with the ball. That was where I hit it best, anyway.''

"You mean you think you had a base hit in your bat, no matter what?''

"I think the chances are damn good I would've gotten a base hit. I was aware of the double-play possibilities. If you look up my record you'll see I didn't hit into very many double plays, not compared to some other guys. That was because when there was a man on first I really tried extra hard to go for those holes. I think I would've likely got it through somewhere.''

"So you don't believe the inning was made possible by that goof by the Dodgers?''

"No sir, I don't. I think once it was started, once Alvin got his hit, it was all momentum after that.''

"Momentum,'' I said looking for a clue. "What do you mean?''

"Well, one thing led to another. Whitey's double, Thomson's home run.''

"Don't you think your hurting your ankle, the game stopping for ten minutes, might have broken the momentum?''

"Oh, it could've gone either way.''

"But my question is, why do you suppose it went the way it did? Would you laugh if I suggested there might've been some kind of outer force that kind of took you all over? Picked you up by the seat of your pants and propelled you over the last hurdle?''

"I wouldn't laugh, but I wouldn't know what you mean either,'' said Mueller.

"Well, look, you had had all these obstacles to overcome through-out the season. The losing streak at the beginning, the batting slumps, the pitching slumps. Then the drive to catch the Dodgers, which you did. Some people say that was the real miracle.''

"It was, in my mind.''

"You mean catching the Dodgers was more important than the last game?''

"No question about it. Anybody can come from behind in one game and win it. There are no odds there. But to come from behind time and time again, to keep winnin' over such a long spell the way we did—well, to my mind that's a mighty big accomplishment. The last game was nothing compared to that."

"Well then, how do you account for that happening?" I said.

"There again, it was momentum."

"No one particular factor? Just a kind of general thing—momentum?"

"Well, momentum is a pretty particular thing."

"Yes, but momentum is an effect, a result of something," I said, trying to narrow Mueller down with science. "The law of cause and effect. You push a ball down a hill, it gathers momentum. But it has to be pushed. So my question is, who, or what, pushed the Giants?"

"This ball of yours," he said after a moment.

"Yes?"

"Sometimes all a ball needs to be started rolling is to have a gust of wind come along. Did you ever think of that?"

A gust of wind! I didn't know whether Mueller meant it as a bit of intentional down-home wisdom or was simply saying it to say something. But mixed in there was a telling point, and it pried itself into the cauldron of theories whirling in my head. Perhaps that was it, after all. Perhaps the *why* and *how* of the miracle at Coogan's Bluff were as ephemeral as a gust of wind.

19

The Black Beauty

EXCEPT FOR MONTE IRVIN, the entire complexion of the final inning might well have been different. "I was swinging for a home run," he told me over lunch in New York. "That was the only thing I had in mind, home run. If I'd of hit it, the ball game's tied. Dressen would've had to yank Big Newk right then and there. Lockman comes up against a new pitcher, Branca or Erskine, who knows what he'd of done? He might have hit the big home run. Or he might've gone out. Then Bobby—who knows what he'd of done? It would've been a different situation, a different pitch."

"The game might have gone into extra innings," I said.

"Right. So how do you figure it? It's all the roll of the dice."

It turns out that of all the players on the Giant club, Monte Irvin was the most nerve-wracked as the miracle at Coogan's Bluff unfolded. Every at-bat, he told me, every chance in the field during the last few weeks of the season and during the playoffs was a shakes-inducing experience for him. "I was thinking too much out there, thinking of all the possibilities, all the things I might do wrong. Like when I went up there thinking home run. I was tight as a drum, thinking I had to do it. Jesus, if I'd just been thinking about hitting the ball I'd of been much better off. Instead I went after that slider of

243

Newk's and popped it up. I was real disappointed in myself, could of kicked myself for being so nervous. When you start thinking like that, you only do yourself harm.''

"At what point during that stretch drive," I asked, "did you begin to believe you were going to catch the Dodgers?''

"I didn't believe it till after that last game was over in Boston.''

"You mean you never thought you'd catch them?''

"Well, maybe some of the guys did. I never really did. None of us ever talked about winning the whole thing. Well, wait a minute. There was a time a few days before the end of the season when I began to think, well, maybe. You see, by then we knew, I knew, we had a chance to catch them. But catching them was one thing, staying caught up, or ahead, was another. I mean, we might have caught them earlier than we did. If they'd lost a game or two more we would've caught them, even gone ahead of them a couple of days before we actually did. And if we did, who's to say we wouldn't've dropped back again in those last two or three days? The whole psychology would've been different for both clubs. So you see, I never thought we'd win it, win the whole thing. But I remember that time Campy got thrown out in Boston a few days before the end. Then I thought, well, OK, now it looks like things are gonna break our way. The Dodgers lost by a run that day. I knew Campanella, and when I'd heard he got thrown out I was sure the Dodgers were cracking.''

"Why did you have so little confidence in the club's ability to do it? Most of the other fellows I talked to say they began to believe it two, three weeks earlier.''

"Well now, I'm not gonna call them liars, but remember, they're looking back at it across, what, twenty-three years. It's easy to say that now. But as I remember it, none of us really believed we were gonna do it. Let me just say this. Man for man, the Dodgers had the best club. There's an old saying in baseball: 'Over the long haul of a season, the best club will always win.' Maybe in a short series the inferior club will beat the better one, but over the long haul the better one will come out on top.''

"You believe that?" I said.

"Yep. I figured the Dodgers were the better club, and even though we might be making a good run at them, I couldn't believe we'd overtake them. I figured them to hunker down those last few days and keep us away from the brass ring.''

"So then, how do you account for the fact that you did catch them?''

"Luck," said Irvin. "Luck, plain and simple.''

"Nothing more than that?''

"Well yeah, one other thing. We were together. The Dodgers were a better club on overall ability. But we were together and they weren't. They had a lot of jealousy over there, a lot of bitching and squabbling. We were smooth as butter, playing every day as a unit. It was something to see. That accounted for a lot of it. You know, I'm a black man. Back in those days the race business was still a big problem for baseball. And we had, what, four or five black guys on the club, all of them from down South somewhere. Even I was born in the South. And then we had all these white guys, and a lot of them were Southerners—Dark, Stanky, Lock, Hearn, Kennedy, at least a dozen others. And yet there was never any 'anti' feeling on the club. Everybody pulled for everybody, no matter the color. In that respect it was a very unusual club. 'Most every other club that had blacks in fifty-one, there were problems. Even the Dodgers had problems. They still had guys on that club who were upset about playing with black men, and there was a lot of resentment and petty bickering going on. My guess is that the Dodgers probably lost six or seven games purely on that alone.''

"What do you mean?''

"Well, say you're in a game and you're a white relief pitcher, and you're brought in to relieve for Newcombe. Say the ball game's tied and potential winning run's on second. Now that run is chargeable to Newcombe on account of he put it there. Now then, let's say you don't like Newcombe because he's a black man. Not because he talks too much or doesn't laugh at your jokes or sleeps with your wife, but simply because he's a black man and you don't like black men. Let's say also that you're pretty secure in your job—I mean, you're not gonna be sent down if you have a bad inning. So you give the batters coming up to face you some easy pitches, you give them every chance you can—without being obvious about it—to get that winning run around from second. That run'll be charged to Newcombe, not you, and the loss will go on his record, not yours. Sure, the club will've lost the game, but you will've gotten your licks in on the black man."

"Are you saying this is what happened on the Dodgers?"

"No," answered Irvin, "not that exactly. I'm just using it as an example of how a club could lose a game out of the racial resentments that existed in those days."

"But you said the Dodgers lost six or seven games because of that."

"That's my guess. Not necessarily in the manner I described, but in other ways."

Irvin worked in the public-relations department of the Baseball Commissioner's Office. Obviously he had to be circumspect in what he said. His boss, Commissioner Bowie Kuhn, had a well-refined reputation for verbal fudgery.

"And the Giants didn't lose any ball games for those reasons?" I asked.

"No, not that year. In fact I'd go so far to say we won a few we shouldn't have because of the racial thing. One, because other clubs lost an occasional game to us on account of the situation in their organizations. And two, because our guys, our white guys, were bending so far backwards to avoid any show of racial feelings that they sometimes had an extra incentive to knock home a Willie Mays, a Monte Irvin, a Hank Thompson with the winning run. And the reverse was true too. If Alvin Dark was sitting out there on second base, I'd have an extra incentive to get him in. I didn't feel any resentment from him 'cause I was black. In fact I always felt he was pulling for me, for Willie, whoever. So I had no reason to resent him. I'd be pulling for him, for Stanky, for Hearn, all of them. I mean, you'd never see me intentionally misjudging a fly ball so that somebody like Jim Hearn would lose a ball game. And if we'd had a black pitcher, you'd never've seen one of our white players do the same thing. That was the kind of thing that went on with other clubs, but not ours. With us it was everybody pulling for everybody, right down the line. Especially that last month. I'll tell you, it was a beautiful thing to be part of. Even if we hadn't caught the Dodgers, it would've been a beautiful thing to be part of."

"I've read that when you first came up to the Giants in 1949 you had a few problems."

"Oh yeah, there were a few. But remember, we—Hank Thompson and myself—we were the first for the Giants. I suppose it took some getting used to for some of them."

"I'd heard that you came up feeling pretty bitter."

"Where'd you hear that?"

"Oh, you know, here and there. I seem to remember reading an interview with you somewhere. You didn't appreciate getting your chance to play in the majors so late in your career. You didn't like the attitude of some of the Giants. You thought the Giants were only interested in you because they were dwindling at the gate. You were pissed off about having to play first base."

"Well," said Irvin, *"that* was true."

"The rest wasn't?"

"I don't know," he said, thinking about it. "Let's just say I've changed. Gotten older. You know how it is when you get older. Right now, hell, I'm grateful I got the chance at all. When I think of all the great black ballplayers I played with in the Negro leagues who didn't get a chance—Ray Dandridge, oh, dozens more—I got to feel grateful. As for that other stuff, well, I'm not so sure I said those things."

"Did you feel them?"

Irvin shrugged. "Maybe I did, maybe I didn't. But I see things a little differently now. I mean, I'm not an Uncle Tom or anything—hell, I suffered from the racial thing just as much as anybody. But I believe in working out problems."

I found it hard to believe Irvin was almost 56. Except for scatterings of gray in his close-cropped black hair and a slight thickening of his girth, he looked much the same as he had 25 years before, when I first saw him in a Giant uniform. When I remarked on his appearance, he said, "Well, you know, it's all in your perspective. When you're young, people in their fifties look old to you. But as you begin to get into middle age, folks in their fifties don't look so old any more."

Missing, however, was the old controlled explosiveness and ferocity I had always associated with him. The only reminder of it came in the brisk, humorless, offhand way he answered most of my questions. When a question came too close to home, his neck would stiffen ever so slightly and his face would turn hard—his mouth set, his large eyes bulging, the muscles in his jaw working furiously. Or had I imagined the ferocity?

"No," he said, "I was a pretty fierce competitor. I still am. But look here, here we are sitting in this fine restaurant, eating all this fancy French food. I know how to relax too."

"How do you account for the lack of any racial tension on the club when you say every other club had it?"

"Don't know what it was. It just seemed to sort of come together on its own."

"Was Durocher responsible for it?"

"In a way, yeah," said Irvin after mulling it over. "Yeah, Leo, he was the kind of guy who didn't give a damn what you were, as long as you could win for him. If you were a winner, he loved you. He wasn't always like that, mind you. It was only after he came to the Giants. A lotta people said he mellowed. Of course he was crazy about Willie."

"How about in his private life? I mean, a man can be color blind around a ball team, but he wouldn't let a black man walk through his front door at home."

"I don't know about that. I don't know what Leo thought privately. You can only go by what a man does when you're dealing with him. Around the club, that's where it counted. Hell, I might not've let a white man walk through *my* front door. But if I got to work with him, I'm not going to worry about whether he's red, white, or blue. All I know is Durocher was always straight with us. Some of that probably rubbed off on the others. Christ, one of my best buddies on the Giants was Whitey, Whitey Lockman. And he was from North Carolina, you know."

"Fifty-four was your last big year with the Giants."

"Nope, I was there in fifty-five."

"You didn't play all that much."

"It was a lousy year for all of us. Except for Willie of course. He hit 51 home runs that year. But we finished third. Leo got fired, and then they tore the heart out of the club. In one year almost the whole bunch was gone. They got rid of Jansen, Maglie, Hearn, Dark, Lockman, myself. They'd already traded Bobby away.''

"Where did you go?"

"Chicago. The Cubs.''

"Who did they get for you?"

"Oh, they didn't trade me. They outrighted me.''

"How did that feel?"

"Not so good. It never feels good to be let go when you've been with a club that long, especially a club like that, in New York and all. But then, with Leo gone, all the old guys going, I didn't really mind. I was having back trouble, I couldn't play too much that last year, fifty-five. With Leo gone, they were looking to rebuild. Youth, you know. That's baseball.''

"What did you do after that?"

"I played a year with the Cubs—hit .271, but my back was getting worse. I was 37, and I figured if I kept on playing, it was really gonna have me in trouble. The back problem developed out of my broken leg. I broke my leg in spring training in fifty-two.''

"I know. That, and Willie Mays being drafted, probably cost the Giants the pennant that year.''

"Yeah, we finished four and a half back. Anyway, I came back too soon. I should've stayed out the whole season, but I came back for the last month and a half, trying to help the club. I was favoring my leg so much I threw my back out of line. That started it. I had a good year in fifty-three, hit .330 or thereabouts, but after that it was all downhill. My back got so bad in Chicago I decided to quit before I ended up in the hospital.''

"So you retired in fifty-six?"

"Yep. Went back to Orange, got a job with the Rheingold organization, stayed with them about twelve years. Then, a few years back, this job came up with the Commissioner's Office. So I took it. Been there ever since.''

We finished lunch and sat waiting for second cups of coffee. "Okay,'' I said, "let's go back to 1951. Do you have any ideas why it happened the way it did?"

"You mean catching the Dodgers? Or Thomson's home run?"

"Catching the Dodgers, yes—a miracle in itself, some say. But you seem to think it had something to do with the fact that you were all so close, pulling for each other, maybe pulling each other along too, like a team of six or eight stagecoach horses used to do. You know—the horses not only pulled the wagon, they all worked together to pull each other as well. If one or two horses were off the pace, they just got pulled along with the tide, so to speak. Now as I understand it, you'd say the Dodgers were doing the opposite, each horse in the team was working against the tide instead of with it.''

''That's more or less the story,'' Irvin said.

''But what about the big miracle, the last inning of the last game, the home run and everything leading up to it?''

''In the first place, it wasn't any miracle. That's just newspaper crap.''

''Well, you've got to admit it had to be just about the most dramatic event in the history of sports.''

''Sure, I'll agree with that, but it was no miracle. The Dodgers gave us a break. And then we went out and did what we had to do, what we'd been doing all along there at the end of the season. We were not a club you could make too many mistakes against and get away with.''

''What was the break? You mean Hodges playing Dark close on first when Mueller was up?''

''Right. Mueller's ball would have been a sure double play if Gil had been in the right position. So we'd of had two down and none on when I came up. Not a very good position to be in when you're three runs behind.''

''Yes, but you know what Mueller says,'' I countered.

''What does Mueller say?''

''He says he hit the ball there on purpose, that he was shooting for that hole because he noticed Hodges was hugging the line.'' Irvin looked doubtful. ''He claims that if Hodges had been playing straightaway he would've gone elsewhere with the ball.''

''Well, I'm not going to doubt the man if that's what he says. But it doesn't really make any difference, because Gil should have had it anyway. He could've gotten to it, he just misplayed it. I remember it because I was on deck and could see everything clearly. Mueller bounced the ball down there and I immediately thought, 'Shit, double play!' The ball wasn't hit that hard, and even being out of position, ninety-nine times out of a hundred Hodges would've had it. He just misplayed the ball. I don't know why, but he just did, which was very unusual for him. I could see him hesitate for just a split second before he began to move. It's too bad he's dead, you could ask him. But I'd swear he'd say he hesitated for just an instant. In other words, he didn't make that reflexive jump after the ball as it came off the bat. And I'm telling you, that was the difference between the double play and the base hit, not so much that he was out of position. Any other time he would've had it. He had a big scoop of a glove, that man. Wasn't often he let balls through down there."

"Why do you suppose that happened?" I asked.

"My guess is this," said Irvin, for the first time showing enthusiasm for our conversation. "Dark's got a short lead off first. Hodges is behind him, just off the bag but close enough so Alvin has got to stay tight. Now, as Newcombe delivers the pitch Hodges drifts further to his right, away from the bag. But he's still behind Dark. In other words, Dark's between him and the plate. Then Mueller swings. As the bat makes contact, Dark is off and running. Just at that moment—as the ball leaves the bat—he crosses in front of Hodges' line of vision. For that split second Hodges' vision is blocked. He knows the ball's coming his way, but he can't see it. That was the instant of hesitation. Then Dark is past his line of sight and he picks up the ball. It's coming down on his right. Now he goes after it. But he's a split second too late, the ball ticks the edge of his glove. And there's your miracle at Coogan's Bluff. It was an eyeblink difference between a double play and the big inning. Now, I can't be certain of it, I never asked Hodges myself. But that's my guess of what happened. Everything else that followed, Whitey's double, Bobby's homer—well, they were both solid hits, professional hits. But that eyeblink of time when Hodges lost the ball coming off Mueller's bat—that's what the so-called miracle was all about. A tiny little accident is all it was. It helped us, hurt them."

First half-inches, then gusts of wind, now eyeblinks. I seemed to be getting further and further away from a definitive answer.

20

The Last Man Up

I'D SAVED BOBBY THOMSON for last. I'd sat with all the Giant regulars now save Eddie Stanky, who told me he was too busy coaching his college team to talk, and anyway had no light to shed, and Larry Jansen, who I was unable to get to see in Oregon. Leo Durocher was saving his theories and recollections for his memoirs, and of course Henry Thompson was dead. So now it was time to get it from the horse's mouth.

I met Thomson in New York a few days after Henry Aaron's historic 715th home run. The irony of it all had not been lost on him. I made reference to the army of newsprint, radio, and television media that had been concentrated in Atlanta, turning the event into a garish promotional circus that had little to do with baseball. "Imagine," I said, "if the media had been able to pre-set the stage in 1951 for your home run the way they did for Aaron's. Why, the Democrats probably would've run you for president instead of Stevenson."

"Yeah," he chuckled, taking a contemplative pull on his pipe. "Either I was born twenty years too soon or television was born twenty years too late."

"I was thinking about that the other night while I was watching," I said. "Your home run and Aaron's were probably the two most dramatic events in the history of baseball. Some people might want to put Ted Williams' last one up there as a pretty dramatic one. Or Gabby Harnett's in 1938. Or the time Babe Ruth was supposed to have pointed to the right-field stands, then hit one in.''

"Yes," Thomson broke in, "and don't forget another big name in baseball, a fellow by the name of Dick Sisler. He hit a pretty important one the year before mine to take the pennant away from the Dodgers. I always like to remind people of that, because he sort of set the precedent for mine.''

"But when you come right down to it, yours and Aaron's will be the two that are the most vividly remembered.''

"Well, thanks," Thomson said. "I thought they overdid the Aaron bit. But you know, times've changed. Baseball's changed. Tell you the truth, I don't follow it much any more. Oh, I check the papers once in a while. But you see, after I gave up the game I found there was more to life than baseball. Work, for instance. Daily nine-to-five work, where you've got real challenges and responsibilities. I never knew what it was to work until I got out of baseball and had to start thinking about the rest of my life. Then I started working and I found out what it was like. And I liked it. I liked the challenges, the responsibilities, the idea of solving problems, of planning things with a group of other people and then working them out until you've succeeded, achieved the goals you set for yourselves.

"Don't get me wrong, I enjoyed my days playing ball. But it's nothing compared to putting in an honest day's work, having to use your brains to deal with all sorts of problems. Some of these baseball players today, they make me laugh. Here you've got a guy who's a leftfielder. His manager says he wants to try him in center. Now this guy's making, what, sixty, seventy thousand a year. And he says, 'Oh, I don't think I can play center field, it's too big a change.' Well, damn, what's the difference between left and center field? This guy's an outfielder, he should be happy to play anywhere out there. In fact center field's easier—you see the ball better off the bat, you don't have to worry about playing the tricky carom, you don't get the ball hooking on you, and so on.''

"You're talking about Cleon Jones?" I said.

Thomson held up his hand. "Let's say I'm not talking about anybody in particular. I don't want to make enemies. I'm just using one illustration, but it happens all over baseball. You've got these guys making four, five, six times what the ordinary working man does, and here they're complaining about playing this position instead of that—it's ridiculous. Let them go out and work for a living for a while, then come back to baseball. I'll guarantee you, they'd play any position they could, and they'd do it standing on their heads if their managers asked them to.''

Thomson's voice was ruminative, gently sarcastic, but good-natured. It contained none of the bitterness of most old-timers who offer the traditional the-game-ain't-played-the-way-it-used-to-be complaint.

As he continued to talk about himself, I discovered that he had a strong, abiding belief, if only lately arrived at, in the old-fashioned American work ethic. He had remained with the Giants through 1953, returning to center field while Willie Mays put in his two years of Army duty. Upon Mays' return in 1954 Thomson was abruptly traded to the Milwaukee Braves. At first it was like being cruelly turned out of the fold for the young man who had originally chosen to sign with the Giants rather than the Dodgers because he had always been a Giant fan. But he learned to like Milwaukee after a while, and was even thinking of settling there permanently when in 1957 he was traded again—of all places, back to the Giants.

The return to the Polo Grounds didn't take, however. It was a ploy by Horace Stoneham to restore some life to the gate after announcing that it was the club's last year in New York. When they moved to San Francisco, Thomson was dumped to Chicago. He'd always liked Chicago as a city, so he didn't mind his two-year tenure with the Cubs. However, in 1960, when he was traded to the Boston Red Sox, he was 36 years old and his skills were diminishing rapidly. Let go by the Red Sox, he was picked up briefly by the Baltimore Orioles and then given his outright release.

It was the end of a curious baseball career, one that was in Thomson's words, "Ordinary in every respect but one." Over a span of fifteen years in the major leagues he compiled a lifetime batting average of .270. The highest he ever hit for a full season was .309—in 1949, the only year he hit over .300. The most home runs he ever hit in a season were 32 in 1951, the last two coming in the postseason playoffs. His home-run average over 15 seasons was slightly under 18 per year. He batted in more than 100 runs four times, but his career RBI average was 68 per season.

Compared to many others, then, it *was* an ordinary career. He was never considered a great defensive outfielder, only a good one, and as a third baseman he had the consistency of foam—although on this score he says, "You hear about all the bad plays I made at third, but you never hear about the good ones. I made a few of those too."

But it was the exception to the ordinariness of his career that defines Robert Brown Thomson, known variously during his playing days as Bobby, the Staten Island Scot, the Hawk and, around the club, Hoot Mon. As a man, a human being, there is something about Thomson that marks him as exceptional—that persuades one upon meeting him that probably only he, among all the members of that team, was capable of executing the exceptional feat that constituted the miracle at Coogan's Bluff. As I sat across from him in the restaurant booth, listening to his wry, humorous, often self-deprecating answers to my questions, this wisp of an idea began to spin in my mind.

Of all his nicknames, Hawk probably fit him best. He was tall and wide-bodied, yet plank-slender, with high, broad, sloping shoulders that suggested a winged creature. The image was completed, though, by his face, an angular face that was at the same time open, wide-eyed, and choir-boy innocent—and dominated by a large nose that was beak-like in the boldness of its curve. His head was small, his forehead sloping back to curly hair, and was attached to the density of his shoulders by a surprisingly thin, slightly cantilevered neck—a bird of prey! For a centerfielder whose job it was to soar great distances swooping up baseballs on the wing, Hawk was a perfect, if somewhat overgenerous, appellation.

At 51 he hadn't changed a great deal. His face was fuller, his neck thicker, his shoulders denser, his hair graying. But he was instantly recognizable, and his familiar plodding walk, which had always belied his considerable speed as a runner, underscored the recognition.

After leaving baseball in 1960, he told me, he began to cast around for a new career, not unmindful of his residual popularity among

New York's business community. "But I wasn't out to trade on my reputation as the guy who hit the home run," he said. "I knew nothing about business. I had a lot of offers from various big companies to come in and talk about a job, but it inevitably came down to them wanting me to be some kind of showcase character. So I held out. I kept looking for something I could get into where I could train for a career, specialize in something, make a real contribution over and above my name."

He feels he was rewarded by his perseverance. He finally joined the West Virginia Paper Corporation as a salesman. He worked hard to learn his new trade and today, fourteen years later, is a high-level sales executive with the same company, which is now known as Westvaco. He works out of comfortable corporate offices on New York's Park Avenue, lives in a pleasant New Jersey suburb with his wife and three children, and views his life with modest philosophical satisfaction.

"One thing I'd like to tell you," he said while we were still on the subject of his post-baseball career. "I only realized after I got out of baseball and into business how little I had utilized my skills. As a ballplayer, I took whatever talents I had for granted. I never worked as hard as I should have. I never exploited them the way I could have. And I'm sad about that. I'm not saying I would've been any better a ballplayer. I may or may not've been. But I cheated myself, and that's what I've come to regret. It took me a long time to mature. That's a thing a lot of ballplayers never realize until it's too late—the value of hard work, the value of perfecting yourself as much as you can. And that's the kick I get out of business. It makes you appreciate your whole self. It makes tremendous demands on your entire being, but it gives you even more tremendous satisfactions. You can't be spoiled, petulant, a prima donna, and get very far in business. You've got to have discipline, a sense of purpose, and a wide range of skills—mental and physical."

"You sound as though you're downgrading baseball," I said.

"No, I'm not downgrading it. If I had to do it all over again, I would. But knowing what I know now, I would've done it differently, much differently. I'm only sorry that baseball tends to keep the kid in a man so long."

"How about your own kid?" I asked.

"Oh, he plays. I'm involved with kids' baseball over where I live. I try to give it a little more meaning—you know, impart a little knowledge to the youngsters, not only about baseball but about life, and work, and learning how to exploit their skills. Without taking the fun out of the game, of course."

"Well, just think," I said. "If you'd approached the game differently, there may never have been a miracle at Coogan's Bluff. How do you weigh that against the other?"

"You're probably right." he said, reflecting for a moment. "But you know, if I had to choose between the two—between hitting the home run and having a more mature outlook on life as I was going through my career—I'd choose the second."

"Do you regret the home run?"

"Oh no, not at all. I mean, how many times does a man have an opportunity in life to rise to an occasion like that? The only time I've regretted it is when I meet people and all they can see in me is the home run. They think that's all I am, it's all I know how to talk about. But really, no, I don't regret it at all. God almighty, I'm eternally grateful for it. And yet if I hadn't hit it, I never would've known what I missed, would I?"

"I guess not."

"But looking back on the whole of my career, I know what I missed there. That's what I meant when you asked me what I'd choose."

"So now," I said, "about that home run."

Thomson laughed as he lit his pipe. "I thought you'd never ask."

"You must be fed up to the teeth talking about it."

"Well, you get to the point where you think, what more can you say about it? But you know, it's there, it's out there for all the world to see. I don't have any private claim to it. And I don't mind talking about it. Sitting here, reminiscing like we've been doing—I always get a kick out of it. That reminds me—something I thought I must tell you coming over here. Little things always come up in my daily life that have something to do with that homer. For instance, as I was leaving my office to come over and meet you, I get on the elevator and this fellow recognizes me and introduces himself. He says he's in the printing business and I made him a lot of money back there in 1951. He says his company had gotten the contract to print the World Series programs for that year. Well, when it looked like it was going to be the Dodgers in the Series, they got the go-ahead to start printing the programs. Then we caught the Dodgers, so this guy gets a stop order. He had the programs all loaded up on trucks and set to be delivered. So he held on to them during the playoffs, and then, when the Dodgers get three runs in the eighth inning of the last game he receives a call saying, 'Okay, send the trucks out.' Then comes the ninth inning, and the trucks are on their way to Ebbets Field and Yankee Stadium. He gets another call, 'Bring back the trucks and reprint the programs. Thomson just hit a home run. It's the Giants in the World Series.' So he got paid for printing two sets of programs, all because of me. Now, how's that for a story, that I should run into this fellow just when I'm coming over to talk to you.''

A light bulb popped on in my head. ''You seem to have a gift for being in the right place at the right time,'' I said.

''But you want to hear the kicker? When the guy introduces himself to me in the elevator, you know what he says his name is? Wouldn't you know, his name is Koslo? I haven't heard that name ever before, except for one other guy.''

''Dave Koslo.''

''Right,'' laughed Thomson. ''Now I ask you—coincidence?''

''That's what I was thinking,'' I said. I explained my quest to Thomson, my search for the *why* and *how* of his miracle home run. And I told him of some of the fragmentary suggestions I'd gotten back—the half-inch, the loss of fear through desperation, the gust of wind, the eyeblink, divine providence. ''Of course, I've been saving you for last. I've never believed it was just coincidence. In fact, it was my inability to accept this that got me off on this project in the first place. I take it you don't believe it was coincidence either. Do you ever wonder about it?''

''I used to a lot,'' he said. ''But no, I don't believe it was just coincidence. Like I say, it's followed me ever since. Too many things have happened in my life that are somehow or other connected with that home run. Like meeting that guy on the elevator today when I'm on my way over to talk to you about it. And the fact that his name is Koslo.''

"Did you have any premonition when you came up to bat? Any feeling whatsoever of what you were about to do?"

"Not a one," he said. "I wasn't even thinking about a home run. All I was thinking about was getting a base hit."

"All right," I said. "I feel I'm within a whisker of an answer. Let me reconstruct things with you."

"All right."

"First, the season." We went over the early part of the season, the losing streak, the Lockman-Irvin switch, the advent of Willie Mays. "Yeah," he said, "the coming of Willie lost me my job, but it enabled Leo to play with his line-up until he got the right combination."

"He sat you down for a while through there."

"I wasn't hitting."

"But then he gave you another chance, this time at third base."

"It was a last-ditch shot for me." Thomson said, and went on to tell me the story of his summons to Durocher's office.

"How did you feel about going to third?"

"Well, I was willing to play anywhere. Remember, I came up as a third baseman. They turned me into an outfielder at Jersey City, but when the Giants called me up in 1946 they were thinking of me as a third baseman. I remember, in spring training in forty-seven, they'd gotten this new boy from out in California—Jack Lohrke. Sid Gordon had been playing a lot of third base for the club. And then there was me. So Mel Ott, he told the three of us he'd give each one a fair chance to win the job, alternate us every third day. But then as we were barnstorming back east with the Indians, we had a problem with Buddy Blattner, our regular second baseman. Mel Ott came up and asked me if I'd consider playing second base."

Thomson chuckled at the memory. "I'd never played second base. But I was just a young, stupid kid, I suppose, so I said sure. So the next day I played second base, and I opened the season there. Of course, I was lucky to have a guy like Joe Gordon of the Indians— Joe worked a lot with me and taught me all he could in a couple of days. At first it was a disaster, but after a while I began to feel comfortable at the position and I think I might've done a pretty good job playing second. But then they discovered I could run, so Mel came back to me and asked if I'd take a crack at center field. And from then on, that was it, center field."

"One thing's always puzzled me," I said. "You were the fastest man on the Giants, one of the fastest in the league. Yet you never stole many bases. Why was that?"

"In forty-seven we weren't a running team."

"But what about after Durocher took over? He was a great believer in the hit-and-run, the steal, the daring play."

"That's what I was saying before. I had all this speed, but I never developed any base-running skills. If I had it to do all over again, I'd like to develop my running."

"You were faster than Monte Irvin. Yet in 1951 he stole home six times, not to mention his steals of second and third. I don't think you even had six attempts at stealing that year."

"I remember one year I stole nine for nine, but you're right, I never ran much. Leo never had me running, and I suppose it had something to do with my aggressiveness. I wasn't very aggressive, you see. I was sort of placid and easygoing. If I'd really wanted to run, I would've been after Leo to let me run."

"Were you an aggressive hitter?"

"Well, that's another thing. I suppose it's because I wasn't that I was able to hit that home run. If I'd been an aggressive hitter I would've gone after that first pitch, but I just let it go by."

"What I meant was, were you a thinking, waiting hitter, in the style of Ted Williams? Or were you a swing-away hitter like, say, Irvin or Yogi Berra?"

Thomson laughed. "Oh, once in a while I fooled myself into thinking I was a thinking hitter. But I really wasn't. I wasn't a free swinger either. If you want to know the truth, thinking back on it I was a pretty dumb hitter. Again, it goes back to what I said before, I didn't work hard enough to develop myself. There were so many things I didn't do that I should have done. I never developed my sliding—I didn't even know how to slide when I got in the big leagues. That's why I used to slide headfirst all the time, I never learned the right way. And that's why I banged up my knee that first season—had to have it operated on. I never developed my bunting."

"With your speed you might have added ten or twelve points to your average," I suggested.

"Sure. I could hit for power, so those third basemen had to play me deep. If I'd learned how to do the running bunt, I'd have been that much better a ballplayer. But I was dumb kid, just a dumb kid."

I have to admit that I was beginning to wonder whether Thomson wasn't being too harsh on himself, perhaps out of some sort of guilt deriving from the fact that he somehow felt he did not deserve the two decades of adulation his home run had brought him.

"OK," I said, "toward the end of the season you're playing third base, and you start hitting like there's no tomorrow."

"Yeah, I did start swinging the bat. I figured, like Leo said, it was my last chance. Leo had ways of getting you psyched up. I guess I began to feel it was all or nothing. I just went up and started swinging, and the base hits and home runs began falling in."

"Now, there's a clue," I said.

"What's that?"

"Well, you said you felt it was all or nothing. You were desperate, it was a last-ditch situation. And instead of getting overanxious, you relaxed up at the plate. You figured you had nothing to lose. As a result, you started hitting the ball like crazy. Now isn't there an analogy between the way you felt then and the way you felt when you went up there in the last playoff game?"

"Hey, you know, I never thought of it that way. You may be right. But I was pretty anxious going up there."

"OK, but before we get to that, there's one other ingredient in that season I'd like to ask you about. Not many people are aware of it, and I wonder if you are. Do you remember back there—it was right after the end of the 16-game winning streak, toward the end of August—when Durocher switched you and Mays in the batting order?"

"Vaguely, yeah, I remember."

"You had been alternating with Mueller between third and seventh, and Mays was batting sixth all the time."

"Yeah, against left-handers he'd move me up to third and move Mueller to seventh. Then reverse it against right-handers."

"That's right. But then—I suppose because you and Mueller both had hotter bats than Mays about then—he dropped Willie back to seventh and moved you two to sixth, depending on the pitcher. For the rest of that year you were batting sixth against right-handers instead of seventh."

"So I came up instead of Willie."

"Right," I said. "Of course no one knew it then, but of all the crucial moves Durocher made that year, that was the *most* crucial. Were you by any chance aware of it when you came up?"

"I'd be kidding you if I said I was," he said. "No, I wasn't aware of it. In fact I never really thought much about it. But you're right again, it was a pretty important thing."

"My point is, probably the two most crucial moves Durocher made throughout the season both involved you. Three, if you count Mays' coming up in the first place. It was as if, somehow, your die was being cast."

"That's interesting," said Thomson, refilling his pipe.

"I mean, these three things weren't any coincidence. Not that they were planned or anything, but they had to be more than just coincidence."

"Well, it still beats the devil out of me," he said.

"OK, but let's take it to the end. I've been clinging to this theory—that the club's incredible comeback that last month and a half got a kind of collective energy going. Now, since the three most crucial moves involved you, and because you more than anyone— with your hitting—had been responsible for bringing the club from behind, I see that energy sort of collecting and becoming embodied in you at the final last-ditch moment. It had to be you, who else could it be?"

"Well, I hit well, but so did other fellows on the club."

"Yes, Mueller was hitting well, Irvin was hitting well, Dark was hitting well. But nobody was hitting like you were those last weeks.

And nobody had figured so importantly in so many crucial events across the season.''

"So you think I became a kind of symbol for everyone else?" Thomson said.

"Not a symbol so much as a kind of magnet for all that energy that'd been building throughout the comeback. I mean, after catching the Dodgers, there was no way you could then lose it.''

Thomson was listening to me attentively, but I don't think he was buying it. In fact he may have been thinking I was a candidate for the loony bin. He chewed reflectively on his pipe. "Mmh, but it's interesting to consider.''

"What were your feelings when the ninth inning started?''

"Total dejection," Thomson said with emphasis. "I didn't think we were good enough. It was the way I'd been thinking most of the way through the comeback. I didn't think we were good enough to catch the Dodgers.''

"But largely because of you, you did.''

"Well, it wasn't only me, there were a lot of other guys doing their bit, too.''

"I know, but you can't deny yours was the biggest bat down the stretch. And you hit the home run that won the first playoff game. Also, you drove in the run that tied the last game up—in the sixth.''

"Yeah, but I did that goofy bit of base-running in the second, and I cost us a couple of runs in the eighth by misplaying two balls hit at me. I was totally dejected. Even after Lock hit his double and I was going up there to the plate, I was still sulking. I wanted to hide my head in the nearest hole. When I think back on it, it was lucky for me Mueller hurt his ankle and the game had to be stopped. At least it gave me time to come back and begin thinking about the present instead of the past.''

"And what were you thinking?''

"Well, I was thinking, gotta get a base hit, gotta get a base hit.''

"No home run?''

"Absolutely not.''

"Were you surprised to see Branca?''

"No, I wasn't thinking about who it was out there.''

"Even though you'd homered off him in the first game?"

"No. All I was thinking was, damn it, you S.O.B., you've gotta vindicate yourself for all those boners you pulled."

"Did you have any idea of the—well, the significance of the moment?" I struggled for the right words. "I mean, did it ever occur to you what a home run would've meant? To the Giants, yes—but especially to you?"

"Nope. Never thought of it."

"Well, then," I said, "and here I go again. Did you have any kind of feeling, any slight hint, or sense, that some power was taking over your body, your reflexes?"

"Absolutely not. I was tight, I was quivering inside. I had everything I could do to calm myself down."

"All right," I said. "What about the famous Durocher statement? I've heard about sixteen different versions of that inning, but everyone agrees that Durocher came up to you while Branca was finishing his warm-ups and said, 'If you've ever hit one, kid, hit one now.' "

"Well," Thomson said, "I'll put you as straight as I can about that, because nowadays Leo's going around telling all sorts of wild stories about what he said to me. Just last month I was out in California doing a television program about the whole thing. Leo was there, and they asked me what he said. And I said, you know, 'If you've ever hit one, hit one now.' The TV thing was called *How It Was,* so Leo pipes up and says he's going to tell us all how it was, how it really was. How he claimed he said to me, 'Remember what he threw that first game when you hit a home run off him, you said it was a slider.' Then he said to me in the studio, 'Remember I told ya, "Don't ya look for that slider, ya ain't gonna get it, yer gonna get this one, yer gonna get the fast one." ' Well, he'd said that to me at an Old-Timers Game at Shea Stadium a few years ago. And who am I," Thomson said wryly, "to disagree with Mr. Durocher?"

"Well, what in fact do you recall him saying?" I asked.

"My recollection is, 'If you've ever hit one, hit one now.' And I—the thought ran through my mind—I didn't even answer him. I was on my way back to the plate after the action was about to begin again after the Mueller thing. As I recall, he came up from behind and put his arm around me, and that's when he said it. And I remember thinking, you're out of your mind. I mean, home run? I was thinking about just getting a base hit some place. Anyway, that's my recollection.''

"So even if he said it—'if you've ever hit one, hit one now'—that didn't put home run in your head."

"No, definitely not. I just wanted to get my bat on the ball. And to tell you the truth, I wasn't very confident of doing that."

"And that first pitch was . . .''

"Right down the middle,'' Thomson said with emphasis. ''Maybe a shade in, but right down the middle. Now, if we want to rationalize on that, on the way to the plate, I was still cursing at myself to get up there and do a good job. I was saying to myself, 'Wait and watch, wait for the ball and watch it, wait and watch, don't become overanxious'—which is the worst thing a hitter can do. 'Sit back and wait and watch.' And 'You S.O.B., get up there and do a good job, give yourself a chance.' And I don't know, all I can think of, I was waiting and watching. Boy, I mean, I watched that thing right down the middle, it was the nicest pitch I ever saw. I took it!''

"Were you taking it because you wanted to swing at it?"

"Hell no. I just had no reason. I should've been hitting the first pitch, it was the perfect pitch to hit. There was no reason, except I was just talking to myself, trying to psych myself, and while all that was going on, here comes this perfect pitch and I let it go by. I was numb.''

"Were you aware of Mays being on deck, that he might be able to do something if you didn't?''

"I wasn't aware of anything."

"Rube Walker was catching for the Dodgers, do you recall that?"

"I couldn't tell you who was catching."

"Well, I talked to him in Florida a few weeks ago, and he said Branca's second pitch—the one you hit—was not a strike. Do you feel that way?''

"It could very well not have been. Yeah, up and in. A good pitch though, it would've been close. I can remember just getting a glimpse of it. And of course you've got to remember, I was pretty quick inside, quick with the bat. All I had to do was get a look at the pitch, especially if it was inside, and I could get the bat on it.''

"Was there any hesitation on your part?" I asked.

"None at all. I just got a glimpse of that ball—in—and I reacted."

"Did you look it all the way into the bat?"

"Oh gee, I don't know about that. I always hit the inside pitch pretty good though, so I guess you could say it was automatic. The next thing I knew, I'd hit it. Now I don't take credit for doing too many things in my life, but one thing I take credit for that day is giving myself a chance to hit and letting the bat go."

"When you hit it, did you know it was gone, as a hitter often does?"

"I thought I had a home run. I really laid into it, really got good wood on it. But then as I got away from the plate, I began to wonder. It started out high and then looked like it was sinking. Durocher, on this show, he said it started out low. Well, I say it started out high. And what it was, it had overspin on it, a slight overspin. I'd seen Johnny Mize really coldcock these low line drives of his through the infield—you know, get over on top of it. And those balls would have this terrific overspin on them and they'd sink like crazy. Well, I'd never hit a ball like that in my life. It started up high and then began to sink. So I began to think, at least I've got a base hit. I figured it'd be off the wall, enough to get Whitey in with the tying run. And then the ball disappeared into the lower stands. By that time I was halfway, three-quarters of the way to first. Of course this was what I saw in the pictures afterward. I really didn't know where I was. I remember, my first thought was, it's a home run, and then, no, a base hit, and then—bingo!"

"Do you recall circling the bases?"

"Oh gee, the only thing I remember was making these funny noises. I was more excited than I ever was in my life."

"Do you remember seeing Stanky and Durocher wrestling down there by third base?"

"No, but I remember pushing Durocher away. Durocher came up to grab me, and I kind of tried to push him away. I missed Stanky and him. I only saw it later, when I got to watch the film."

"And then what?"

"Well, it was pure pandemonium. There was just this fantastic mob scene at home plate, and then it kind of turned into a riot. The next clear thing I remember was people trying to rip pieces of my uniform off. I thought, hey, I could get killed. Those fans were absolutely out of their minds. So I took off for the clubhouse. Never ran so fast, I guess, weaving my way through all those people, all of them trying to get a piece of me.''

"And then?"

"Well, it took some time to sink in. I went out there that day thinking about getting my RBI total over a hundred. I think I had 97 up to that last game, and the playoff statistics were going to count as part of the regular season. So one of my ambitions was to get over the hundred mark, and I guess I was sort of happy about that. And of course I was happy we'd won the pennant. But at first I wasn't able to digest it all, connect it to me. Later that evening they had me on the Perry Como show, and I got a standing ovation. Then everywhere I went people were cheering me. That's when it started to sink in. And when I finally got home that night, my brother Jim was waiting up for me. And he said, 'Bob, do you realize what you've done?' We talked about it, about how it was more than just a home run to win a ball game, to win a pennant. That's when it began to sink in, what it really was. So I went to bed that night, and I wondered what I had ever done to deserve this. . . .''

Epilogue

I HAD COME FULL CIRCLE in my quest. I had, I thought, gained an understanding—albeit an abstract and barely comprehensible one—of how the miracle at Coogan's Bluff had come about. But the *why* of it remained buried in the *how*.

Not that I deluded myself into believing that knowledge of the *why* could ever be gained with any certitude. After almost a year of trying, I was more positive than ever that the answer I sought would require nothing less than an apocalyptic vision. So, like Moses to the Burning Bush, I returned once more to Coogan's Bluff—hoping not for visions but for perhaps just the one intuition I imagined might still be lingering there like an invisible, residual wisp of smoke in the air.

The day of my second return was gray and cold. Nothing had changed except for the graffiti; where the year before it had been a series of mazes across the high foundations of the brick apartment houses, now it was a solid coagulation of iridescence, like an exhibit of abstract paintings lacking the slightest hint of form or detail.

I retraced my steps through the housing complex and poked into its every corner in the half-expectation of sniffing the wisp of smoke. Nothing. The tiny asphalt baseball diamond was still there, its faded foul lines now invisible under an inch or so of yesterday's dirty, wet, late-spring snow. I climbed the bluff again, finding the wide, black-railed stairway empty. The idlers were elsewhere this bleak, frigid day, but they'd left reminders of themselves in the wind-bunched piles of litter that plugged the creases of the steps.

I stood at the top of the bluff for a while, waiting for the wisp of smoke to drift up. Nothing came but the smell of dank cellars. I saw another change, though. Across the river, Yankee Stadium looked like a bomb had hit it. It was being torn apart and rebuilt, a fate denied the Polo Grounds.

I listened for the rustle of a jam-packed stadium, the crack of a bat, the whoosh and roar of a crowd. All I heard was the shrieking voice of a woman through a window opposite, yelling at a child, then the impatient hooting of a tugboat on the river as it approached one of the Harlem River bridges.

I made my way back down to the housing project. I lingered for a few moments, earning a suspicious glare from a woman passing by, then gave it up as a bad job. No use, I thought, it's not here. There's no shrine here, no monument, no plaque. And no memory. Perhaps there was no miracle. Perhaps it was all imagined.

As I left the grounds of the project and began the short walk down Eighth Avenue to the subway, I turned back for one last look. Something caught my eye. Something was awry, not the same as it had been. It wasn't just the graffiti. What was it?

Then I saw. The signs. The signs that had proclaimed, ''Positively No Ball-Playing Allowed.'' They were gone.

	POS	G	AB	R	H	2B	3B	HR	RBI	SB	AVG.
Whitey Lockman	1b-of	153	614	85	173	27	7	12	73	4	.282
Eddie Stanky	2b	145	515	88	127	17	2	14	43	8	.247
Al Dark	ss	156	646	114	196	41	7	14	69	12	.303
Hank Thompson	3b	87	264	37	62	8	4	8	33	1	.235
Don Mueller	of	122	469	58	130	10	7	16	69	1	.277
Willie Mays	of	121	464	59	127	22	5	20	68	7	.274
Monte Irvin	of-1b	151	558	94	174	19	11	24	121	12	.312
Wes Westrum	c	124	361	59	79	12	0	20	70	1	.219
Bobby Thomson	of-3b	148	518	89	152	27	8	32	101	5	.293
Ray Noble	c	55	141	16	33	6	0	5	26	0	.234
Bill Rigney	3b-2b	44	69	9	16	2	0	4	9	0	.232
Davey Williams	2b	30	64	17	17	1	0	2	8	1	.266
Spider Jorgensen	of-3b	28	51	5	12	0	0	2	8	0	.235
Sal Yvars	c	25	41	9	13	2	0	2	3	0	.317
Lucky Lohrke	3b-ss	23	40	3	8	0	0	1	3	0	.200
Clint Hartung	of	21	44	4	9	1	0	0	2	0	.205
Artie Wilson	2b-ss-1b	19	22	2	4	0	0	0	1	2	.182
Jack Maguire	of	16	20	6	8	1	1	1	4	0	.400
Earl Rapp		13	11	0	1	0	0	0	1	0	.091
Totals		157	5360	781	1396	201	53	179	734	55	.260

Pitchers:	T	G	IP	W	L	PCT	SO	BB	H	ERA
Sal Maglie	R	42	298	23	6	.793	146	86	254	2.93
Larry Jansen	R	39	279	23	11	.676	145	56	254	3.03
Jim Hearn	R	34	211	17	9	.654	66	82	204	3.63
George Spencer	R	57	132	10	4	.714	36	56	125	3.75
Dave Koslo	L	39	150	10	9	.526	54	45	153	3.30
Sheldon Jones	R	41	120	6	11	.353	58	52	119	4.28
Al Corwin	R	15	59	5	1	.833	30	21	49	3.66
Roger Bowman	L	9	26	2	4	.333	24	22	35	6.23
Al Gettel	R	30	57	1	2	.333	36	25	52	4.89
Monte Kennedy	L	29	68	1	2	.333	22	31	68	2.25
Jack Kramer	R	4	5	0	0	.000	2	3	11	14.40
Alex Konikowski	R	3	4	0	0	.000	5	0	2	0.00
George Bamberger	R	2	2	0	0	.000	1	2	4	18.00
Red Hardy	R	2	1	0	0	.000	0	1	4	9.00
Totals		157	413	98	59	.624	625	482	1334	3.48

APPENDIX B
LEAGUE STANDINGS

	Won	Lost	Percentage	Games Behind
New York *	98	59	.624	
Brooklyn	97	60	.618	1
St. Louis	81	73	.526	15½
Boston	76	78	.494	20½
Philadelphia	73	81	.474	23½
Cincinnati	68	86	.442	28½
Pittsburgh	64	90	.416	32½
Chicago	62	92	.403	34½

* Defeated Brooklyn in playoff 2 games to 1.

APPENDIX C
BOX SCORE
OCTOBER 3, 1951

BROOKLYN DODGERS

	At Bats	Runs	Hits	Put Outs	Assists	Errors
Furillo, rf	5	0	0	0	0	0
Reese, ss	4	2	1	2	5	0
Snider, cf	3	1	2	1	0	0
Robinson, 2b	2	1	1	3	2	0
Pafko, lf	4	0	1	4	1	0
Hodges, 1b	4	0	0	11	1	0
Cox, 3b	4	0	2	1	2	0
Walker, c	4	0	1	2	0	0
Newcombe, p	4	0	0	1	1	0
Branca, p	0	0	0	0	0	0
Total	34	4	8	25 *	12	0

NEW YORK GIANTS

	At Bats	Runs	Hits	Put Outs	Assists	Errors
Stanky, 2b	4	0	0	0	4	0
Dark, ss	4	1	1	2	2	0
Mueller, rf	4	0	1	0	0	0
Hartung [c]	0	1	0	0	0	0
Irvin, lf	4	1	1	1	0	0
Lockman, 1b	3	1	2	11	1	0
Thomson, 3b	4	1	3	4	1	0
Mays, cf	3	0	0	1	0	0
Westrum, c	0	0	0	7	1	0
Rigney [a]	1	0	0	0	0	0
Noble, c	0	0	0	0	0	0
Maglie, p	2	0	0	1	2	0
Thompson [b]	1	0	0	0	0	0
Jansen, p	0	0	0	0	0	0
Total	30	5	8	27	11	0

* One out when winning run scored.
[a] Struck out for Westrum in eighth.
[b] Grounded out for Maglie in eighth.
[c] Ran for Mueller in ninth.

Brooklyn.... 1 0 0 0 0 0 0 3 0 — 4
New York... 0 0 0 0 0 0 1 0 4 — 5

Runs batted in—Robinson, Thomson 4, Pafko, Cox, Lockman, (Reese scored on Maglie's wild pitch in eighth).

Two-base hits—Thomson, Irvin, Lockman.

Home run—Thomson.

Sacrifice—Lockman.

Double plays—Cox, Robinson, and Hodges.

Left on bases—Brooklyn 7, New York 3.

Bases on balls—off Maglie 4 (Reese, Snider, Robinson 2); off Newcombe 2 (Westrum 2).

Struck out—by Maglie 6 (Furillo, Walker 2, Snider, Pafko, Reese); by Newcombe 2 (Mays, Rigney).

Hits—off Maglie 8 in 8 innings; off Jansen 0 in 1; off Newcombe 7 in 8$^1/_3$; off Branca 1 in 0 (pitched to one batter in ninth).

Wild pitch—Maglie.

Winning pitcher—Jansen (23-11).

Losing pitcher—Branca (13-12).

Umpires—Lou Jorda (plate), Jocko Conian (first base), Bill Stewart (second base), and Larry Goetz (third base).

Time of game—2:28. Attendance—34,320 (paid).

Index